ECONOMIC STUDIES OF INDIGENOUS AND TRADITIONAL KNOWLEDGE

EDITED BY

NIRMAL SENGUPTA

ACADEMIC FOUNDATION

NEW DELHI

First published in 2007
by

ACADEMIC FOUNDATION
4772-73 / 23 Bharat Ram Road, (23 Ansari Road),
Darya Ganj, New Delhi - 110 002 (India).
Phones : 23245001 / 02 / 03 / 04.
Fax : +91-11-23245005.
E-mail : academic@vsnl.com
www. academicfoundation.com

in association with:

Indian Economic Association Trust for Research and Development

Cataloging in Publication Data--DK
Courtesy: D.K. Agencies (P) Ltd. <docinfo@dkagencies.com>

Economic studies of indigenous & traditional knowledge / editor, Nirmal Sengupta.
p. cm.
Contributed articles.
Includes bibliographical references (p.)
Includes index.
ISBN-13: 9788171885862
ISBN-10: 8171885861

1. Ethnoscience--Economic aspects--India.
I. Sengupta, Nirmal. II. Title: Economic studies of indigenous and traditional knowledge.

DDC 500.89 22

Typeset by Italics India, New Delhi.
Printed and bound in India.

Contents

List of Tables, Figures, Boxes and Appendices

TABLES

FIGURES

BOXES

APPENDICES

सत्यमेव जयते

अध्यक्ष
प्रधानमंत्री की आर्थिक सलाहकार परिषद्
विज्ञान भवन सौंध 'ई' हाल
मौलाना आज़ाद रोड
नई दिल्ली–110 011

डॉ. सी. रंगराजन
Dr. C. RANGARAJAN

CHAIRMAN
Economic Advisory Council to the Prime Minister
Vigyan Bhavan Annexe, 'E' Hall
Maulana Azad Road
New Delhi-110 011

Foreword

The Indian Economic Association Trust for Research and Development has been bringing out monographs and readings in select themes of economics. The objective is to enable the teachers, students and researchers in various colleges, universities and research institutions as also the policy makers have at one place, access to the concepts, theories, policy issues and empirical analysis of the subject.

This volume is a compilation of 13 papers on economic studies of indigenous and traditional knowledge in India by experts in this field. These papers cover the importance of indigenous and traditional knowledge in meeting the basic needs of people and policies about indigenous medicine and traditional knowledge.

In 1992, the UN Conference on Environment and Development proclaimed, "Indigenous people and their communities and other local communities have a vital role in environmental management and development because of their knowledge and traditional practices. States should recognize and duly support their identity, culture and interests and enable their effective participation in the achievement of sustainable development" (Rio Declaration: Principle 22). A major challenge for the global community is the design and enforcement of an appropriate international regime for access to and sharing of the benefits resulting from the use of indigenous and traditional knowledge.

Dr. Nirmal Sengupta, Professor, Indira Gandhi Institute of Development Research, Mumbai has done a commendable job in bringing out this valuable compilation. The IEA Trust is grateful to him for this effort.

C. Rangarajan
Chairman, IEA Trust

Contributors to the Volume

Madhulika Banerjee did her graduation in Economics and Ph.D. in Political Science from Delhi University. At present she is a Reader, University of Delhi. She was Visiting Fellow, Queen Elizabeth House, Oxford. Actively involved in issues of traditional medical systems in public health she has published several articles particularly in the area of politics of pharmaceuticals industry and state policy.

Aparna Bhagirathy is M.A. (Economics), Madras University; MPIA (Masters in Pacific International Affairs), University of California, San Diego. At present she is a Research Associate at the Centre for Micro-Finance Research, Chennai. She has published a couple of articles in newsletters, magazines on Intellectual Property Rights and Traditional Knowledge. She was also the co-organiser of a series of workshops on traditional knowledge and is principal investigator on a project on traditional knowledge and IPR

Mouchumi Konwer Borgohain is M.A. (Economics) from Gauhati University with specialisation in econometrics and mathematical economics. She has 25 years teaching experience in colleges. At present she is Head, Department of Economics, D.C.B. Girls' College, Dibrugarh University, Assam. Her other areas of research and interest are women's studies, ecological economics and environmental economics. She has written several articles on Assam and has worked as resource person for training programmes on gender sensitisation.

Pushpam Kumar Ph.D. in Environmental Economics from the University of Delhi. Currently Reader in Environmental Economics, Institute of Economic Growth (IEG), Delhi. Earlier, he was Lecturer in Economics in the Department of Business Economics in the University of Delhi. Some of his recent publications are a book: *Economics of Soil Erosion: Issues and Imperatives from India* (2003) and articles "Does Environmental Kuznets Curve Exist for Changing Land Use: Empirical Evidence from Major States of India", (in *International Journal of Sustainable Development*, 2003) and "Corporate Social Responsibility: Some Issues" (in *Global Business Opportunity*). His book (co-author) *Economics of Ecosystem Services of Wetlands* is in press.

G. Badri Narayanan, B.Tech(Textile Technology), Ph.D. at Indira Gandhi Institute of Development Research, Mumbai. At present he is a Fellow,

Indian Council for Research in International Economic Relations (ICRIER). His broad area of research is Economics and Management of Textile Industry. His article: "Garment Exports–A Mission with Vision" was published in the *Journal of Textile Association*.

P.S. Ramakrishnan, M.Sc. (Botany); Ph.D., Banaras Hindu University, is an internationally renowned Ecologist, is currently associated with the School of Environmental Sciences, Jawaharlal Nehru University, as a U.G.C. Emeritus Professor. He was Professor of Ecology at Jawaharlal Nehru University; Founder Director, G.B. Pant Institute of Himalayan Environment and Development; and Professor of Botany/Eco-development, North Eastern Hill University. For his work in the area of population ecology, Professor Ramakrishnan was elected to the Fellowship of National Academy of Sciences (1972), Indian Academy of Sciences (1975) and Indian National Science Academy (1980). For his researches in the area of sustainable management of biodiversity and natural resources, with concerns for sustainable livelihood/development of traditional societies, comprising of about 400 research publications and 17 research volumes, he has received many national and international recognitions including fellowships of the Third World Academy of Sciences, and the Honorary Fellowship of the International Association of Tropical Biology (ATB). Development projects in Nagaland to conserve biodiversity in shifting agriculture affected areas, through an incremental build-up of the Traditional Ecological Knowledge (TEK), were based on over 20 years of research effort of Professor Ramakrishnan, scientifically validating his theory.

T. Ramasami, after obtaining his Bachelor and Masters degrees in Leather Technology from the University of Madras carried out his doctoral research at the University of Leeds, UK. He worked for six years in the United States at the Ames Energy research laboratory, Iowa, and at Wayne State University, Detroit; he was Visiting Fellow at the University of New Castle upon Tyne, joined the Central Leather Research Institute (CLRI) in 1984 as a senior scientist, and was appointed later as Director of CLRI. At present he is the Secretary, Department of Science & Technology, Government of India. He is co-author of over 100 publications in refereed journals and more than 50 technical reports. Dr. Ramasami has a broad range of scientific interests and represents a combination of strengths in chemistry, with the capability to develop technologies from first principles. He is a member of several professional scientific and academic bodies in India and abroad, and is a recipient of several awards, including the Shanti Swarup Bhatnagar Prize for Chemical Sciences, special award of honour from the Indian Leather Technologists Association and Coleman Research Prize. In 2001, National Civilian Honour Padma Shri was conferred on him by the Government of India. He is an elected fellow of the Indian Academy of Sciences and Indian Leather Technologists Association.

Aromar Revi, formally trained as a technologist and civil engineer, Indian Institute of Technology (IIT), is a consultant, researcher and practitioner in development, public policy, technology and sustainability. He is a founding Director of TARU, a leading South Asian research consulting firm and has lectured and taught widely in India and the West. He is also internationally recognised in the areas of systems and cybernetics. He has made a significant contribution to human settlements development in India, for which he was awarded the Ashoka Fellowship in 1990. This includes a key role in the design of India's national public housing programme, serving on high-level committees of the Government of India and developing housing and urban development sectoral plans for half of India's states in the early 1990s. This provided him through extensive fieldwork and travel, a unique insight into the immense complexity and diversity of the country. He is one of South Asia's leading disaster mitigation and management experts and has led emergency teams to assess, plan and execute recovery and rehabilitation programmes for 10 major earthquake, cyclone, surge and flood events affecting over 5 million people.

Nirmal Sengupta Master of Statistics (M. Stat.), Diploma in Econometrics and Planning, Ph.D. (Indian Statistical Institute), is Professor, Indira Gandhi Institute of Development Research (IGIDR), Mumbai. Before joining IGIDR he was Malcolm Adiseshiah Professor for Policy Studies (former Director) at Madras Institute of Development Studies. He has also worked at the Indian Statistical Institute, Calcutta; A.N. Sinha Institute of Social Studies, Patna, as Deputy Director of State Planning Board Bihar; Expert and Consultant to UNDP, FAO, Netherlands Ministery for Development Cooperation, World Commission on Dams and Visiting Scholar at National Institute of Rural Development (Hyderabad), Institute of Philippine Culture (Manila), and Indiana University (Indiana). Sengupta's varied interests cut across disciplinary boundaries. His writings like "Irrigation: Traditional *versus* Modern" (1985) and "Traditional Water Management Systems: Primitive or Precious?", Keynote Address, First Congress on Traditional Science and Technologies of India, initiated research works in indigenous irrigation. His recent books include *The Economics of Trade Facilitation* (Oxford, 2007), *Biodiversity and Quality of Life* (ed. Macmillan, 2005), *A New Institutional Theory Of Production–An Application* (Sage, 2001).

Meera M. Hira Smith is M.Sc., Ph.D. (Sc.) in Geography, Calcutta University. Presently she is Director of Project Well, California, USA and researcher at the School of Public Health, University of California, Berkeley. Her thesis was on *Impact of Air, Water and Sound Pollution on the People of Calcutta: A Geographical Analysis*. Her articles have been published in *Geographical Review of India, Environmental Health Perspectives* and *Epidemiology*. Engaged in health research since 1993, her involvement in the field of Arsenic Crisis relief began in 1996. She is the international coordinator and founder of Project Well and maintains a website on this. Besides, she has co-authored a book *Easy Way to Learn Bengali* consisting of 100 chapters and accompanied by four compact disks (*http://www.geocities.com/learnbengali2003/*).

Nori Tarui, M.A. (Economics) at Keio University, Tokyo; Ph.D., Department of Applied Economics, and a Scholar at the MacArthur Interdisciplinary Program on Global Change, Sustainability and Justice at the University of Minnesota. Till recently a Fellow at the Earth Institute, Columbia University he is now an Assistant Professor, Department of Economics, University of Hawaii-Manoa. Research areas include common-property resource use, non-market institutions in rural villages and environmental regulation.

K.T. Thomson, graduated with a first class in Mathematics, later did his M.A. (Economics) from Dr. John Mathai Centre, University of Calicut and Ph.D. (Economics) from Madras University. He is a Resource Economist in the School of Industrial Fisheries of Cochin, University of Science and Technology. He is also associated with the Centre for Integrated Coastal Zone Management of the School of Marine Sciences and the Centre for Rural Development and Appropriate Technology (RUDAT) of the Cochin University. He has been associated with Food and Agricultural Organization, Asian Development Bank and the World Bank as consultant fisheries socioeconomist and has done field works in Bangladesh, Maldives, Sri Lanka, Malaysia, Thailand and Indonesia in a variety of issues related to small scale fisheries management. He has finished several projects on coastal biodiversity management and sustainable development. At present he is the co-investigator of two international projects on fisheries, one on co-management in South Asian fisheries and another on estuarine management.

Acknowledgements

The editor and publisher gratefully acknowledge the following for permissions to reproduce copyright materials.

Sage Publication, New Delhi for: (a) Excerpts from book of Nirmal Sengupta, *User-Friendly Irrigation Designs*, Sage publishers, New Delhi, 1993, and (b) Article by Madhulika Banerjee, "Power, Culture, Medicine: Ayurvedic Pharmaceuticals in the Modern Market" in *Contributions to Indian Sociology*, 36(3), September-December 2002, pp. 435-467.

P.S. Ramakrishnan for article, "Tribal Man in the Humid Tropics of the North-East" in *Man in India: Quarterly Journal of Anthropology*, 65(1), March 1985: pp.1-32. Publisher, Seminar for article by Aparna Bhagirathy and Nirmal Sengupta, "Surviving in a Globalizing World", *Seminar*, Issue No. 523, March 2003.

Indian Institute of Geomorphologists, for article by Meera M. Hira Smith, "An Assessment of Alternative Methods of Providing Arsenic Free Water in Villages of North-24-parganas, West Bengal, India", published in the Proceedings of the International Seminar of *Changing Environmental Scenario of India and Adjacent Countries since Independence* and XII Annual Conference of Indian Institute of Geomorphologists (IGI), 2000.

The editor also acknowledges his gratitude to the authors for their contributions to this volume; to Indira Gandhi Institute of Development Research, Mumbai and Madras Institute of Development Studies, Chennai for extending necessary facilities; and to the Indian Economic Association Trust for Research and Development; to Professor Vadiraj Panchamukhi; Professor C. Rangarajan; Professor U. Sankar and the editorial team of Academic Foundation.

1

Introduction

NIRMAL SENGUPTA

Interest in traditional knowledge has increased in recent years. The objects of attention are certain parts of existing agriculture, food practices, medicinal systems and the likes. Why are they called 'traditional'? People have been building houses, cultivating fields and treating patients since millennia. Nor did they invent, once in a remote past, some techniques for doing these works, and thereafter repeated those year after year, generating traditions. In all ages knowledge has been enriched, new techniques have been added, and some of those have faded into oblivion. What is so distinct about the present era that led to compartmentalisation of our existing knowledge and practices into traditional and modern?

No doubt, transistors or computers are unique to the present era. These are knowledge and technology truly modern and without any tradition. No doubt, great strides have been made in our epoch in the fields of science and technology. But that does not enable dividing the activities with long history into compartments marked 'traditional' and 'modern'. Modern technology invented steam engines and computers but did not invent agriculture or medicine. One may say that there is a lot of difference. Modern agriculture uses HYV seeds; medicines are available as tablets and capsules. Indeed, that is the difference. In agriculture and medicine, in housing and irrigation, modern science has enriched the earlier technology and knowledge, just as in the past. But it did so only partially. The spheres that were touched by the magic wand are now called 'modern'. Those that were not are regarded as 'traditional'.

This would not have been a problem if the normal process of development would not have been vitiated by a prejudice accompanying the notion of 'traditional'. Progress is a gradual process and all spheres of an activity may not experience improvements at the same time. It is reasonable to find that some spheres of continuing activities received the benefits of modern science and technology at an earlier date, some others later. But this possibility, of gradual transition, has been frustrated by a presumption that all those termed 'traditional' are not worth developing. Human knowledge and productive activities have been divided into two spheres, the one called 'traditional' has been condemned before trial. This intolerance discourages further efforts to apply modern science and technological knowledge for improvement of yet-untouched spheres, thus creating a vicious circle. Recently, the development agencies have woken up to the great divide and noted with awe that a very large section of human activities have been bypassed by modern science and technology. World Bank found that after several decades of massive developmental efforts two-thirds of the world's population still could not survive without foods provided through indigenous knowledge of plants, animals, insects, microbes and farming systems (UNDP, 1994). The World Health Organization noted that up to 80 per cent of the world's population depends on traditional medicine for its primary health needs (WHO, 1998). The Bank (1998) declared: Traditional knowledge is an underutilised resource in the development process. Its dissemination can help to reduce poverty.

There is another reason why traditional knowledge is drawing considerable attention in recent years. A new dimension has been added to the notion of development, that of sustainability. Historical evidence shows that many local communities have utilised natural resources over centuries without impairing their capabilities to support them and their successive generations. Their ways and their knowledge is therefore, immensely valuable for learning sustainable ways of development. At the 1992 Earth Summit in Rio de Janeiro, world leaders agreed on a comprehensive strategy for 'sustainable development'. One of the key agreements adopted at Rio was the Convention on Biological Diversity, which has been ratified by 178 countries. The Convention established three main goals: conservation of biological diversity, sustainable use of its components, and fair and equitable sharing of the benefits from the use of genetic resources. In the Preamble, the Convention recognised in clear terms "The close and traditional dependence of many indigenous and local communities embodying traditional lifestyles on biological resources." States were asked to "respect, preserve and maintain knowledge, innovations and practices of indigenous and local communities embodying traditional lifestyles relevant for the conservation and sustainable use of biological diversity and promote their wider application."

Neglected knowledge deserving attention may be found anywhere, though in varying degrees. Therefore, assigning a name for the group is a serious problem. Way back, in the 1980s, the pioneering scholars felt that the term 'traditional' was commonly equated to 'extinct or redundant' (e.g. Sengupta, 1980; Sen, 1992) or 'simple, savage and static' (e.g. Brokensha, Warren and Werner, 1980; Howes and Chambers, 1980; Banuri and Apffel-Marglin, 1993). They therefore, favoured an alternative term:[1] 'indigenous'. Use of this term is not without problems. Indigenous knowledge need not have a long history or tradition; petty innovations by local people of a very recent date qualify for being called 'indigenous'. Also, over the years the so-called tribal communities have come to be known as 'indigenous people'. Today, the notion of indigenous knowledge may exclude valuable traditional knowledge of 'non-tribal' people. The Convention on Biological Diversity used both indigenous and traditional.[2] Both the terms are in currency. Different agencies show preference for one or the other. In this book we have used both the terms and interchangeably.

Everywhere in the old colonies, colonial rulers were keen to denigrate history and society of colonial people.[3] In the past, this was the root cause of negligence of indigenous knowledge. Yet, this is dwarfed by the happenings in the post-colonial period. The development process that was initiated in the newly independent

1. e.g. Sengupta, Nirmal (1980). "Indigenous Irrigation Organisation of South Bihar", *Indian Economic and Social History Review*, April; Brokensha, D., D. Warren and O. Werner (eds.) (1980). *Indigenous Knowledge Systems and Development*, University Press of America, Lanham; Howes, M. and R. Chambers (1980). "Indigenous Technical Knowledge: Analysis, Implications and Issues", in D. Brokensha *et al.*, (ed.), *op cit*: pp. 329-340; Sen, Geeti (ed.) (1992). *Indigenous Vision,* Sage and India International Centre, New Delhi; Banuri, T., and F. Apffel-Marglin (eds.) (1993). *Who Will Save the Forests? Knowledge, Power and Environmental Destruction*, London, Zed Books.

2. Article 8(j) refers to knowledge, innovations and practices of indigenous and local communities embodying traditional lifestyles.

3. Colonial period had also seen several great scientists and engineers like Sir Arthur Cotton, in the field of irrigation or J.A. Voelcker, in agriculture, who were diligent students of indigenous Indian knowledge and technology and made ways for their developments. Their works show the great potential of development created by the contact with modern Western knowledge system, a potential that was not realised in many spheres.

countries, was unbalanced. In India for example,[4] during the independence struggle, rationalisation of social and cultural practices and glorification of past achievements was a method for contesting colonial propaganda. Several of our patriotic intellectuals were committed to this counter-propaganda often conducted at the cost of factual correctness and analytical rigour. It may be possible to justify those 'compensatory delusions' on the ground of necessity 'to boost up our morale' during the freedom struggle.[5] But then, the situation changed after independence. No longer there was any need of such delusions. One could be critical of social and cultural traits of Indians, like superstitions and backward-looking character, without the fear that their criticisms would be misutilised for colonial purpose. In post-independence India, science and technology was seen as the prime mover of development. Reformers set forth the agenda for creating a new society ready to embrace science, technology and development.[6] Unfortunately, the agenda they set shared with global development agenda of that period all the limitations that we have already discussed. A very large section of intelligentsia in the post-independence India believed and preached that only by rejecting everything traditional anything worthwhile could be built in India.

While this was the overwhelming trend, some feeble streams of dissidents continued. Militant nationalism with glorification of past had its proponents in scholars like Dharmapal (2000). Orthodox nationalism including religious fanaticism was another stream of intellectuals that cared little about factual correctness and analytical rigour. It is now clear that there was a third stream of dissidents who had quietly pursued constructive agenda using traditional and indigenous knowledge. When, in the 1990s, a science activist organisation[7] organised three Congresses of Traditional Science and

4. There were some sane voices. For details see Nirmal Sengupta, 2005.

5. In the Preface of his popular book on Indian philosophy (Chattopadhyaya, 1964).

6. E.g. statement on 'scientific temper' made by several leading scientists, *viz.* Haksar *et. al.*, (1981).

7. Named Patriotic and People Oriented Science and Technology (PPST) formed around the late seventies primarily by some former IIT students. PPST organised three Congresses on Traditional Science and Technologies of India. The First Congress was held at the Indian Institute of Technology, Bombay in 1993 and the Second one at the Anna University, Madras on 1995, and the third at the Gandhian Institute, Varanasi two years later. The Congresses were the culmination of several years of campaign for recognising the importance of traditional knowledge. I was not a member of this group.

Technologies in India, they found that thousands of Indian professionals and technologists have been working on these areas. There were hundreds of papers, grouped under heads such as: architecture and building materials, agricultural and biodiversity, bamboo, fisheries, food and nutrition, forestry, health care, metals and materials, navigational technologies, pottery, textiles, traditional industries, vermiculture, and water resources, even mathematics (Sengupta, 1995). Still it was far from a complete list. About a thousand participants, engaged in promoting one or the other field, attended each Congress.

The Congress brochures introduced the problem of traditional knowledge as: In spite of remarkable progress in many fields, we have still not been able to feed, clothe, shelter, educate or employ all our people. While the size of our population has been held out as the main reason for scarcity of all resources, it appears that there is another very important dimension to this phenomenon. This has something to do with the very image we have of what constitutes resources for development in our context. If houses can be built only with cement and steel, then it is quite possible that there may be no way in which we can think of housing for all. The picture changes substantially if we include in the list the wide variety of materials and techniques traditionally employed by our people in different parts of our land in making houses for themselves. If we include in our plans the wide variety of proven medicines, practices and principles that have been indigenously evolved for health care in our society, then the resource position on the health care front may not appear as bleak as it now seems to. If the wide range of materials and techniques that our farmers have traditionally employed to ensure land fertility, pest control, high yield, etc. are included in the list of resources at our command, then the prospect of enhancing food production in an ecologically and economically sound manner may not appear as daunting as it seems to be now. There is a wide variety of skills and knowledge that our people possess, which, if properly understood and recognised, can make substantial contributions to all our productive efforts and endeavour. This theme, which was the basis of the Traditional Science and Technologies Congress of India, was not a romantic exaggeration. By now, the immense potential of these neglected resources has been noted from all over the world.

This volume is a compilation of some economic studies of traditional and indigenous knowledge in India. Needless to say, it is neither an exhaustive account nor a comprehensive collection dealing with different dimensions of the issues. What the scientists and technologists can do with traditional and indigenous knowledge is obvious. Sociologists and anthropologists, among the social scientists, have also noted the appropriate areas where their works may make a difference. Economists often wonder whether they have anything to do here. This is a collection of articles showing the wide variety of research on indigenous and traditional knowledge that can be done by economists. Some of these are written by economists themselves. The rest are valuable economic studies by scholars from other disciplines. The first 4 chapters were published within the last 20 years. Although the significance of their contents has only increased over time, they may show the limited range of inquiries in the past. The last 8 chapters are very recent works. They show the proliferation of issues and efforts to analyse those by using varieties of analytical tools. A reader may get a taste of the evolution of research issues and analytical frameworks during these two decades of increased interest and intense activities in this field.

The first two chapters are studies of communities, using three different approaches: ecological, political economic and anthropological. In "Tribal man in the Humid Tropics", P. S. Ramakrishnan explained the ecological principles on which the rural-ecosystem of the North-east is based, and the judicious management of the natural resources in this extremely fragile ecosystem. By now, the modifications of the *jhum* system that he had suggested have been put into practice. In "Marine Fisheries: Knowledge, Production and Distribution", K.T. Thomson introduced the nature of traditional ecological knowledge systems, property relations and the consequent modes of distribution of fisherfolk in the east coast. He argues that the social organisation of traditional fishing communities needs to be considered in evolving a strategy of good governance in the fisheries sector that is undergoing a rapid structural transformations.

The next four chapters show the continued importance of indigenous and traditional knowledge and techniques in meeting basic needs of people. The first two of these are countrywide studies. Aromar Revi *et al.* and Nirmal Sengupta assessed the current importance of traditional knowledge in housing and irrigation sectors respectively, bringing out the policy imperatives for 'housing for all' and 'water for every corner'. Some of their recommendations are now widely discussed, although radical changes in policy, as they suggest, are still awaited. The next two chapters are of specific regions. In recent times, the occurrence of arsenic in drinking water on an extensive scale in West Bengal and Bangladesh has become a national and global catastrophe. From a comparative study of different methods of providing arsenic free water Meera M. Hira Smith explains why the experts now tend to agree that the best way to cope with this gigantic tragedy should be based on traditional knowledge and wisdom. The last chapter of this section is about food economy. As already noted, a very large section of the world's population still relies on foods provided through indigenous knowledge of plants, animals, insects, microbes and farming systems. The methods change from place to place adapting to locally available resources. One example is here in the chapter, "The Economy of Homestead Garden", where Mouchumi Konwer Borgohain discusses this little known feature of Assam.

The next two chapters address different dimensions of a hotly debated current issue: global policies about indigenous medicinal and genetic knowledge. The estimated market value of plant-based medicines sold by pharmaceutical companies in OECD countries in 1985 was US$ 43 billion (Principe, 1989). Most of these were based on traditional knowledge; of the 119 plant-based compounds used in medicine worldwide, 74 per cent had the same or related use as the medicinal plants from which they were derived (Farnsworth, 1988). The custodians of these knowledge were in most cases, poor and indigenous people. They did not receive any share of these billions of dollars of sale proceeds. Instead, the developing countries are required to engage in costly legal battles to retain their rights over their traditional knowledge; India had to spend millions of dollars for preventing patents on *neem* and turmeric in the USA. A greatly cost-efficient way is to develop legal frameworks for recognition and protection of traditional knowledge. In recent years, frantic efforts are being made all over the world along this line. In 1992, the Convention on Biological Diversity (CBD) highlighted the need to promote and preserve traditional knowledge. In its Ministerial Conference at Doha in 2001, WTO mandated review of relationship between the TRIPS

Agreement and the CBD and protection of traditional knowledge. Several global and national agencies are now engaged in designing appropriate intellectual property rights (IPR) for indigenous and traditional knowledge. Until now, the exercise has thrown up more questions than satisfactory answers. The two contributors here use tools of economic analysis to answer a couple of questions. Aparna Bhagirathy argues that there is a case for increasing patent length and breadth in IPR on traditional knowledge. Pushpam Kumar and Nori Tarui explore the economic value of indigenous knowledge in discovery of new drugs, which will ultimately be the basis of benefit sharing arrangements.

The last three chapters: deal with some issues in industry and commerce; innovation, production, marketing, and export activities. With a case study of the Dabur company, Madhulika Banerjee analyses different aspects of modern marketing of traditional India medicine. G. Badri Narayanan assesses comparative advantages of using synthetic dyes and traditional knowledge based natural dyes in textiles industry in India. T. Ramasami tells how modern science and technology succeeded in reorganising traditional leather industry and improving the social and economic conditions of the depressed communities traditionally engaged in this activity. The last chapter by Aparna Bhagirathy and Nirmal Sengupta brings out the necessity of intellectual property protection for the craft sector in India, a sector that comes second in employment generation, outranked only by agriculture.

Unlike a couple of decades back, traditional is not anymore a pejorative term. But even enlightened discourses on traditional knowledge in India do not go beyond *Vedas* and *Upanishads*, Aryabhatta, Panini and Charaka, or peaks of excellence such as the invention of zero. Those who speak high of Indian traditional knowledge speak only of Sanskrit sources. Rarely is it realised that material knowledge has continued to develop and flourish in India and elsewhere, uninterrupted over the centuries. There is very little understanding or appreciation of the achievements of traditional Indian sciences and technologies in meeting the current material needs of our people. The chapters included in this volume are in stark contrast to this popular discourse of the greatness of Indian tradition. They deal with the traditional and indigenous knowledge of villagers of India, that of its tribal and Dalit population, fisher folk, craftsmen, artisans and leather workers, their agriculture, housing and irrigation methods, medicinal knowledge, drinking water collection, arts and culture. The chapters describe the continuing, ever increasing economic significances of such knowledge in the modern world and introduce a wide variety of ways for utilising those knowledge.

2

Tribal Man in the Humid Tropics[1]

P.S. RAMAKRISHNAN[2]

Introduction

The continued existence of biological populations depends upon the available natural resources that could sustain them. For example, a herbivore animal population would continue to grow up to a point of time when the plant resources on which it depends becomes limiting. In-built control mechanisms that operate within the animal population would check its further growth (Wynne-Edwards, 1962), unless the population itself becomes extinct.

What is applicable to a typical biological population is also applicable to man. However, man's ability to manipulate nature has added a new dimension to exploitation of natural resources around him. Because of his special abilities, man has sometimes brought down the resources around him below the critical level. The replacement of non-renewable resources is difficult and even renewable ones is slower than the heavy demand often placed upon it by man and come under severe stress. Breakdown of human society as man is often a non-prudent predator upon his natural resources have resulted in the past in wiping out of human civilisations such as that of Mesopotamia due to desertification. Apart from such extreme cases, as farms and human settlements spread to desert-prone areas, it resulted in barrenness as in Spain, but also helped to create desert such as Sahara in Africa and Rajasthan in India. The inescapable conclusion is that human population has multiplied and its life resources have shrunken (Moore, 1975).

---

1. First appeared as "Tribal Man in The Humid Tropics of the North-East", in *Man in India: Quarterly Journal of Anthropology*, 65(1), March 1985: pp. 1-32.

2. The help from my pupil, K.S. Rao in organising the illustrations and the references is acknowledged.

The rural society in India has always been very close to and in harmony with his natural setting. This has contributed to the health of the Indian civilisation through ages. Starting from the stage of hunter-gatherers in the remote past through various stages of development of agriculture and pastoralism by about 500 BC (Kosambi, 1965) the low density of population permitted judicious use of the natural resources. With gradual increase in population pressure, restrictions imposed upon the society through religion and cultural taboos helped in conserving the natural resources. The division of labour associated with the caste system, perhaps, further contributed in maintaining an equilibrium state of the rural man with his environment through self-imposed restrictions on varied activities. It is with the exposure to western civilisation through the British rule over India that large-scale exploitation of natural resources for an industrialised society tended to upset the steady state. This got further accentuated in the recent past with explosion of the human population in the Indian subcontinent.

Humid Tropics—A Unique Ecosystem Type

The humid tropics cover all three regions of the tropical and sub-tropical zone where the dry season is less than four months and where the mean annual rainfall is at least 1200 mm. It covers a vast tract of land spread over many continents—Southeast Asia, Africa and Latin America and is characterised by evergreen forests. In the Indian sub-continent, these rain forest types are confined to the Western Ghats in the south and to the north-eastern region.

With a rich species diversity in these forests that have evolved over many hundred years, the stability of all the diverse living organisms including man has been maintained by nature most effectively than any human planning and 'developmental' activities could achieve. The maintenance of the soil cover and its fertility in these high rainfall areas is crucial for agriculture which is the basic economic activity of man all over the world and of the humid tropics. In the humid tropics, the soil fertility needed for agriculture is best maintained through a species-rich forest cover. This empirical knowledge developed through intuitive experience of the tribal farmer, through his 'rotational bush-fallow agriculture' (commonly known as *jhum* in India) (Ramakrishnan, 1984b) has brought him closer to his natural environment than anywhere else making him a well integrated whole with nature.

The forests of the humid tropics are very fragile because of the high rainfall, extremely leached and nutrient deficient soil and the long time span involved in the development of a dense virgin forest. In fact, the living biomass is the chief storage compartment for the mineral nutrients, rather than the soil (Table 2.1). In contrast to this, in a more stable forest ecosystem type, the soil acts as a more important storage compartment for the mineral elements so that even if the forest is clear-cut over large areas, regeneration is quick. With the elements stored in the living biomass, after clear-cutting the nutrients would soon be flushed out of the ecosystem due to high rainfall and rapid decomposition of the dead litter. Therefore, the relationship of man with his humid tropics environment could be fragile indeed, if the perturbations are of a larger magnitude.

Consequently, the humid tropics offer two contrasting situations: (i) where the dependence of man on his environment is closest and (ii) yet this inter-relationship between man and nature is so fragile. In the following pages we shall consider this dilemma from a variety of angles and shall look at the possible measures that need to be incorporated into our developmental strategies for the tribal people of this geographical zone, a strategy which could enable them to be in harmony with their environment.

Table 2.1

Biomass and Potassium Content of Tropical Forest

Components	*Biomass Kg/Ha*	*Potassium Kg/Ha*
Leaves	11,989	135
Stems	355,829	2,846
Fruits & Flowers	139	1.3
Roots	9,850	81
Litter	17,554	39
Soil to 30 cm	—	353
Herbivores	13	0.05
Carnivores	8	0.01
Detritivores	52	0.14
Total	**395,434**	**3,445.5**

Source: MAB, UNESCO 1979.

Forest Farming

One of the important economic activities of the tribal man in the Northeastern hills which has kept him so close to nature is the age-old practice of shifting agriculture (commonly known in the country as *jhum*). Essentially this form of agriculture depends upon harvesting solar energy through the forest and a variety of crops grown on a plot of land. Thus the solar energy captured by the forest cover is released in the form of manure during the slash and burn operation for use by a variety of crops sown together which also offer a well organised canopy cover for efficient capture of solar energy.

The Practice

The practice in its typical form (Toky and Ramakrishnan, 1981a) essentially involves clear-cutting of a plot of 2 to 2.5 hectares of land on steep slopes of 30° to 40° angle, by a family of 5-6 members, allowing the slash to dry during the dry winter season, followed by burning the slash in March-April. The more difficult operations are done collectively by more than one family; otherwise the family unit is independently responsible for cropping a plot of land. Though the land is owned by the village through the village headman who regulated its use, the plots allotted to a family for *jhum* normally remains with that family after a token payment. The typical *jhum* is practiced extensively all over the Northeast.

Where the forest cover is sparse, the soil is even more infertile and forest regeneration is slow because of low temperature and high soil acidity as at higher elevations, modifications have been made by the tribals in following this practice. Thus at higher elevations of the Khasi hills of Meghalaya (Mishra and Ramakrishnan, 1981) clear-cutting of forest is no longer feasible. Therefore only a few branches of the scattered pine trees along with the undergrowth is slashed. To conserve the nutrients in short supply the slash is arranged in parallel rows, covered over by a layer of soil before burning. Crops are sown only on the ridges while the alternating furrows are compacted.

Imitating Nature through Mixed Cropping

Diversity is the law of nature. Nowhere is this more evident than in the forests of the humid tropics. A rich species diversity in a tropical rain forest not only ensures relative stability of this otherwise fragile ecosystem but also helps in conserving the precious mineral elements of the soil through a perennial plant cover. A variety of species also help in effective capture of light energy and optimisation of production.

By raising a variety of crop species all together on the same plot the *jhum* farmer has adapted the nature's way of diversity to optimise production from his *jhum* plot. The number of crop species may be more than 30 on a single plot. The farmer raises a variety of cereals, tuber crops, legumes, vegetable crops, etc. to meet his varied needs of food and even fibre. The larger pieces of wood during slashing the forest along with bamboo, at least in part, would meet the fuel, wood and timber needs of the farmer. As far as the crops are concerned, the aim is to obtain his varied needs from the same plot and be self-sufficient. The rich species diversity on the *jhum* plot ensures maximum protection to the soil cover, only after the crop cover is established (Toky and Ramakrishnan, 1981b; Mishra and Ramakrishnan, 1983a); in the earlier phase of cropping the losses of sediment, and nutrients through water is heavy indeed. Crop diversity ensures stability of the system by checking large-scale damage through pests and disease attacks. A variety of crops positioned in different layers above ground ensure optimising productivity through efficient light capture, and different layers below-ground ensure a stratified root system to obtain maximum nutrition from the soil. In fact the spatial distribution of the different crop species along the slope itself is based on the empirical knowledge developed through long experience. Thus, some of the tuber crops which are more efficient in nutrient uptake and use are toward the top portion of the slope which is relatively poor in soil fertility whilst those which are less efficient in nutrient uptake and use like some of the cereals often are placed down below where the soil fertility obviously would be high.

The mixture of crops are sown at the same time after the rains but harvesting is sequential, spread over many months as crops mature (Table 2.2). This has many advantages in terms of the *jhum* ecosystem function. A multi-layered crop canopy with extensive root system developed early during the monsoon would help in conserving the nutrients that would otherwise be lost from the steep slopes through run-off and infiltration of water, as the rainfall is heavy. As one crop matures and is harvested, it creates more space for the next crop which is at its peak growth. This helps in optimum use of the light resource by the crop canopy and the soil nutrients by the root system. This is important under an extremely transient environment with rapid depletion of soil nutrients (Ramakrishnan and Toky, 1981; Mishra and Ramakrishnan, 1983b). The sequential harvesting of crops also helps the nutrition of the remaining crop species through recycling of the dead biomass of the crop harvested. The crop biomass that is ploughed back into the soil improves the physical quality of the soil through the humus produced and nutrients released into the soil when completely decomposed.

Table 2.2

Sequential Harvesting of Crops on Jhum Plots under 30-Year Cycle at Lower Elevation of Meghalaya

Species	*Sowing Time*	*Harvesting Time*
Setaria italica	April	mid-July
Zea mays	"	mid-July
Oryza sativa	"	early September
Lagenaria spp.	"	"
Cucumis sativa	"	"
Zingiber officianalis	"	early October
Sesamum indicum	"	"
Phaseolus mungo	"	"
Cucurbita spp.	"	early November
Manihot esculenta	"	"
Colocasia anticorum	"	"
Hibiscus sabdariffa	"	early December
Ricinus communis	"	(Perennial crop)

Source: Ramakrishnan *et al.*, 1981.

The Non-weed Concept

Weeds are plants that grow in disturbed sites (Baker, 1965) and are considered to be undesirable and adversely affecting crop yield when growing in agricultural systems. Therefore considerable effort has gone into developing technologies for controlling them through various methods. The useful role of weeds in agricultural systems is being recognised more and more in recent times and therefore the management of weeds in this direction would receive more attention in future. The *jhum* farmer has always realised the importance of the weeds in his *jhum* plots under a highly transient environment. In the *jhum* system of the Northeast, weeding by the tribal farmer is never a total operation. The tribal farmer knows exactly when to stop weeding his plot and therefore he does weeding only to the extent that it may not adversely affect crop yield. Even these weeded plants are used by him for recycling of nutrients in the *jhum* plots. Therefore the weeded biomass is ploughed back into the soil or channelised through the compost pit in the village (Mishra and Ramakrishnan, 1982). The standing crop of weed left on the plot would help in conserving nutrients in the soil that would otherwise be lost through run-off and infiltration water (Swamy and Ramakrishnan, unpublished).

While the tribal farmer has a use for the weed standing on his field for conserving nutrients in the soil and that hand-hoed as an organic manure, this often contrasts with a Nepali *jhum* farmer who has adopted *jhum* as a practice after recent immigration into the tribal community. Invariably he would do a more thorough weeding of his plot and would use the weed for feeding the cattle. It may be noted that cattle farming is an introduction into the region and is not part of the tribal culture.

Apart from the above uses of the weed, the weed on the *jhum* plot may find other uses. The broom grass, a part of the *jhum* system is even exported out of the region as broom. Another species, the thatching grass, is used for hut construction.

Lesser Known Plants of Food Value

A viewpoint shared by a number of scientists all over the world is that with rapid explosion of the population, by the turn of the century, conventional food resources of the present may not be able to meet all the needs of man. By this time about four-fifths of the world population would be living in the under-developed parts of the world, chiefly in the tropics. It is in this context that there is a growing realisation that man may have to depend more and more upon new food resources, what we may broadly classify as 'lesser known plants of food value'. The humid tropics is a repository of a variety of food crops as yet used only by the rural population. This is apart from the rich germ plasm resource of the conventional food crops such as rice, maize and such others.

These lesser known food plants are either obtained from the wild or even cultivated by the farmer in his *jhum* plot. In the Mokokchung district of Nagaland, the Naga tribes use two weedy species known as *Gnetum montanum* and *G. gnemon* as important food sources. In the higher elevation of Meghalaya, the Khasis cultivate at least two wild plants—*Pesilla ocimoides* and *Flemingia vestita,* the latter locally known as 'Sohphlang.' We are currently in the process of quantitatively evaluating these and many others used by different tribes of the Northeast as food source.

Forest farming is considered to have been operating always at a subsistence level. In order to have an objective assessment about it one ought to consider the system as it operated in the past when it was in harmony with the environment, and the working of the system as it operates now under increased population pressure and reduced acreage caused by irreversible damage to site quality. The chief difference between the operation of the system now and then lies in the length of the *jhum* cycle (the length of the fallow period between two successive croppings from the same site).

Figure 2.1

Crop Yield Pattern under Jhum Cycles of 30,10 and 5 Years at Burnihat, Khasi Hills

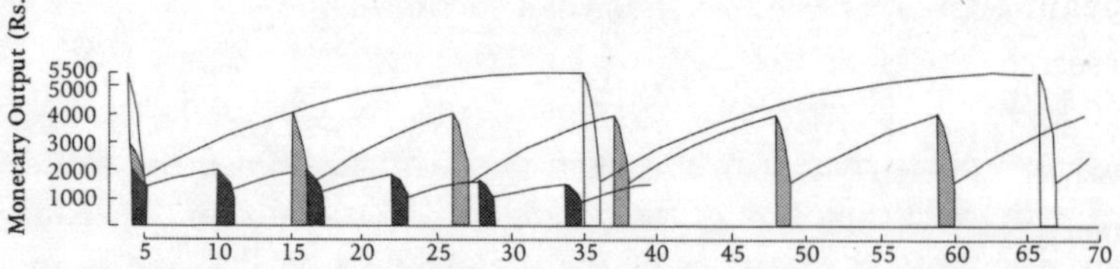

Source: Based on the data of Toky and Ramakrishnan, 1981a.

The yield under *jhum* depends upon the length of the *jhum* cycle (Figure 2.1). The chief function of the fallow period is to recover soil fertility through a natural process as vegetation develops. Cropping results in rapid depletion of soil fertility. The initial phase of vegetation development further depletes soil nutrients. It is only with the release of nutrients as the vegetation or leaf litter is cycled back into the soil does nutrient recovery start. In the Northeastern region a reasonable fallow interval (Ramakrishnan and Toky, 1981; Mishra and Ramakrishnan, 1983b) would be about 10 years. A longer cycle than this would improve economic yield but more than that, it is important for the ecology of the region. A shorter cycle than this would reduce economic yield as the soil would never be able to recover all the nutrients lost during the cropping period.

All the earlier studies on the economics of *jhum* in the Northeast has been confusing as they failed to define the parameters in terms of location of the plots, the *jhum* cycle under consideration and the tribals involved in it. These studies often expressed yield in terms of rice and failed to specify the conversion factor for expressing mixed crop yield in terms of rice. Even inputs such as fertilisers were ignored particularly when *jhum* was shown down in terms of terrace cultivation which has been suggested as a viable alternative, but has failed to find favour with the farmers.

The Agro-Economic Research Centre, Jorhat conducted surveys and showed an average yield of 800-900 kg ha^{-1} in the Garo Hills, Mizoram and Arunachal Pradesh which compared favourably with the average rice yield of 1145 kg $ha^{-1}yr^{-1}$ for the country as a whole for 1971-1972. On the other hand, the rice yield under *jhum* in Tripura was reported to be around 1200 kg ha^{-1} (Misra, 1976). At Burnihat in Meghalaya, the *jhum* rice yield was 853 kg ha^{-1} as compared to 3428 kg ha^{-1} under valley cultivation and 738 kg ha^{-1} under terracing (Sahu, 1978). A more recent report of the Indian Council of Agricultural Research (Borthakur *et al.*, 1978) suggested an amazingly low yield of 190 kg $ha^{-1}$of rice under *jhum* compared to 1860 kg ha^{-1} under terrace.

It is in the above context our studies on comparative yield under *jhum* (Toky and Ramakrishnan, 1981a; Mishra and Ramakrishnan, 1981) become significant. A 5-year cycle (common at present) has been compared with longer cycles of 10 and 30 years (more prevalent in the past) at Burnihat at lower elevations in Meghalaya (Table 2.3). Though terrace cultivation gives as much returns to the farmer as a 10 year *jhum* cycle, a major fraction of the input into the terrace system is in the form of inorganic fertilisers which are expensive and in short supply. A 30 year cycle gives better returns to the farmer but is impractical because a larger land area is required to sustain a 30 year cycle which is just not available in the present context. Therefore, from an economic viewpoint, a cycle length of 10 years could be more feasible than a 30 year cycle.

Table 2.3

Monetary Input-Output (Rs./ha/yr) into Jhum, Terrace and Valley Agro-ecosystems

	Jhum			*Terrace*	*Valley*
	30 Year	*10 Year*	*5 Year*		*Crop I & II*
Input	2616	1830	896	2542 (4544)	4843
Output	5586	3354	1690	3658	5565
Net Gain/Loss	2970	1524	794	1116 (-886)	722
Output/Input	2.13	1.83	1.88	1.43 (0.80)	1.14

Note: In parentheses are values for first year terracing.

Source: Toky and Ramakrishnan, 1981a.

An aspect of the economics of *jhum* that needs a special mention here is that the *jhum* farmer shifts his crop mixture towards perennial and tuber crops under short cycles where the soil fertility is low. Even in the high elevation *jhum* where the soil fertility is generally low under an acid soil and low temperature, the farmer has caught on to potato, a tuber crop that came along with the British. This shift in cropping pattern is often an adaptation by the tribal farmer to maximise yield under low fertility levels in the soil (Ramakrishnan, 1984b). In fact we have come across a variety of cropping patterns even under identical conditions and are currently evaluating the economic implications of a shift in emphasis in crop mixtures even under the same *jhum* cycle.

Energy Efficiencies

There is considerable interest in *jhum*, in the recent past, as it is being held out as a model from the energy efficiency point of view. Compared to an energy output of less than one for every unit energy input into the mechanised agriculture (Steinhart and Steinhart, 1974) and an average output of about 7 for Indian agriculture (Mitchell,

1979), the energy efficiency of *jhum* could be up to about 50 (Table 2.4). Qualitatively, the energy input into *jhum* is labour energy which is provided by the family members and therefore does not come from outside whereas in modern agriculture the energy for fertiliser and farm machinery comes from outside the system. However, considering that the frequency of use of a given plot under 5, 10 and 30 year cycles are very different, for calculating real energy efficiency, one ought to use a factor of 1/5, 1/10 or 1/30. Even from this view point a 10 year cycle is sustainable (Toky and Ramakrishnan, 1982).

Table 2.4

Energy Ratios in Agricultural Systems—Jhum, Terrace and Valley Cultivation

Agricultural System	*Energy (MJ ha^{-1} $year^{-1}$)*		*Output/Input Ration*
	Input	*Output*	
Jhum—30 Year Cycle	1665	56766	34.1
Jhum—10 Year Cycle	1181	56601	47.9
Jhum—5 Year Cycle	510	13858	46.7
Terrace	6509 (8003)	43602	6.7 (5.4)
Valley—I and II Crops	2843	50596	17.8

Note: In parentheses are values for the first year of terracing.

Source: Toky and Ramakrishnan, 1980.

Socio-cultural Aspects

Jhum is often described as a way of life for the tribals. This way of life is imposed by the environment of the humid tropics, particularly because maintenance of soil fertility is possible only through forest regrowth. However the cultural life of the people has had its own evolution centred around *jhum*. Therefore the rich and diverse dance and music forms of the different tribes could be related to varied *jhum* operations. Dance and music form part of minor or major festivals associated with the *jhum* calendar. These festivities are always associated with feasting and drinking of rice beer. Slaughtering of pigs, an animal associated with shifting agriculture all over the world, form an important and essential component of the festivities. Starting with the slash and burn operations through the last harvest of the crop, the festivities associated with the *jhum* system provides a means for ensuring a co-operative effort among the members of the village community.

All festivities relate to propitiating and honouring the key elements of nature—fire, rain, sun, etc. Thus among the Garos, the Wangala festival—the 100 drum dance is performed to propitiate the Sun God at the time of harvest of rice, their staple food. How appropriate indeed it is when the *jhum* system itself is essentially harvesting the sun through the forest and the balanced mixture of crops in the jhum plot!

Starting from the Vedic times, nature worship has been an important aspect of Indian civilisation. Starting with a holistic approach to nature worship, in the present day Hindu society, it has come down to specific trees such as *Pipal* (*Ficus religiosa*) and *Bel* (*Aegle marmelos*).

In more traditional societies such as the tribal societies of the Northeast, the concept of sacred grove is very prevalent. Thus, in the Khasi Hills of Meghalaya at one time each village has had a small patch of forest preserved in a virgin state. It is believed that the deities, representing various elements of nature such as sun, rain, fire, etc. reside in these sacred groves. Besides, the spirits of dead persons who are revered by the community are often said to reside in these forests. Often there is a reigning deity for each of these sacred groves such as 'U Basa' or 'U Ryngkew' for the 'Mawphlang' sacred grove locally called 'Law Lyngdoh'. Such groves also exist in Upper Shillong and at Mawsmai in Cherrapunji. Apart from regular religious functions organised to propitiate the Gods residing in these sacred groves which include sacrificial offerings, any damage done to these forests is compensated only through elaborate ceremonies involving sacrifice of prescribed animals.

In any case, the significance of the concept of sacred grove within each village boundary is two-fold: (i) it speaks of the value system of the tribals who are very close to nature and whose every survival is dependant upon the natural resources around them. Even the uninitiated youngster in a village is thus taught to respect nature from the very beginning through the sacred groves, (ii) through superstitious beliefs, the sacred groves have been an effective method for preserving patches of virgin forests easily accessible to the village community (Boojh and Ramakrishnan, 1983).

Animal Husbandry

The chief animal husbandry practice of the tribals of the North-east is swine husbandry. It is part of the shifting agricultural system in many parts of the world. The main advantage of this linkage between the *jhum* and swine husbandry lies in the fact that it forms an important linkage in the detritus food chain, the animals feeding upon the vegetable waste and food that is unfit for human consumption. The maintenance cost of pigs is minimal.

Figure 2.2

The Energy Flow and Energy Efficiencies through Animal Husbandry Compartment of a Khasi Village at Setthliew

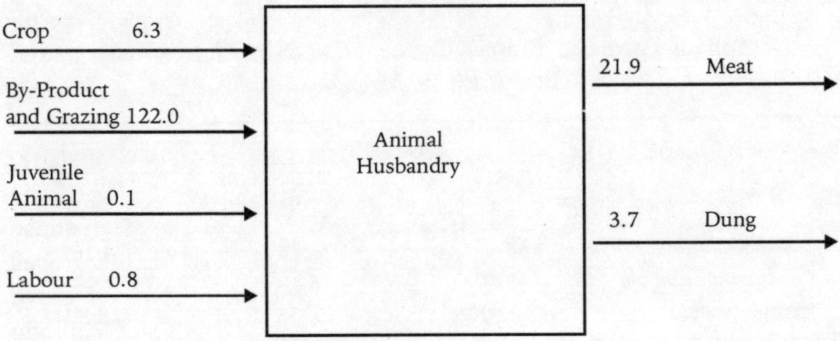

Output : Input Ratios
Meat (+By-product + Grass) = 0.17
Meat (-By-Product + Grass) = 3.04
Meat + Dung = 0.20

Source: Mishra and Ramakrishnan, 1982.

In Figure 2.2 the energy flow diagram of the animal husbandry compartment of a small Khasi village with 12 adults and 8 children at Setthliew near Shillong is shown (Mishra and Ramakrishnan, 1982). Apart from 16 pigs, the village had 9 goats and 20 fowls. Being nearer to a city centre at Shillong, animals other than pigs are also maintained; in more interior regions the animal husbandry system has only pigs or pigs along with fowls. The input into this system is negligible. Grazing and crop by-products are freely arising out of the *jhum* system. Labour is from within the family unit

Pork is the chief source of animal protein to the tribal farmer and a sizeable fraction of the total protein consumed is obtained from this source (Table 2.5). Much of the energy out of this is exported outside the village boundary. About 1/4th of the total annual income of Rs. 103000 generated within this village comes from the animal husbandry unit.

Poultry is another important activity in the tribal village. The indigenous fowls need practically no maintenance, and is not as important an activity as rearing pigs. During festivities which has a link with the *jhum* calendar, slaughter of pigs is a major function. Therefore these animals form part of a system that is ecologically and economically viable and at the same time is well integrated into tribal culture.

Table 2.5

Annual Food and Protein Consumption in a Khasi Village Ecosystem in Meghalaya

Category	*Food*		*Protein*
	Quantity (Kg)	*Energy Equivalent* (MJ)	*Equivalent* (Kg)
Solanum tuberosum	88.96	1288	4.16
Colocasia antiquorum	43.30	629	4.23
Ipomoea batatus	360.00	5965	15.59
Zea mays	342.80	5685	44.02
Oryza sativa	2567.00	42538	213.57
Phaseolus vulgaris	10.78	169	2.55
Cucurbita maxima	28.00	430	6.00
Pork	112.50	8560	93.49
Total		**65264** (67383)	**383.61** (321.20)

Note: Values in parentheses are the standard requirements.

Source: Mishra and Ramakrishnan, 1982.

Distortions in the Relationship between Man and Nature

The rain forest ecosystem of the Northeast has always been subjected to a certain degree of disturbance, since the tribal man has always been dependent upon these for his food, fuel, fodder and timber. These minor disturbances have always maintained the disturbed phase of the ecosystem at a low key that the stability of the system was always maintained. It is only with the increase in population pressure in the recent past, with increasing pressure on the land for food through *jhum*, and larger needs for fuel wood and timber that distortions in the relationship between man and his environment and instability in the ecosystem has become apparent. This has been further accentuated by the large-scale exploitation of forests by the industrial man.

Timber Extraction

A large part of the timber and plywood needs of the country as a whole is being met from the humid tropical forests of the Northeast. Apart from the fact that timber extraction through contractors results in removal of more than the sanctioned quantity of timber from an area, the extraction procedure itself results in much greater damage to the forest ecosystem than envisaged. Until recently, commercial operators have been interested in only a few selected species, often less than 20 out of over 400 species present per hectare. Many of the remaining trees are damaged beyond recovery during extraction. While no comprehensive data are available on the magnitude of damage to natural forests of the North-eastern region, Table 2.6 shows the annual timber extraction from two of the states of Manipur and Tripura. These projections are only indicative of the problem.

Table 2.6

Annual Availability of Forest Products from Manipur and Tripura (Units in $m^3 \times 10^3$, Bamboo in $t \times 10^5$)

Product	*Manipur*	*Tripura*
Saw Timber	10.0	7.1
Plywood	110.0	19.8
Pinewood	23.9	—
Hard Wood for Industry	147.0	—
Pine Wood for Industry	9.1	—
Pulp Wood	—	66.0
Poles	—	1.8
Match Wood	—	1.6
Bamboo	1287	5.5

Source: Ministry of Agriculture (study reports).

Man and Land

Three major needs of the tribal man is met from the land: (i) food, (ii) fuel wood, and (iii) timber. The pressure on land on these counts is related to the population density. The population trends in the Northeastern region (Figure 2.3) suggest that with the exception of Tripura, population has slightly more than doubled in the first 50 years since the turn of the century. In Tripura, during the same period, there was a four-fold increase chiefly due to influx of people from outside. During the subsequent 20 years between 1951-1971, the population all over again doubled. The impact of such rapid increase in population in the Northeast on the rain forest is not difficult to visualise.

Figure 2.3

Population Trends in the Northeastern States of India

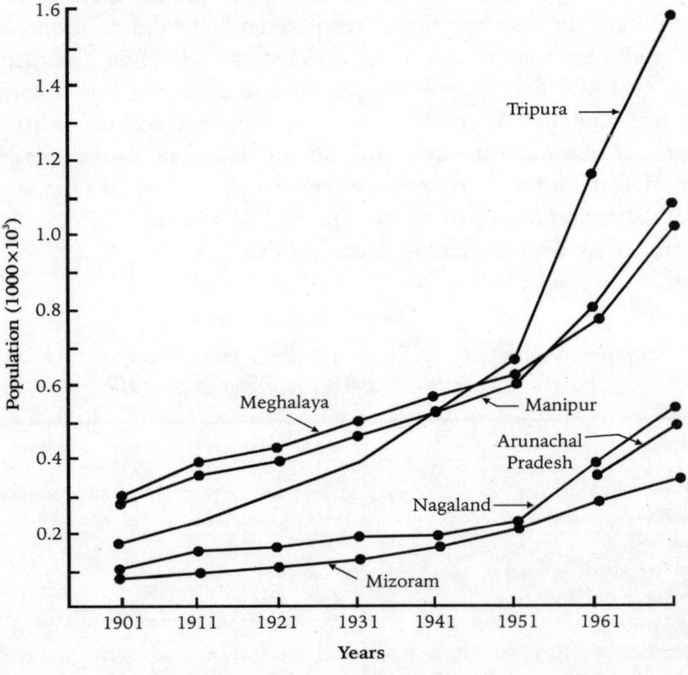

Much of the firewood consumed in the region come from secondary forests; only a small fraction comes from the primary forest.

In India, it has been observed that about 70 per cent of the firewood comes from the peripheral zones of the forest, decreasing rapidly beyond the 10 km zone until there are no extraction beyond 15 km (Myers, 1980). However, the increased population pressure and rapid depletion of forest cover is rapidly changing this situation.

In one of the studies on village ecosystem function (Mishra and Ramakrishnan, 1982), the firewood import from outside the village boundary for a village population of 20 members was estimated as 3060 kg (52455 mega-joules of energy) accounting for about 58 per cent of the total annual consumption. For this 58 per cent import into the village, in the present situation, it is not uncommon to trek a distance of up to 15-20 km. If about 5000 kg of fuel wood is considered to be the average annual consumption by 20 individuals, then the consumption for a total population of 19.58 million in the North-east (according to 1971 census data) would work out to about 489 x 10^7 kg. It may be realised that the population during the last 10 years has gone up by about 30 per cent. Therefore the impact of man on the natural resources just on this account alone is alarming.

Jhum, as discussed earlier, is a major link between the tribal man and his land. Due to rapid increase in population pressure and extensive damage to land due to shortened *jhum* cycle in the past the land is laid barren and the *jhum* cycle has been reduced to a short cycle of 4-5 years or sometimes even less, in most of the areas in the region. The shortened *jhum* cycle is neither ecologically nor economically viable. The economic returns are so low that the farmer is not able to obtain enough for the whole year round and yet he has no options in terms of alternatives. The losses of sediments through run-off water and through percolating water is heavy and more frequent than it would be under longer cycles (Toky and Ramakrishnan, 1981b; Mishra and Ramakrishnan 1983a). The soil fertility, even to start with, is very low compared to that possible under longer cycles and the physical qualities of the soil are very much damaged (Ramakrishnan and Toky, 1981; Mishra and Ramakrishnan, 1983b). The first five years of a fallow developing after cropping of a *jhum* plot consists only of weeds. When a short *jhum* cycle of 4-5 years is imposed again and again on the same site, the fallow gets permanently arrested at the weed stage. This has two consequences: (i) forest cover is totally eliminated from vast tracts of land which now have only a weed cover, and (ii) the weed potential under a short cycle is very high that seriously interferes with economic yield from the *jhum* plot (Saxena and Ramakrishnan, 1984).

Present Forest Cover

National Remote Sensing Agency (1983) has made an estimation of the forest cover in the Northeastern region for 1980-1982 and has contrasted it with the period 1972-1975 (Table 2.7). The present total forest cover for the region is estimated at 48.28 per cent which represents a reduction of 2.81 per cent over the 1972-1975 estimate of 51.09 per cent. Of this, 40.94 per cent is estimated as the closed forest cover with an actual reduction in closed forest area of 14708 km^2 during the last 7-year period. What is reported through the Landsat imagery itself is a high rate of conversion of forest cover. However, I suspect that even this is an overestimate of the forest cover, from an ecologic viewpoint. Thus for, e.g., the Khasi Hills has very little forest cover older than 50-70 years still available. In this high rainfall region, a closed forest cover with a fairly high species diversity would develop within about 30 years after clear felling a plot. In fact, a dense bamboo forest of *Dendrocalamus hamiltonii* in the Khasi Hills of Meghalaya is just about 10-20 years old, developed after clear felling for *jhum* (Toky and Ramakrishnan, 1983). All these would be a 'closed forest' from the point of view of satellite imagery. Ecologically speaking, therefore, further classification of this 'closed forest' is warranted. Fifty years could hardly be considered a reasonable age for a tropical rain forest, as the process of forest

Table 2.7

Landsat Data for Forest Cover in the Northeast

	1972-1975	*1980-1982*	*Change*
Total Area Under Forest Cover in Percentage of Total Geographical Area	51.09%	48.28%	(-) 2.81% Reduction
Categories			
Closed forest	46.72%	40.94%	(-) 5.78% Reduction
Open/Degraded Forest	4.37%	7.34% Degradation	(+) 2.97% Increased

Source: National Remote Sensing Agency, 1983.

development to the mature stage could well run into a few hundred years. Apart from the fact that bamboo forests have economic value, a mixed rain forest of about 40 or 50 years age would have very little to offer from the point of timber yield.

Desertification

Desertification in its broadest sense encompasses the processes through which vast tracts of land are rendered useless through over-exploitation of the natural resources. Apart from that due to aridity in the environment, this could occur due to improper water management resulting in salinity conditions as is happening in the northwestern parts of India in UP, Haryana and Punjab—what are termed as Usar or Khallar soils. Desertification in the Northeast is due to deforestation of fragile forest ecosystems due to various causes discussed earlier. The degraded areas at Mawphlang in the Khasi Hills, a few kilometres away from Shillong which has small patch of luxuriant prime forest in the form of the 'sacred grove' standing out as a small oasis in a vast desertified landscape is a vivid testimony to the rapid deterioration of the ecology of the region upsetting the delicate equilibrium of man of the humid tropics with nature. This process of desertification sometimes may often have a long gestation period of overexploitation of the forest resources or it may happen at a single stroke as it has, perhaps, happened at Cherrapunji sometimes in the distant past. Exceptionally high rainfall, extremely nutrient deficient soils developed on limestone rocks and the extensive network of underground caves (Krantz topography) have been additional factors for this instant desertification at Cherrapunji. In extreme cases of desertification the bare rock is exposed with practically no soil except in the crevices of rocks that would support a few scattered grasses. The more common situation in the region is development of grassy meadows with a mixture of weeds both native and exotic. When such a level of degradation is reached the land is unfit for *jhum*. Such degraded sites at the arrested weed stage will not regenerate a forest cover through natural processes as the germ plasm of trees have been totally eliminated from the vicinity. Artificial regeneration of forest cover here could be only at a great cost which we can ill afford. Perhaps, the immediate strategy should be to check further expansion of the process of desertification in the region. It may be mentioned here that the National Remote Sensing Agency

(1983) data given in Table 2.7 would suggest that in most of the hill states other than Assam the desertified areas range between about 40 to 50 per cent. This evaluation could be a slight overestimate as some allowance needs to be made for valley lands used for wet cultivation of rice.

Man and Nature: Building The Bridge

Modification of Jhum

Traditionally *jhum* with long cycles of 20 years or more, as was common in the past, involved shifting of human settlements from one place to another. In the present context of 4-5 year cycles the village settlements are permanent. The land is collectively owned by the village community under the overall direction and control of the village Headman. If a family is involved in a five year rotational bush fallow agriculture, that family is allotted five plots on payment of a token sum of money. As long as that family is involved in *jhum*, those plots of land remain under its control.

In the above situation it is possible to introduce suitable modifications in the *jhum* system in order to recover the lost soil fertility of the cropping period by suitable plantations of shrubs and trees in the fallow phase. Normally a 5-year cycle is too short for recovering the lost soil fertility. Thus, in one of our studies (Mishra and Ramakrishnan, 1984), we have shown that during a cropping year the *jhum* system would loose about 600 kg of nitrogen per hectare from the soil. In order to replace this lost nutrient a fallow re-growth period of 10 to 15 years would be needed. During a 5-year period only about half of this nutrient lost from the system would be replaced through natural processes. In other words, if a 5-year cycle is imposed continuously on the same site for a 20-year period as was the case in one of our study sites, then the system would lose about 1200 kg of nitrogen from a hectare. In such a *jhum* plot if native legumes which can fix nitrogen in the soil could be introduced along with the natural regrowth soon after the cropping phase, then the recovery of nitrogen fertility could be hastened. These trees and others would also improve the physical qualities of the soil through litter in the soil. This would also cut short the early weed stage during fallow development. Such a biological control would check the uncontrolled take-over of vast tracts of land by weeds such as *Eupatorium* and *Imperata* due to shortened *jhum* cycle as it is happening now. In some parts of Nagaland, a non-legume nitrogen fixer such as alder is part of the *jhum* system. The chief objective here should be to supplement forest regrowth at a faster rate through scientific manipulation.

Jhum as it is practised now is subject to much loss of nutrients through blow-off of ash soon after the burn because of the strong winds during the dry month of April. Subsequently, loss of nutrients through rain water is very heavy before the crop cover is established (Toky and Ramakrishnan, 1981b; Mishra and Ramakrishnan, 1983a). A modification in the *jhum* system that could check to some extent these losses is to have a permanent tree belt around the *jhum* plots. This tree belt could also be judiciously exploited for fuel wood and timber. Bamboo which is used extensively by the rural people for construction of huts and which is a commodity sold out of the village could replace the tree belt. Such a bamboo belt, apart from performing the ecologic functions could also contribute to the economy of the village.

A New Approach to Plantation Economy

Our studies discussed earlier suggest that a 10-year *jhum* cycle is the minimum for making it ecologically and economically viable. Of course, longer the cycle the better it is from an ecologic viewpoint. In order to lengthen the *jhum* cycle to 10 years or more the present 4-5 year cycle, the pressure on the land has to be taken off. This can be done by going for plantation crops such as rubber, tea, or coffee which have been tried successfully on an experimental basis. Horticulture has also a great scope in the Northeastern region. Apart from providing an export-oriented economy, the perennial plant cover would protect the soil more effectively. Annual cereal cropping would necessitate frequent disturbance to the soil and exposure of the bare soil at least for part of the year. Plantation crops are generally considered to be economically viable only as large-scale enterprises. An example of this is the large tea plantations of Upper Assam. However, I do believe that such a large-scale plantation could be in the form of 1 or 2 hectare plots managed by each family of a network of villages in a geographical area with 100 or so families organised on a cooperative basis. Such a cooperative philosophy already exists in the tribal society which only needs to be strengthened further. Large-scale plantations imposed from above, otherwise, would result in virtually reducing the tribal farmer to bonded labour, only adding to his misery (Ramakrishnan, 1984a).

Forest Management

As far as forestry in the region is concerned, the developmental activities have to be, again, multi-pronged. The two important functions of the forestry programme should be: (i) to generate enough fuel wood and timber for local consumption in the villages and (ii) to meet the ever-increasing needs of the urban and the industrial man. While the tree/bamboo belt around *jhum* plots and the tree re-growth in the *jhum* fallows would meet part of the needs of the villagers, small wood lots may have to be created in each village to meet the family needs. These wood lots may have fast growing native trees which could be harvested at regular intervals on a sustained yield basis. Such 1/2 hectare or 1 hectare wood lots may be managed by individual families alongwith their *jhum* and plantation plots.

Cash crops such as black pepper, tuber crops, cardamom and others could form part of an agro-forestry system appropriately integrated along with indigenous or introduced fruit trees or fast growing fuel wood/timber trees. Such a multiple land use developed considering village as the unit of development would meet a variety of needs of the local community for which it is designed and would also provide additional income through export outside the village.

An aspect of forestry which needs to be taken up urgently is the reclamation of desertified areas within and outside the village units. Normally the process of forest development to a mature stage could extend to a period of a few hundred years through a natural process of successional development. Our studies on tree architecture (Ramakrishnan *et al.*, 1982) has opened up the possibility of a condensed succession for relatively quicker development of a natural forest cover. An appropriate mix of architectural designs of trees to exploit different levels of solar radiation ranging from sun to shade conditions could achieve quicker results over a few decades. These theoretical possibilities based on tree growth patterns needs to be developed on the basis of actual field trials. The dependance of the country on the Northeast for plywood and timber would only increase in the future. Further the industrialisation of the Northeastern region itself is to a great extent to be based on forest resources. Thus the demand on bamboo and pulp wood tree species would be very high indeed with the establishment of the already sanctioned giant paper mills. Many more such enterprises may be inevitable on socioeconomic and sociopolitical considerations. All these needs of the industrial man cannot be met from the natural forests which are dwindling at a rapid rate. A well though out mixed forestry plantation programme and reclamation forestry programme as discussed above should be the immediate concern of the governmental agencies. Bamboo forest development and their management needs special attention to meet the needs of the paper industry. While it is easy to be tempted to introduce better known exotics, such as Eucalyptus, extreme restraint is warranted when one is dealing with the fragile ecosystems of the Northeast. The adverse effects of such introductions based on immediate grains may have repercussions in the long term, which may not be foreseeable at this stage. For the humid tropics, the native species (of which we have a variety of choices, about which we have not cared to know enough) would be a safer bet from an ecologic point of view.

Introduction of New Technology

The first step in technological innovations should be with respect to the traditional activities in the village. This would create the necessary confidence and acceptance of totally newer technologies that may come later. There is much scope for innovations in swine husbandry and valley cultivation of rice through better varieties of animals/crops.

However, extreme caution needs to be exercised while introducing economic activities alien to tribal culture. Thus cattle farming which is not a part of tribal culture, but has made incursions with the migrant Nepali population and the plains people like Biharis, could cause environmental damage as has happened through overgrazing in the western Himalayas. Rearing of goats is also a recent phenomenon due to contact of tribals with the outside world. Large-scale introduction of goats could also pose environmental problems through browsing. I emphasise this here because introduction of dairy technology is one of the things often talked about for the tribals.

Low level technology could be for semi-processing of the primary produce. Extraction of plants for lemon grass oil or processing of rubber latex into sheets could be done at the village level or for a cluster of villages. Energy efficient *choolahs* for each family could save much on the consumption of fuel wood. Other possibilities are introduction and support for artisan activities such as blacksmithy, leather processing, etc.

The Philosophy for Development

Tribals by their very nature are independent. Yet they have a rural society on a cooperative basis. The mechanism through which the land is collectively owned by the village community, yet maintaining an incipient family ownership of land for *jhum* is indicative of the fine blend between dependence *versus* independence. The contribution of collective labour when required for heavy operations such as slash and burn and contribution of family labour for all other maintenance operations in *jhum* is yet another example of a reconciliation between these two contrasting social tendencies. Any developmental strategy should take into consideration this independent spirit of the tribal farmer, at the same time fully exploiting the cooperative spirit in a village unit.

The micro-environmental variations are of a great magnitude in the Northeastern region because of the topography. This, is further accentuated by socioeconomic and sociocultural diversities of the people. It is uncommon to have tribal differences over a distance of just a few kilometres. With a large number of tribes of major and minor sorts inhabiting this region of the humid tropics, the developmental needs are different. Each tribal community has its own emphasis and finer variations in village organisation and socio-economic activities based on diverse cultural attitudes. Even within the same tribe, the proximity of the village to urban society or major road network systems have brought about changes due to outside influences. We have been able to show through our, as yet unpublished, studies the manner in which alien communities such as Nepalis and Biharis have brought about changes in village organisation and function. The mutual avoidance for coexistence of migrants with the native population has resulted in diversification in economic activities—an aspect of study by itself is interesting indeed.

With all these micro-environmental differences, no one single developmental solution could be conceived for the region as a whole. Each village or cluster of villages will have to be treated separately. An area development plan needs to be prepared tailor-made to suit local needs. Such a developmental strategy cannot be individual task-oriented, as for e.g., exclusive programmes for piggery, agriculture, forestry or plantations, treated independent of one another. A co-ordinated multi-pronged approach is important, as it should be to make the village system self-sufficient, as far as possible through recycling of resources from one sub-system to another, as for e.g., agriculture and piggery. If this is based on an understanding of the village ecosystem function with which the tribal could identify and understand, then it would ensure his participation. This would then also ensure the kind of diversity in village function with which the tribal farmer is familiar.

Village should be the unit of development, with a broad strategy worked out for a cluster of villages. In this approach, the family should be the focal point. This would ensure peoples' participation and would ensure a kind of development that the people would accept and suited to their needs. The aim should be to develop and polish a value system that people already have, rather than impose from outside a value system that we consider is the best for them. This would ensure harmony between the tribal man and his natural environment, a philosophy which has been the basic tenet of his traditional religious beliefs and the very way of life.

3

Marine Fisheries: Knowledge, Production and Distribution[1]

K.T. THOMSON

Introduction

Traditional production systems of the Indian fishing communities have been undergoing rapid structural transformations during the last few decades, mainly due to the introduction of capital-intensive mechanised technologies. Although these developments have brought in a variety of economic benefits to the nation, the process of modernisation has been criticised for causing economic disparities, resource degradation, environmental degradation and social conflicts (Kurien, 1985; Platteau, 1989; Thomson, 1989; Bavinck, 2001). It is however, believed that an understanding of the social organisation of traditional fishing communities would provide useful directions towards evolving strategies of good governance of these natural resources as these resources had been managed by them locally for centuries. Unfortunately, very few attempts have been made to understand the traditional production systems especially how traditional fishing communities ensured sustainability and equitable sharing of resources among various producer groups. The purpose of this chapter is to highlight how traditional fishing communities of Colachel, socially organised their fishing activities with the knowledge they acquired both from the nature and their fellow producers.

---

1. Extracts from the doctoral thesis of the author titled *Political Economy of Fishing: A Study of an Indigenous Social System in Tamilnadu*, Madras University, 1989.

The Study Area

Colachel is a natural seaport town located about 23 kilometres west of Nagercoil, the district headquarters of Kanyakumari district.[2] About 24 per cent of the population of Colachel belongs to the fishing caste called 'Mukkuva'. The fishing village has a coastal belt of two kilometres with a total population of 9167 in 1996. There were 662 catamarans, 54 canoes and 1100 fishing gears in the village in 1986 (Directorate of Fisheries, 1986a). The social life in the village is centred around the church, which involves in the socio-economic life of the village people in many ways. Apart from performing the spiritual functions, it is directly involved in resolving the conflicts among individual households and acts as a supreme legal institution. The entire village is now divided into six communities by the local church. They are named as the Simon Colony, Onram Number, Irandam number, Moonram number, Nalam number and Maramadi.

The characteristic feature of traditional social systems is the close connection between the physical and social features in terms of their specificities. That production, is primarily in relation with nature is all too evident in economies like that of fishing. Not only fish itself in its free condition but also the natural features like wind, currents, temperature, monsoon and migratory characteristics of fish, exist independent of people and limit people's capacity to dominate nature. This opposition between nature and people is resolved by developing productive forces. This includes using their physical capabilities like using their own hands, developing new instruments, organising the instruments in a productive manner and using their mental capabilities to shape these natural features into their advantage. Production is a social process too and can be understood by analysing property relations and the various political and legal relations. The existence and development of individual private property within the boundaries of

---

2. Colachel was an important port town in the erstwhile Travancore state. Before independence, the port was famous for the export of coir, sugar, and many other primary commodities. It was busy for about eight months in a year. Today, the importance of Colachel as a port town has considerably reduced. Monozite is the only item that is handled through this port now. Ships reach the port during November and February to transport the cargo from the Indian Rare Earth Factory at Manavalakurichi. Although this provided a subsidiary income to the bulk of the population during these months, the major activity in Colachel, even now, is fishing.

communal property is the basic contradiction that produced gradual moments of change in the system

I. TRADITIONAL KNOWLEDGE SYSTEMS OF COASTAL ECOLOGY OF COLACHEL VILLAGE

The ecology of any coastal village comprises of varieties of fish and the marine habitat/environment in which they live. The marine environment consists of monsoon, salinity of water, temperature, aquatic plants, and seabed specificities, nature of wind and currents, etc., which are integral parts of the coastal ecology. In the present section, we shall discuss only a few of these features that are relevant in shaping the labour processes in the fishing economy of Colachel. They are the location of fish in terms of the depth of the sea, their seasonal availability, and the nature of the seabed. These features are important because the evolution of the basic instruments as well as the extent and nature of cooperation depend on them.

Location of Fish

Marine biologists argued that east coast of the Indian subcontinent has a much diverse distribution of fishes compared to its western coastal zone. Since Colachel village lies near the tip of the Indian peninsula, this coastal ecozone was marked by a high degree of species diversity. In 1956, about 19 major varieties of fish were caught in Colachel (Chacko *et al.*, 1960). These species of fish, in general, can be divided into bottom living ones and surface living ones. In scientific terminology, the bottom living species are known as 'demersal' fish and the surface living species as 'pelagic' fish. In 1956, seven varieties of fish caught in Colachel fell into the pelagic category, 12 of them into the demersal category.[3] Since pelagic species are shoaling ones and are highly influenced by the nature of wind and currents, they are caught by using different surface setting nets (Kawasaki; 1985: 133). Demersal species, on the other hand, live at the bottom of the sea, at fishing grounds, locally known as 'madais'. Table 3.1 shows the important *madais* accessible to Colachel fishermen.

---

3. See Figure 3.1 for details.

Table 3.1

Important Fishing Grounds of Colachel Village

Name of the Madai	*Depth in Maar**	*Distance from Shore (in Km)*
Naruva Madai	12	within 4
Vilangu Madai	12	within 4
Puthenthurai Pudicha Madai	12	within 4
Annakallupudicha Madai	12	within 4
Pallipudicha Madai	12	within 4
Mechallilpudicha Madai	20	within 4
Mullur Madai	20	within 7
Cheyyakudi Madai	22	within 8
Puthu Madai	18	within 9

Note: * A Marr is about 1½ to 2 metres approximately.

Source: Based on author's calculations.

The table reveals two important ecological features of fishing in Colachel. First, the fishing grounds where fishermen go for fishing lie well within 10 kilometres from the shore. It means that the area of the communal property, which is accessible to active fishing teams, was determined by the level of productive forces. Secondly, even within this range, the depth of the grounds varies considerably. This means that the location of fish is not the same for all the demersal fish. Given this fact, as we would see subsequently, Colachel fishermen have to combine various elements of the labour process like crafts, gears and human cooperation differently to trap different species of demersal fish.

Seasonal Distribution of Fish in Colachel

Fish is a moving biomass which does not stay permanently in one particular location. Consequently, the availability of individual species of fish in any location is seasonal. We have already noted that different species of fish, in the process of fishing, necessitate the use of different implements, gears and different extent of human cooperation. Thus the seasonal availability of different species calls for varied sets of productive forces to maintain fishing as a viable occupation throughout the year. Let us now see the calendric availability of different species of fish in Colachel in 1956 (Table 3.2).

Based on Table 3.2, we have prepared a Figure (Figure 3.1) to

Table 3.2

Fishing Calendar for Colachel, 1956

Month	*Varieties Available*
January	Sea Bream, Seer, Shark, White Bait, Lobster and Balistes.
February	Seer, Perches, Rock Cod, Horse Mackerel, Tuna and Lobster.
March	Seer, Perches, Sea Bream, Rock Cod and Tuna.
April	White Bait, Lactarius, Shark, Sardine, Pomfret, Perches and Rock Cod.
May	White Bait, Ribbon Fish, Lactarius, Horse Mackerel, Shark and Sardine.
June	Ribbon Fish, Shark, Horse Mackerel, Prawn, Rock Cod and Sardine.
July	Ribbon Fish, Sabre Fish, Shark, Cat Fish, Horse Mackerel, Prawn and Sardine.
August	Sabre Fish, Ribbon Fish, Lactarius, Cat Fish, Shark and Sardine.
September	White Bait, Ribbon Fish, Sabre Fish, Seer, Lactarius and Shark.
October	White bait, Ribbon Fish, Sabre Fish, Seer, Lactarius and Shark.
November	White Bait, Seer, Lobster, Silver Belly and Lactarius.
December	White Bait, Shark, Seer, Lobster, Dossumerai and Perches.

Source: Chacko, Kurien and Sherief (1960).

show the duration of the availability of important pelagic and demersal groups of fish landed in Colachel. The figure shows that out of the 19 varieties of fish landed in Colachel, 15 varieties (ribbon fish, sardine, horse mackerel, tuna, sabre fish, rock cod, lobster, perches, pomfret, prawn, catfish, silver belly, sea bream, balistes and dossumerai) were available not even for six months in a year. The other four varieties (seer, white bait, shark and lactarius) were available from 6-8 months in a year. No species was available throughout the year. The figure also shows that at least 3-8 varieties of fish were available during every month. This shows that, despite the seasonal variations, fishing was possible throughout the year in Colachel.

However, the important feature of the fishing activity is its seasonality. When natural factors like monsoon, wind, currents and the up—welling of planktonic masses, etc. increase the fertility of the sea, more fish will be available near the in-shore fishing spots. As the above factors change, the availability of fish also changes. Consequently, three important seasons can be identified in Colachel. The best season—when fish is available in larger quantities—ranges

Figure 3.1

Seasonality of Important Fishes in Colachel in 1956

Fish Caught	*Months*												*Months*
	J	*F*	*M*	*A*	*M*	*J*	*J*	*A*	*S*	*O*	*N*	*D*	*Available*
Pelagic													
Sardine				×	×	×	×	×					5
Seer	×	×	×						×	×	×	×	7
White Bait	×		×	×	×				×	×	×	×	8
Ribbon Fish					×	×	×	×	×				5
Horse Mackerel		×		×	×	×	×						5
Tuna		×	×										2
Dossumerai												×	1
Demersal													
Sabre Fish						×	×	×	×				4
Rock Cod	×	×	×		×								4
Shark	×		×	×	×	×	×	×	×				8
Lobster	×	×									×	×	4
Perches	×	×	×									×	4
Lactrius			×	×				×	×	×	×		6
Pomfret			×										1
Prawn				×	×								2
Catfish						×	×						2
Silver Belly											×		1
Sea Bream	×	×											2
Balistes	×												1
Number of Fish Varieties Appearing on the Shore during Each Month	8	7	8	6	7	6	6	5	6	3	5	5	

Source: Based on author's calculations.

from April to September. The next three months—October to December—are normal months while the last three months—January to March—are the lean period of the year. Thus knowledge about the specific features of the nature has led to the division of the fishery into various seasons and the consequent socio-economic adaptation of local fishing activities.

Major Instruments of Production

In the previous section, we have seen the important features of the coastal ecology of Colachel. Most of these factors are fixed and exist independent of fishermen. To that extent, the instruments which they used for fishing have evolved in correspondence with these natural parameters. This section provides a detailed description of the important instruments of production in the indigenous social system and also indicates how these instruments evolved in conjunction with the natural features described in the above section. In order to perform fishing operation, fishermen need certain instruments, known as crafts and gears. Crafts are a platform like instrument which enable fishermen to reach the fishing grounds. Gear is an instrument which enables fishermen to trap the fish.

Fishing Crafts

Indigenous non-mechanised fishing crafts in Colachel may be divided into two: *viz.* catamaran and canoe. Evolution of fishing crafts is related to the nature of the sea. The sea in Colachel is rough for about 6-8 months during a year. Waves during this period are very strong making the launching of crafts extremely difficult. Under these circumstances, a craft which is light and easy to launch is essential. Consequently, catamaran[4] evolved as the best suitable seagoing craft in this region. It easily floats over the rough waters and is launched from the shore by cutting even the high waves. Since the craft is an open one, people working on board can easily escape in case of any damage of the craft.[5]

4. Catamaran is the simplest craft made by tying together a number of light rough woods and enable small groups of fishermen to reach the fishing ground. It is, in fact, the most suitable craft to the coastal ecology of this area. The size of the craft is determined by the number of wood used for making the craft. For example, *Cherumarams* are made of tying together only three logs. A four log *maram* is known as *Periamaram* while a five log *maram* is known as *Irukkamaram* of *Thoondilmaram*. The largest *maram* is made of seven logs and is known as *Kulamaram* (Hornell, 1927). Some of these types of catamarans do not exist in Colachel at present.

5. Hornell (1927) has given a detailed account of the fish catching methods of Madras Presidency and indicated their relation to the natural features, especially the roughness of sea. He divided the entire coastal belt into the Telungu Coast the Coromandel Coast, the Palk Bay, the Gulf of Mannar and the West Coast. The fishing crafts used along these coasts are different. For example, in the Coromandel Coast, the major craft is the catamaran while in the Palk Bay, it is the canoe. In the Gulf of Mannar, a combined form of the canoe and the catamaran called the boat catamaran is used for fishing. Accordingly, Hornell named these coasts as the Catamaran Coast, the Dhoni Coast, and the Boat Catamaran Coast.

The catamaran which is normally found in Colachel and nearby villages of the Gulf of Mannar eco-zone is popularly known as 'boat-catamaran'. This is made in such a way that the side logs are placed higher than the upper surface of the central piece giving the catamaran a dish like appearance similar to that of boats. An average catamaran is of 15-20 long, square on one edge. The other end curves into a conical shape. This end rises slightly above the sea level and forms the stem of the catamaran. The working space for hauling, storing fish and for the resting of the crew depends on the size of the *maram*. It is found that the boat catamaran found in Colachel are slightly wider at the back than at the front end (Menon, 1980).

Local fishermen distinguish catamarans by two names: *viz*. the 'chalathadi' and the 'madimaram'. Chalathadi is in fact the smallest Catamaram which can accommodate only a crew of two and is usually used for *thoondil* (hook and line) fishing. *Madimaram* is a bigger catamaram having more space available for working crew and is used in pairs with a bag net locally known as 'thattumadi'. Catamaram is normally used from April to December when the sea is very rough.

By mid-October, the sea becomes relatively calm and fishermen start using cones for fishing as well as loading monazite bags onto the ship. However, the exact number of days for which canoes and catamarams are used, cannot be obtained due to instantaneous changes in the behaviour of the sea. When the sea becomes rough again, with the onset of the southwest monsoon, fishermen replace their canoes and use catamarans.

Two types of canoes are seen in Colachel. The first type called 'dug-out canoe' is made by scooping out wood from a single log. The second type, called the 'plank-built canoe', is made by building its body using wooden planks. Dug-out canoes are not common in Colachel now. The biggest canoe which is found in Colachel—sometimes called 'padagu' or 'masula boat'—runs from 26 to 35 feet long, 5-8 feet wide and 3½ feet deep; it is used for launching shore seines. This canoe is made by joining together planks with coir ropes. The canoe is internally divided into different columns, using planks, and can take a crew of 20.[6] When the huge shore seine is loaded, the

6. See Mathur (1978) for a detailed description of the division of the canoe and corresponding division of labour in the Malabar Coast.

boat can carry a crew of maximum 10 people. During November and February, if at all the sea is calm, a relatively smaller size canoe is used for fishing. This canoe can carry a crew of nine to twelve depending on its size.

Fishing Gears

Crafts enable fishermen to reach the fishing grounds. But the actual act of fishing is done by work teams using certain gears. The basic factor behind the evolution and use of indigenous fishing gears is nature and its specificities. For example, the availability of different species of fish at different depths of the sea necessitates a large number of bottom and surface setting gears in the economy. According to the 1978 fishery census reports, more than 40 varieties of nets are used in Tamil Nadu (Directorate of Fisheries, 1982). Despite a wide variety of gears used for fishing different varieties of fish, it is possible to group these gears into four basic types: (1) seine nets, (2) bag nets, (3) gill/drift nets, and (4) hook and lines.

Seine nets and bag nets are made of cotton. Seine nets, used in Tamil Nadu, are known by various names like 'peria-valai' and 'dara-valai'.[7] The basic feature of this class of nets is the presence of a conical bag at the end of the net to contain fish. The important shore-seine in Colachel is called the 'karamadi' and the bag net is called 'thattumadi'. Gill net, on the other hand, is a wall like net which can be set at various depths using proper weights.[8] Unlike in the bag netting method, in this method fish are caught at their gills, while they try to enter the other side of the wall like net. The most important gill nets used in Colachel are: *sala valai, ayila valai, nethili valai, iral valai, calral valai, vazhi valai* and *vala valai*. *Iral valai* is used by traditional fishermen for catching prawn during the months of June, July and August. *Sala valai, ayila valai* and *nethili valai*—as the names indicate are—used for catching sardine, mackerel and white bait respectively. *Vazhi valai* and *vala valai* are used for catching big fish. *Calral valai* is used for catching lobster. Hooks and lines are generally used for catching big fish in the off-shore and in the deep

7. In Andhra, it is known as the 'alivi' net and in Goa and Karnataka, it is known as the 'rampani' net (Govindan, 1916). The important bag nets used in Tamil Nadu are, 'thuri-valai', 'era-valai' and 'kola-valai' (Hornell, 1927).

8. The major difference between the bag net and a gill net is that while a bag is attached at the end of the bag net, no such bag is attached in the gill/drift net.

sea during normal weather. They are also used at the rocky patches of the sea bed. The important lines are known as the hand line, the trolling line and the long line (Kurien and Sebastian, 1982). Hooks are attached to the lines with baits tied to lure the fish. While attempting to swallow the prey, the fish is caught on the hook.

Cooperation and the Labour Processes

So far we have described certain important natural features and indicated their relation to the evolution of a large variety of instruments of production. Although, 'nature' and instruments are essential components in social production activity, they become a productive force only when they are combined by human labour in the actual labour process. In this sense, cooperation is a productive force. It is important here to quote Marx and Engels (1964:49) "... a certain mode of production, or industrial stage, is always combined with a certain mode of cooperation or social stage, and this mode of cooperation is itself a productive force."

However, nature imposes a number of constraints on the continuous use of different nets and crafts and fishermen do overcome these limits by changing the level of cooperation. For example, the seasonal changes in the availability of different species of fish lead to a change in the use of fishing nets. Similarly, a behavioural change of the sea from rough to calm leads to a change in the use of canoes instead of catamaran. Thus, as the natural features change, people have to change labour processes by changing the level of cooperation. In this section we shall show how human labour combines nature and instruments in the non-mechanised labour processes.

According to the mode of combining nature and instruments of production, four non-mechanised labour processes can be identified. They are listed below:

Name of the Process	*Craft Gear Combination*
Process 1	Plank-built canoe-*Karamadi*
Process 2	Catamarans—*Thattumadi*
Process 3	Catamaran—Gill nets
Process 4	Catamaran—Hook and line

For the sake of convenience, we shall refer to these processes hereafter as *karamadi* fishing, *thattumadi* fishing, gill netting and *thoondil* fishing respectively.

Organisation of Karamadi Fishing

Karamadi fishing is extensively undertaken by fishermen in the Kanyakumari district of Tamil Nadu even today. An ordinary *karamadi* made of cotton/nylon has a length of 1000 to 2000 feet. It is normally operated in early morning in calm water while a shoal of fish is seen near the shore. *Karamadi* is very sensitive to the roughness of the sea. Being a drag net, *karamadi* cannot be operated on the rocky patches of the sea bottom. This conditions the operations of *karamadi*. Before the introduction of mechanisation, *karamadi* was operated from September to June, especially from the Maramadi shore (Figure 3.2). This is because the sea beds of the other communities in the village are rocky. During the monsoon season, *karamadi* could not be operated.

Having discussed how the natural features condition *karamadi* operations, we shall now explain the internal organisation of *karamadi* operations. *Karamadi* operations are technically divided into three phases—launching, pulling and drying the net. *Karamadi* fishing needs the active cooperation of about 60 to 100 labourers. According to the active involvement of labourers in the work process, the *karamadi* group may be divided into two. The 'core group', which consists of 8-10 healthy men, acts as the nucleus of *karamadi* operations. The success of *karamadi* operation lies with this group. This team is responsible for launching *karamadi* into the sea on time. The second group, exclusively used for pulling *karamadi* back to the shore, comprises of men up to the age of 90 and even children of the school-going age.

The whole work is organised under a leader called 'thalaivar' or 'thaleiyali'. Major decisions regarding the operations of the net are taken by the 'thalaivar' in consultation with the members of the core group. Every morning, during the season, the core group reports at the shore and makes arrangements for the launching operation. While the core team pushes the 'padagu' into the sea, members of the second group start gathering in. Those who report first at the shore hold one end of the rope of the net which is taken into the sea by the 'core team'. The 'padagu' makes a circular journey, launches the net and comes back to the shore. By this time, all the members of the team should have reported for the pulling operations. The other end of the rope is taken by this team while the core group takes the 'padagu' back to the shore. The members of the core group join the subsidiary group immediately in the pulling operations. The two pulling teams are expected to keep the mouth of *karamadi* open. The number of labourers required for *karamadi* operations is influenced by the 'neerotams' (current) and wind. The *thalaivar* evaluates these parameters and allocates workers on either side of the net. The net is then slowly pulled towards the shore with the help of the incoming tides. When the net reaches the shore, about 5-8 men jump into the sea and close its mouth. The whole operation lasts for about 2½ to 3½ hours, depending on the nature and strength of the currents, wind, tides and the amount of fish caught inside the net. The entire operations need the active cooperation of about 60 to 100 workers.

Members of the 'core group' gather again on the shore after the fish was auctioned and the nets were spread out for drying. They discuss the next day's strategy by evaluating the current day's performance in comparison with those of the other units. In the mean time, somebody will report the details of the catch in other *karamadis*. This information is also evaluated in order to arrive at the next day's strategy. After making a tentative evaluation of that day's fishing operations, the 'core group' disperses. This process is repeated until the season ends.

Organisation of Thattumadi Fishing

In *karamadi* fishing, most of the workers, except the core team, need not go to inshore waters for fishing operations. In *thattumadi* fishing, the whole fishing team has to go inshore waters for fishing. *Thattumadi* fishing needs the cooperation of 7-8 workers. This means that *thattumadi* unit is smaller than *karamadi* team. The crew works under the leadership of a *thalaivar*, who himself is the owner (or one among the owners). *Thattumadi* fishing needs two catamarans,[9] a net and in total 7-9 active fishermen on the board.

The actual work process of *thattumadi* fishing is controlled by a 'thalaivar' who is responsible for the organisation of the production team. The production team is divided into two groups. Once a big

9. The second largest fishing group on the Coromandel Coast of Tamil Nadu uses either 'mada valai' or 'paindi valai'. In both cases, four catamarans are needed for fishing. *Mada valai* unit consists of four catamarans, a *mada valai* and 14 men, while a *paindi valai* unit is composed of four *marans*, a net and 12 to 14 men. *Thurivalai* operation seen on the Coromandel Coast is similar to the *thattumadi* fishing in Colachel. For details, see: Hornell (1927).

catamaran is loaded with net a team of four fishermen will push the catamaran into the sea. This is then followed by the other team in a second catamaran. The place of fishing is determined after an evaluation of the nature of currents, tides and other related information by the *thalaivar* himself in consultation with the team. On reaching the fishing ground, the team in the big catamaran, hands over a portion of the rope to the second team. After receiving the rope, the second group rows far, while workers in the first catamaran launch the net, trawling starts after sufficient distance is attained between the two catamarans so as to keep the mouth of the *thattumadi* open. The team terminates its fishing operations after catching sufficient fish. The above description shows that active cooperation of two groups is essential for the success of *thattumadi* fishing. *Thattumadi* is used in the rough season of the year from the middle of April to October (Figure 3.2). The net is so designed as to catch all types of fish in inshore waters during these months.

Organisation of Gill Netting

As mentioned earlier, the important gill net that were on use in Colachel during the pre-mechanisation period, were *nethili valai, ayila valai, sala valai, vazhi valai, vala valai, iral valai* and *calral valai*. Since most of the gill nets have a common *modus operandi*, we shall provide a general picture of cooperation in gill netting rather than taking up different types of gill nets for elaborate analysis. Unlike *thattumadi* fishing (which needs two catamarans and a net), gill netting needs only one catamaran. The production unit consists of a single work team with a crew of 2-4 men. Gill nets are used as and when individual species appear in the coastal belt of the village.

Organisation of Thoondil Fishing

Thoondil is used by fishermen in all seasons except rough weather. The production team for *thoondil* fishing consists of a small catamaran (*chalathadi*) and a crew of two to three persons. The team will in no case exceed four fishermen. This shows that the level of cooperation under *thoondil* fishing is lower than other methods

In Table 3.3 we summarise the major features of the different non-mechanised labour processes in Colachel.

Table 3.3

Major Fishing Methods in the Non-mechanised Economy in Colachel

Process No.	Name of Process	Name & No. of Craft	Name of Gear	Fish Caught	No. of Crew
P(1)	*Karamadi* fishing	Padagu (1)	*Karamadi*	All Varieties Near Inshore	50 to100
P(2)	*Thattumadi* fishing	Catamaran (2)	*Thattumadi*	-do-	6 to 7
P(3)	Gill netting	Catamaran (1)	Gill nets	Sardine, Mackerel, White Bait, Ribbon Fish, Cat Fish, Shark, Prawn, Lobster, Seer, etc.	3 to 4
P(4)	*Thoondil* Fishing	Catamaran (1)	*Thoondil*	All Big Fish	2 to 3

Source: Based on author's calculations.

The purpose of such a detailed discussion of the non-mechanised labour processes in the economy is to reveal the dynamics of the work organisations in the village. The discussion so far had brought out the following points. The *karamadi* operation needs the largest fishing group in the indigenous economy. *Thattumadi* unit is smaller than the *karamadi* unit. This is followed by the gill netting unit and the *thoondil* unit respectively. In other words, the intensity of cooperation is the maximum in the first unit and cooperation decreased across the other units.

So far we have discussed how the natural features and the instruments of labour were combined in various labour processes with the help of human cooperation. However, an important point to be noted is that all these processes are not applied simultaneously during a year. The selection of a particular process is dictated by the season and the execution of the process changes as the season changes. In the following section, we will discuss this aspect of the problem.

Seasons and the Natural Selection of Labour Processes

According to a survey of the fishing industry in Kanyakumari in 1956, shore seines (*karamadi*) were operated here during September and June, whereas, *thattumadi* was operated during April and October. Gill nets were operated during August and April and *thoondils,* on all seasons except during the rough monsoon season. A diagrammatic representation of the duration of fishing of important processes is presented in Figure 3.2 below.

Figure 3.2

Duration of Fishing of Major Non-mechanised Labour Processes in Colachel, 1956

	Months											
Process	*Jan.*	*Feb.*	*Mar.*	*Apr.*	*May*	*June*	*July*	*Aug.*	*Sep.*	*Oct.*	*Nov.*	*Dec.*
Karamadi	—	—	—	—	—	—			—	—	—	—
Thattumadi					—	—	—	—	—	—		
Gill Netting	—	—	—	—				—	—	—	—	—
Thoondil	—	—	—	—	—	—				—	—	—

Source: Department of Fisheries, 1958: 106.

This figure shows that none of the labour processes is used throughout the year due to the limitations imposed by nature. The fact that different species of fish cannot be caught by using single type of net and that no single type of labour process be executed throughout the year, implies that communities have to combine any two or more labour processes to engage themselves in fishing throughout the year. But the selection of this combination is complicated due to the availability of a large number of species of fish in the sea and the investment necessary to procure the necessary combinations of processes.

In order to understand how exactly fishermen select these processes during a year, it is necessary to analyse the month-wise distribution of the species of fish available and the corresponding process of extraction in the economy. Table 3.4 shows the distribution of fish and the corresponding processes used for catching them.

Table 3.4

Fishing Cycle and Important Processes of Extraction in Colachel, 1956

Month	*Fish Caught*	*Process of Extraction*
January	Sea Bream, Seer, Shark, White Bait, Lobster and Balistes	*Karamadi*, gill nets and thoondil
February	Tuna, Lobster, Seer, Perches, Rock Cod, Horse Mackerel,	*Karamadi*, gill nets and thoondils
March	Seer, Perches, Sea Bream, Rock Cod and Tuna	*Karamadi*, gill nets and thoondil
April	White Bait, Lactarius, Shark, Pomfret, Perches, Rock Cod and Sardine	*Karamadi, thattumadi*
May	White Bait, Ribbon Fish, Lactarius, Horse Mackerel, Shark and Sardine	*Thattumadi*, gill nets *thoondils* and *karamadi*
June	Ribbon Fish, Shark, Horse Mackerel, Prawn, Rod and Sardine	*Thattumadi*, gill nets and *thoondils*
July	Ribbon Fish, Saber Fish, Shark, Cat Fish, Mackerel, Prawn and Sardine	*Thattumadi*, gill nets and *thoondils*
August	Saber Fish, Ribbon Fish, Shark, Cat Fish, Mackerel, Prawn and Sardine	*Thattumadi*, gill nets and *thoondils*
September	White Bait, Ribbon Fish, Lactarius, Cat Fish, Shark and Sardine	*Karamadi, thattumadi* and *thoondils*
October	White Bait, Lactarius Seer and Saber Fish	*Karamadi*, gill nets and *thoondils*
November	White Bait, Seer, Lobster, Silverbelly	*Karamadi*, gill nets and *thoondils*
December	White Bait, Shark, Seer, Lobster, Dossumeria and perches.	*Karamadi*, gill nets and *thoondils*

Source: Chacko, Kurien, and Sherief (1960).

The distribution of work activities corresponding to the labour processes, as shown in the table confirms that fishing communities in Colachel cannot survive for a year by resorting only to any one of the processes. As seasons change, the processes also change. It is interesting to note that *thattumadi* is the only basic process which can be operated in the rough season of May, June and July. Organisation of this process needs better skills and ability than other fishing units. After the rough rainy season, this unit breaks into different gill netting and *thoondil* units. Fishermen cannot go for *thoondil* fishing due to high tides and wind during these months. Therefore, during this rough season, *thattumadi* emerges as a basic process—the only viable technique. As far gill nets are concerned, they are applied as and when the specific types of fish appear. For example, during the sardine season, fishermen use *sala valai*, when white bait comes; they use *nethili valai* and so on. Consequently, four basic combinations of various processes, *viz.* (i) *karamadi-thattumadi*, (ii) *thattumadi*-gill netting, (iii) *thattumadi-thoondil* and (iv) thoondil-gill netting, emerged as viable combinations of work in Colachel. The above discussion shows that a certain amount of specialisation in any one combination is necessary for the viable and economical organisation or work by the fishing communities in Colachel. It is noted that the selection is generally made from the combinations listed above. These aspects will be discussed again later in the chapter.

So far we have discussed how fishermen in Colachel shaped nature and the instruments of labour to appropriate various fisheries. Fishermen possessed a high degree of ecological knowledge which was used by them for evolving various labour processes. The presence of a high degree of fish species diversity in this eco-region necessitated in the evolution of a variety of craft gear combinations for trapping these different varieties of fish. Seasonal variations in the availability of individual species have also led to different ways of catching them. Consequently, four basic non-mechanised labour processes existed in this economy. It is noted that different levels of cooperation are necessary for the execution of these non-mechanised labour processes. The most important feature of the fishing activity in Colachel is its seasonality. Consequently, fishing communities had to combine two or more processes in order to make a living from fishing. The selection of these processes synchronised perfectly with the seasonal variations and maintained the ecological harmony of the social system.

Communal Property and the Community

The analysis of productive forces, as presented in the previous sections, helps one not only in understanding 'nature', but also enables to establish its connections with the instruments of labour. We have also seen how cooperation equips the communities to overcome the limits imposed by 'nature'. However, when people cooperate, they enter into various social connections among themselves, the most important of which is the production relations. In order to understand production relations, one has to analyse the property connections, because it is property that determines access to basic means of production. In the context of our study, property has two dimensions. The first one relates to the access to various fishing grounds and the second to the ownership of instruments of labour. This section provides an account of the basic production relations that prevailed in Colachel prior to the beginning of the process of mechanisation.

We begin our discussions by examining how the communities enforced their collective claims over a specific fishing territory as communal property, explain the norms for sharing 'communal property' among the members and describe the nature of possible conflicts in the process of sharing resources. We then introduce the nature of the ownership on the instruments of production—nets and crafts—in Colachel. Here we shall indicate the relationship between the communal property on fishing territory and the individual private property on various crafts and gears and shows how community and class were complexly related in the indigenous economy. We shall then identify the various claimants of the social product and show how the product got distributed across them and shows the institutions and mechanisms which ensured the reproduction of the indigenous social system despite the inherent contradiction arising out of the private property component of the property relations.

Communities in Colachel

Communities which depend on marine fish for a living constitute a distinct social formation and have existed in Colachel from time immemorial. These communities settled primarily near the most fertile fishing ground and then gradually moved towards less fertile fishing grounds along the coast. The elders recalled that the first settlement in Colachel village was just opposite to the rocky portion of the sea because it was only from this portion of the shore that fishing crafts (catamaran) can be launched even in times of rough weather. Inhabitants of this settlement together enforced a territorial claim of about two kilometres on the shore and the corresponding inshore water space. The resources were abundant compared to the requirements of the settlement and there was no need for appropriating them fully for meeting the need of the settlement.

Consequently, permission was usually granted to 'outsiders' in the rough season to appropriate village property.

The basic cause for division of the original settlement was primarily related to the ecological features of the original property claim itself. Since the seabed of the original settlement is rocky, beach seines (locally known as *karamadi*) cannot be operated there. The bed is therefore relegated to the specialisation of the hook and line technique. As the knowledge related to the use of *thoondil* technology was the property of the community, and is transferable only to the members of the community, people specialising in one particular technique settled in a particular location. Staying together is also necessary for the viability of group formation. However as the population increased, even within the original settlement, certain 'clusters' of households specialising in a particular technology started going for fishing operations more frequently than others purely on economic grounds. These clusters of the original settlement are locally known as Onram number, Irandam number, Moonram number and Nalam number. The point we are making is that the rocky nature of the sea bottom led to the evolution of *thoondil* technique and that even within this settlement rules of exclusion (the basic feature of their property claims) evolved purely on economic grounds.

Nalam number and a few households close to it had an added reason for making more rigid norms for excluding other clusters. This is related to the ecological difference in the sea bottom. As one moves towards the east from the original settlement, the sea bottom becomes sandy making the operations of the large beach seines possible. This also implies that *thoondil* technology was less productive for the Nalam number and to those Moonram number household staying close to Nalam number. Consequently, their interest was to exclude others from the beach seine fishing spots (*karamadi padus*). Therefore the division of the property of the original settlement into sandy and rocky led to the evolution of different ways of catching fish and accordingly antagonistic relations developed among different group in the process of enforcing territorial claims on different fishing spots.

We have already pointed out that Colachel port used to provide some job opportunities in the cargo loading activities especially in the lean fishing season. Availability of work attracted a large number of fishermen from other villages to Colachel. At least some of these immigrants who were regular workers on cargo loading boats then settled in the village itself leading to its spatial expansion. The pace of this expansion was accelerated by a social practice related to marriage. It was noted that fishermen or women from the village after marriage settle down in the village itself. This is especially true in the case of Colachel women. Similarly, breaking down of joint families and differentiation among fishermen families (either due to marriage or other economic pressures in the initial settlement impoverished many families. Growth of the population and increased rate of differentiation led to the spatial expansion of the village settlement towards east and west. The number is named after the founder president of the Colachel fishermen cooperative society as Simon colony. The settlement at the east of Nalam number is known as Maramadi.

During the early stages of the formation of the Maramadi community, most of the settlers were mere *karamadi* pullers—coolie workers—of the big *karamadi* owners of Nalam number and Moonram number. There are two important reasons for the simple reproduction of labour households in Maramadi. Since there were large number of labour absorbing *karamadis* in Colachel, those who originally came to the village as cargo loading workers could settle in the village itself. The situation aggravated due to the overall increase in the population forcing the impoverished households to move from the initial settlements to Maramadi. Simon colony, on the other hand contains settlers from Onram number and Irandam number communities who have settled there either due to the partition of their families or due to impoverishment.

In short, the Colachel settlement had broken into six communities namely Onram number, Irandum number, Moonram number, Nalam number, Maramadi and Simon colony. These communities had come into existence much before the introduction of the mechanisation programme. These communities together could enforce a territorial claim on about two kilometres along the shore and corresponding inshore water spread. Fishing operations were confined to this area. None of the non-mechanised production units from any of these communities in the village used to go outside this territory during any time of the year.[10]

Rules of Property Access

The question is whether there existed any social norms for sharing the communal property in the village. Our enquiries confirmed that a variety of norms existed in the village for sharing the property. Fishing right was exercised by the local communities at various levels. Fishing instruments were kept within the boundaries of individual communities during normal months of the fishing cycle. Fishing crafts were operated from the respective shore areas of individual communities. Fishing units normally worked on fishing grounds opposite to their shore to catch demersal fishes. Pelagic fishes were caught within their respective boundaries when the necessary water currents 'neerotams' were set. Fishermen know the time and directions of the 'neerotams', the nature and direction of winds and the consequent migration habits of the fish shoals. The calculations for trapping the shoals then depend on an evaluation of the above parameters. An expert fisherman was the one who evaluated these

10. Territoriality refers to a system of informal rules which regulate access to the critical means of production. In many pre-capitalist economic formations property is conceived as a form of territoriality rather than as individual ownership of means of production (Newman, 1983:142). Individual anthro-pological enquiries among fishing communities confirmed that fishing resources are not free-access/common property resources. Several authors have noted that fishing spots are not formally owned: communities could effectively enjoy the rights of property by controlling the secrecy of the fishing grounds and other related information (Anderson, 1972; Forman, 1967; Suster, 1980), or by the exclusive nature of technology known only to them (Cordell, 1974; Lofgren, 1972). Mc Cay (1979: 399) has pointed out that in most societies fishing rights involve control over 'fishing space' and not on the resource itself. In some cases, temporary use rights to 'choice spots' are allocated to the boat that reaches the ground first (Britain, 1979) and in other cases, the boats share 'choice spots' by taking turns. In many fishing communities, fishing territories are defended in various ways to exclude 'outsiders' (Acheson, 1972 and 1979). For example Acheson (1979) has shown that 'Mass Hagan' fishermen have traditionally claimed all the waters within the two kilometres from the island as their fishing area. They do not go for fishing outside their territory at any time of the year nor do they permit others to fish from theirs. Any one attempting to violate their boundary is very apt to meet with the coordinated persistence of all men fishing on the island (Acheson, 1979: 254-55). An important dimension of the problem which emerges from these studies is that the notion of 'property' is specific to an ecological zone and the modes of managing property vary according to the specificities of the ecological features. In the case of out village, territoriality is not so strictly practised. We will show later, that inter-community cooperation is the major community characteristic of the fishing communities in this ecological zone. Similarly the Goan beach seine fishermen on the west coast of India were reported to operate their nets within the well defined village boundaries (Gadgil, 1987:27). For a detailed documentation about the nature of communal rights on the pearl fishing grounds of the Parava fishermen of the Coromandel Coast in South India, see: Development Department (1929:161) and Roche (1984:18).

features and took decisions to trap the fish. Knowledge about these features again, was not an individual private property shown by the fact that this was something which was discussed in the production unit itself while the team prepared for fishing operations. Owners and non-owners could learn how exactly these features were combined in the labour processes. In catching the demersal fish, communities obeyed certain informal norms. Production units from one community launched their nets without enmeshing the nets of other communities. They waited until space was made available for launching their nets. In case the nets got entangled, the total catch was shared among the production units. In addition to these norms the use of different type of nets on the same fishing ground (*madai*) was customarily banned. The rules and customs laid down by these communities were respected and obeyed by all concerned without any compulsion. Violation of these norms was viewed as an offence and whenever such violation took place it was promptly thwarted.

However, the rules on exclusion/territoriality practiced by the Colachel communities were not very rigid. When fishing becomes extremely difficult or impossible during the rainy seasons of the fishing cycle, social sanction was granted to all the village communities (Simon colony, Onram number, Irandam number, Nalam number, and Maramadi) to use the shore space of Moonram number from where launching crafts is easy due to protection offered by rocks. It is also noted that the local communities allowed outsiders' too to use their fishing spots during the rough seasons of the fishing cycle. Even today, communities from Kottilpad, Puthur, Chinnavilai, and Kadiapattinam fish in Colachel fishing grounds during May, June July and August. Communities from these villages migrated to Colachel with their instruments of labour during the rough season in search of livelihood. The decision to grant permission to 'outsiders' to stay in the village and use domestic fishing grounds was purely internal. However, the interests of the local communities were well protected.[11]

11. This tendency is seen in the case of the organisation of the subsidiary activity also. Monazite loading is a subsidiary activity in the village during the lean season of the fishing cycle. Colachel communities have well defined norms for allocating the loading activities among the 'local' and 'outsider' communities. Local communities do not allow 'outsiders' to bring their 'cargo loading *vallams*' (CLV) to the village. *Vallam* launching rights are *vested* with the local fishing communities. However, each *vallam* can employ *coolies* either from local communities or from the 'outsider' community. This means that the four inter-community cooperation is very restrictive and does not include owners of the 'outsider' communities have well defined social norms for property sharing and the right is properly protected as and when required.

Domestic production units got priority in launching nets. This was enforced by a local ruling to keep the fishing instruments of the 'outsiders' behind the instruments of the local communities. This enabled the local communities to start their fishing operations earlier than the 'outsiders' and this ruling was not violated under normal circumstances. 'Outsiders' had to vacate the village as soon as the natural conditions in their villages become favourable for fishing.

Two inferences may be drawn from the above discussion. First, fishing grounds and territories were not freely accessible to all. Local communities in Colachel together used an inshore area corresponding to two kilometres shore as their communal property. However communities did not practice strict territorial rules in order to overcome the limitations of 'nature'. Secondly, inter-community cooperation was the major community characteristic of the fishing population in this eco-region. It is important to note that a social sanction was needed for this inter-community cooperation to become operative. The local church still collects a small amount from the 'outsiders' for the sanction offered to them for fishing in the domestic fishing grounds. This clearly establishes the fact that the local communities in the village have collective rights on the domestic fishing grounds and these rights are legitimised by the highest legal-political authority within the village, namely, the church as an organisation is a decisive factor.

Resource Conflicts

Sharing of the communal property was never a smooth process. Conflicts did arise during the process of sharing. Two kinds of conflicts were particularly noted. In the first type, the local communities of the village were pitched against those from outside the settlement. Whenever necessary, all the communities in the village together used to defend their territorial claims. This obviously means that this village had to enter into an antagonistic relation with the settlements surrounding it. In the past, many such fights occurred between Colachel village and the settlements of Kodimunai in the west and Kottilpadu in the east. These conflicts generally arose from the violation of certain social norms by the fishing teams of these settlements and were settled by the local churches. The decisions and rulings of the local churches were respected and obeyed by all those involved in the disputes.

The second type of conflict normally occurred among the local communities within the village itself. We shall call this as inter-community conflict. Inter-community conflicts in the village normally arose out of disputes in fixing/casting/launching nets in the inshore fishing territories/grounds or in the process of sharing shore for launching *karamadis*. Although territorial rights of each community were respected by others, open clashes had occurred many times among the local communities regarding launching rights. It is interesting to note that these conflicts were immediately dissolved by the intervention of the local church.

Ownership of the Instruments of Labour

In the previous section we have seen that the access to the fishing space was open to all who belonged to the native communities during the whole year and to some outsiders also, during the rough season of the fishing cycle. Individual members had access to the communal property only as members of any one of the communities. In this sense, inter-community cooperation provided only a social sanction to all those actual and potential asset owners within the community to appropriate the communal property. However, the actual capacity of an individual or a household to appropriate the resource depended on nets and crafts at his or its disposal. The minimum condition for an individual/household in a community to set a labour process in operation was that it should own at least a catamaran and a net. This gave him/it the status of an owner. Since the modes of distribution were biased in favour of the owner of instruments, those who did not own any of the instruments could join only as 'coolie labourers' in the production units of the owners.

Differential Ownership

An individual household should own at least two labour processes to engage itself in fishing throughout a year. Table 3.5 shows the cost of acquiring important labour processes for each community as in 1956. This table reveals many interesting dimensions of the social organisation of fishing in the village. The division of the village into two distinct groups is clearly seen from the type of specialisation evolved and adopted over time by different communities in the village. Simon colony, Onram number, Irandam number and a portion of

Moonram number were settled on the shore near the rocky portion of the bottom of the sea. They specialised in a *thattumadi-thoondil* combination or in a *thattumadi* and gill nets combination.

Table 3.5

Cost of Acquiring Nets and Craft Combinations in Colachel Village in 1956

Name of Community	*Combination of Processes*	*Cost Per Combination in Rs.*
Simon Colony	P(4,2); P(4,3)	3100; 3200
Onram Number	P(4,2); P(4,3)	3100; 3200
Irandam Number	P(4,2); P(4,3)	3100; 3200
Moonram Number	P(4,2); P(4,3) P(2,3); P(1,2)	3100; 3200 3000; 5000-8000
Nalam Number	P(2,3); P(1,2)	3000; 5100-8000
Maramadi	P(1,2); P(2,3)	8000; 5100

Note: The numbers in parentheses indicate the non-mechanised labour processes in Colachel as described in Table 3.3. For example P(4, 2) refers to a *thoondil-thattumadi* combination while P(4, 3) refers to a *thoondil* hill nets combination. Similarly, P(1, 2) refers to a *karamadi-thattumadi* combination and P(2, 3) is a *thattumadi*-gill net combination.

Source: Based on author's calculations.

Nalam number, Maramadi and a portion of the Moonram number on the other hand were specialising in *karamadi-thattumadi* combination or in the *thattumadi*-gill nets combination. However, due to the high levels of investment involved in acquiring these combinations, not all households could invest in all the instruments of production. This, in fact led to the differentiation of the community into various classes. For example, to acquire a *karamadi-thattumadi* combination i.e. P(1,2) a household had to invest Rs. 8000 in 1956. The cost of owning a *thattumadi*-gill net combination i.e. P(2,3) was Rs. 3000 to Rs. 5100. Similarly P(4,3) cost Rs. 3200 While P(2,4) cost Rs. 3100. Investment decision of individual households was obviously constrained by this cost factor.

Since the investment for a *karamadi-thattumadi* combination was much higher than that of the other combinations; very few households in the village could invest on this combination. Consequently, there were only a limited number of *karamadis* in the village. Investment on a *karamadi-thattumadi* combination was made by the richest households in the Moonram number and Nalam number communities. The other households invested on other processes also. An important aspect of this investment was that the local community's investments were very much consistent with the respective gear specialisation. Many households in Onram number, Irandam number, Moonram number invested on the inexpensive combination P(2,4) or P(3,4)—and became owners. Only a few households in Simon colony and Maramadi could invest on fishing crafts and gears. Most of them were either *karamadi* pullers or pure *coolie* labourers. Households which could not invest in any of the combinations, invested on individual processes like a gill net or a *thoondil* or a *thattumadi* and a catamaran. This means that these households could organise fishing (as owners) only during that season when the individual processes at their control could be employed. During other months, they had to join as *coolie* labourers in other production units. People who did not own any of the non- mechanised labour processes were pure *coolies*. They usually worked for a share in the production units of the owners of their respective communities. The incidence of these labourers was very high in Maramadi and Simon colony, and the other communities also had many labour households.

Let us now discuss the type of ownership that existed in the non-mechanised economy. During our enquiry we found joint partnership, family proprietorship and sole ownership to be the important forms of ownership in the village. In the case of *karamadi*, joint partnership and family proprietorship were the two important forms.[12] In the case of *thattumadi*, the major form of ownership was family proprietorship.

12. The available secondary information also confirms out findings. Based on a detailed survey on the economic conditions of fishermen in the east and west coasts of the Madras Presidency, Govindan (1916) reported: "To acquire an 'alivi net' (shore seine) and a boat costing Rs.1000 in 1915, in Kanapapapeta, some 30 fishermen enter into joint partnership and one among them is selected as the headman. He then goes to various money lending persons and obtains from them the necessary money for acquiring an 'alivi net'. In Uppda (in the Godavari delta of Andhra Pradesh) the 'alivi net' is owned by a joint group of fishermen; the headman of the group contributes the central piece of the net as well as the boat rope and other tackle; each of the men contributes the side pieces of equal value" (p.130). In Malpa I, (West Coast) a 'rampani' net (shore-seine) is operated on a cooperative basis i.e. "each man brings three or four pieces and also contributes his daily labour" (p.46). Vijayan and Kurien (1980: 2-3) have shown that this "Collaborative Community ownership of the *rampani* nets was replaced later by a company set up where the net was used by a small group or even by an individual family. However, it was generally found that *karamadi* owners were economically better off than others in the village.

Thoondil units were either family property or individual (sole) property.

Social Hierarchy

The above discussion reveals the nature of rural classes in the fishing economy. According to the capacity of individual households to invest on a combination of non-mechanised labour processes the following classes (the rich fishermen, the middle fishermen, the poor fishermen and the *coolie* fishermen) could be identified in Colachel village. *Karamadi* owners were the local elites. This was so not only because of their economic superiority over the other asset owners but also due to their ability to control a large number of *coolie* fishermen in the village. They never hired out their labour to other production units. The rate of surplus appropriation was higher in *karamadi* fishing than in other units.[13]

The second class consists of households who had direct access to the communal property throughout the year by owning a proper combination of instruments like *thattumadi*-gill nets, *thattumadi*-thoondils or *thattumadi*-gill nets-*thoondil* combinations. They never hired out their labour; but hired in enough labour in order to operate their production units round the year. We call them the 'middle fishermen'.

The third group (class) consists of fishermen who had only a partial access to the communal property because of their inability to own the necessary combinations for the further appropriation of communal property. They usually owned instruments necessary for organising only one process. We call them the poor fishermen. They had direct access to the communal property only during those season they hired in labour to operate their production units. When the season changes, they hired out their labour because they did not own the necessary gears for organising a fishing operation of their own. Majority of the fishermen in Colachel belonged to this category.

Finally we have another group (class) of people who did not own any instruments. They obviously had to join as *coolie* labourers in other production units in order to make a living. We call this class of fishermen 'the coolie fishermen'. Needless to say, this class of

13. As can be seen from Table 3.6, the *karamadi* owner gets a share 25 times higher than the *coolie* labourer.

fishermen had to hire out their labour throughout the year in order to make a living. It is noted that they work in all the processes and in the cargo loading activities also. Table 3.6 below summarises the basic classes in the non-mechanised fishing economy of Colachel.

Table 3.6

Stratification of Rural Classes in Colachel in 1956

Class	*Ownership of Assets*	*Nature of Labour Absorption*
Rich Fishermen	P(1,2) or P(1,2,3)+CLV*	Hire in labour
Middle Fishermen	P(2,3) or P(2,3,4) P(2,4)	Hire in labour
Poor Fishermen	P(2) or P(3) or P(4) or P(3,4)	Hire out partly
Coolie Fishermen	P(00) No assets	Hire out fully round the year

Note: * CLV is cargo loading *vallams*.

Source: Based on author's calculations.

Cooperation, Hierarchy and Economic Organisation of Work in Colachel

In the last two sections, we discussed two important connections under which fishing was organised in Colachel. These are the essential conditions for the active cooperation of people in the labour processes. However, "as a general rule, labourers cannot cooperate without being brought together; their assemblage in one place is a necessary condition of their cooperation" (Marx, 1984: 312). In the pre-capitalist, fishing economy, this was the responsibility of those who owned instruments of labour. In this section, we shall discuss how the owners of the means of production brought the labourers together in different labour processes in the non-mechanised economy. While discussing this problem, we concentrate mainly on the modes of labour absorption and the hierarchy of organising the labourers. The role of a directing authority and the modes of controlling labour are highlighted.

As mentioned in section IV (a) above, this was most labour intensive fishing organisation in the indigenous economy. The crew

14. In other places also, recruitment of crew for fishing operations was based on kinship relation. See, Acheson, (1981: 279-280).

was selected on the basis of kinship relations.[14] The immediate relatives of the owners who did not own any instruments obviously were the first choice. Relatives staying in other villages who could regularly participate in *karamadi* operations also got preference. The second preference was given to those who belong to the community of the owner himself. Finally those who were from outside the community were also considered for recruitment.

After recruiting the entire labour for *karamadi* fishing, the owner then organised them under the directing authority of a 'thalaivar' or 'thaleiyali'. In Colachel, it was found that the thalaivar was either the owner or one of the close relatives of the owner. He employed a small group of 8 or 10 men—mostly relatives—to launch the net into the sea. This team was known as the core team and acted as the nucleus of the entire fishing operations. The remaining labourers were mere *karamadi* pullers and were not involved in any way in the decision making process of the fishing operations.

After ordering the entire fishing team into different strata as a first step to maintain an internal order in the organisation, the immediate task of the team was to acquire the necessary shore right for launching the *karamadi*. In Colachel, acquiring a shore space for launching *karamadi* was competitive because the number of *karamadi* grounds ('padu') in the village was less than the actual number of *karamadis*. There are only three 'padus' located in front of the Maramadi community shore and therefore *karamadi* could be launched only from the Maramadai shore. There were about 20 *karamadis* in the village before mechanisation; in all these nets the nature of hierarchy was as shown above. Out of the 20 *karamadis* in the village in 1956, two *madis* were owned by Moonram number community and the remaining by Nalam number. The other communities did not own any *karamadi*. Three nets were simultaneously launched to cover the three *padus*. The shore area was generally reserved for the group which pushes the 'padagu' first towards a particular spot (*padu*) on the shore. As soon as the first batch finished launching operations and starts pulling the net towards the shore, the second batch could start their operations. This was done carefully by the respective core groups without enmeshing the nets already launched.

Thattumadi fishing team comprised members of the family, relatives and *coolies* from the owners' community. During the season, a large number of *thattumadis* go to the sea. This situation led to a high demand for labour in the village. Since there was no uncertainty regarding the availability of fish in the sea during this season, no owner would risk missing a single working day. In order to ensure the stability of the fishing team, money was advanced to the *coolies*. It was insisted that those who got money as advance, should work with the owner for the period during which the net was in operation. The entire team was divided into two groups and was controlled by a leader called the *thalaivar*.

Gill netting and *thoondil* fishing units involved relatively smaller groups and were managed by the owners themselves. The owner works with the *coolies* and shares the product according to accepted norms.

The above discussions show that kinship and territoriality in labour absorption were methods employed by the owners of the means of production to recruit labour force for organising different labour processes.

Distribution of the Social Product

Having discussed the nature of production relations in the non-mechanised fishing economy of Colachel, we now turn to the distribution of the social product therein.

Major Claimants

Before entering into the discussion of the modes of distribution of the social product, we have to mention the major claimants of the social product. We have identified four major claimants of the social product, *viz.* the *elakaran*, the local church, the owner and the *coolie* labourer.

The *Elakaran*

'Elakaran' is an intermediary between the actual producer and the merchant. The involvement of *elakaran* as an intermediary in the process of exchange is necessitated by the uncertainty in transactions between the direct producer and the buyer. He is the leading financier in the village. Fishermen borrow money from the *elakaran* either for meeting their subsistence requirement during the lean season or for replacing their capital equipments during busy with an informal contractual obligation to sell fish through him. Traditional fishermen do not see their relationship with the *elakaran* as exploitative; instead it was often visualised as a patron-client relationship (Acheson, 1981; Stirrat, 1974). The 'elakaran' auctions the fish landed on the shore by individual production units and consequently links together producers and buyers. He collects the auction money from the merchant and hands it over to the owner of the production unit.

There were about 20 *elakarans* in the village in 1956. Auction rights of a particular production unit were taken by an *elakaran* by advancing money. The auction rights were shared by these intermediaries according to their capacity to advance money to the owners. If the owner had taken advance, a commission of five per cent of the sale value was deducted by the *elakaran* from the total sales proceeds. Even if the owner had not taken any advance, the auction was done through the *elakaran*. In this case the *elakaran's* commission was only three per cent of the total sales proceeds. As a normal practice, the *elakaran* deducted the commission before settling the account with the net owner.

The Local Church

The second claimant on the social product was the local church. Periodic collection of money from the production units was an important feature of this organisation. We shall now explain how the church extracted money from the production units. Money was collected for festivals and for the creation of common goods and services like school buildings, water tanks, market places and common wells. Contribution to the church funds is not voluntary, although it is claimed to be so. It is siphoned off from the production units as and when required, using the 'elakaran' system.

When money is needed for any specific purpose, the priest announces the need in the church and requests everyone to cooperate with him. Collection of this amount is the responsibility of the 'Kariastans'[15] who are either the *Karamadi* owners or their close relatives. The total amount to be mobilised is divided among the communities proportionate to their relative economic conditions. The responsibility to collect this money rests with 'Koorukaran'. 'Koor' responsibility normally vests with the local merchant or

15. *Kariastan* is a lay-leader who helps the parish priest in running the day-to-day administration of the village.

karamadi owners. *Koorukaran* then prepares a list of asset owners and divides the total amount to be collected among them. Rates are fixed separately for *karamadi, thattumadi,* gill nets and *thoondil* units. He then approaches the 'elakarans' and requests them to collect the amount from each production unit. The *elakarans*, in turn, divide the amount into easy instalments and deduct it from the daily catch. Thus, one can see that church enforces its claim on the social product by legitimising the 'elakaran system'. In this way the money collected by the local church is the contribution of all members of the community. However, an important point to be noted is that this money is used mainly for the creation of common goods and services, and thus, the benefits flow back to each and every member of the community in the village.

The Owners

After deducting the commission and the 'voluntary' contribution to the church, the 'elakaran' will hand over the balance to the *thalaivar*/owner of the production unit. This money is then divided among those who participate in the actual fishing operation. It is noted that mode of distribution of the sale value varies from process to process. In certain operation capital gets a share equal to that of labour (*thattumadi* gill net and *thoondil* units), but increases where the capital investments is higher, as in the case of *karamadi*. The owner's share may rise accordingly. In most labour processes, the owner works with the fishing team and hence is eligible for an additional share equal to that of an ordinary worker.

The Non-owners/*Coolies*

The most important aspect of the organisation of labour in Colachel was that production units were organised on the basis of share system. Pure wage forms were not usually found. It is argued that the existence of the share system in the pre-capitalist fishing economy is the reflection of the desire of the community to share among themselves the benefits/losses flowing from unusual fluctuation of the fishing activity. The share system increases the motivation of the crew by making them feel that they are the owners of the production unit (Acheson, 1981). However, in all the non-mechanised labour process, differential modes of sharing exist. The owner rewards individual skills by paying an additional share. In the next section we shall show the exact modes of sharing the social product in the economy.

The Sharing Process

The mode of distribution of the social product varies from process to process.

Sharing under *Karamadi*

Among the four basic non-mechanised processes, the most unequal mode of distribution of the social product was seen in *karamadis*. It was reported that *karamadi* operations in general were organised under the authority of the owner himself. If he is physically weak to go the sea, he authorises one of his close relatives as the *thalaivar*. If the owner works with fishing team, he is customarily eligible for an additional share from the said product. Table 3.7 below shows the major heads of sharing the sale value under *karamadi*.

Table 3.7

Norms of Produce Sharing under Karamadi

Items	*Rs.*
Total Catch	100
Less	
Deduction by Merchant	7
Church Contribution	5
Commission to the *Elakaran*	5 (3 if not tied)
Pulling the *Vallam*	8.25
Launching the Net	50.00*
Thalaivar for Keeping Accounts	1
Liquor	2
Barber	1½ **
Total Deductions	30.25
Balance	69.75
Owner's Share 1/3rd	23.25
Share of the Labourers (for 50 Persons)	46.50

Note: * Those who launch the net are paid Rs. 50 whether there is any catch or not. The advance later adjusted when the catch is good.

** The barber cuts the hair and performs some rituals in case of a death in the village.

Source: Based on author's calculations.

This table shows the extent of inequality in the sharing mechanism under *karamadi*. A *coolie* labourer got only Rs. 0.93 for every 100 rupee worth of fish landed. The owner of the net got Rs. 23.25, the *thalaivar* got Rs. 3.00 and the member of the core group got Rs. 2.00. Apart from this they also got Rs. 6.25 for launching operation. This means that the owner's share was 23 times higher than the coolie's share. The *thalaivar's* share was 10 times higher while the share of a member of the core-group was about 9 times higher than the coolie's share. The table also reveals that the reward to the participants in the production process was proportional to hierarchical status.

Sharing under *Thattumadi*

The mode of distribution of produce under 'thattumadi' was much more equal than under *karamadi* fishing. In a *thattumadi* group of seven members, the produce was divided into eight. Each participant got a share and the remaining one share went to the owner of the net. This pattern of distribution shows that a *thattumadi* was profitable (viable) if and only if it was owned and operated by the members of a family from which at least two or three men could actively participate in the actual work process. Our enquiry revealed that in many cases, irrespective of the communities, 'Thattumadi' was operated as a family enterprise.[16]

Sharing under Gill Nets and *Thoondil*

The pattern of distribution under gill nets and hook and lines was similar to that of *thattumadi* sharing. In a three member gill netting team the produce was shared into four equal parts. Three shares go to the workers. The owner got an additional share for his instruments. In a two member *thoondil* team the produce was divided into three. Two shares went to the labourers while one to the asset owner.

Evolution and Diffusion of Conflicts

The nature of distribution of produce between owners and workers in different processes shows that a non-owner in *thattumadi*, gill-net

16. No family was reported to rent out thattumadi nets. It is interesting to note that since majority of the workers in *thattumadi* nets were from one family, it could easily invest on mechanised boats.

and *thoondil* units got better from the produce than *karamadi coolie* labourer. This means that *karamadi coolie* labourers belong to the lowest strata of village population. Their absolute standards of living were also very low as there were no opportunities to earn additional income other than *karmadi* pulling. This certainly would lead to moments of frictions between *karamadi* owners, the local elites, and the *karamadi coolies*. Thus the distribution of social product under *karamadi* was the prime factor responsible for the sharpening of class antagonism in the system. Conversely, the other processes contributed little towards this process.

Anyhow this class antagonism had never been so sharp because of the existence of various socio-economic checks. Let us explain these socio-economic factors in some details. First, most of the labour processes, except the *karmadi* absorbed less labour. These production units were profitable only when they were owned and operated as family enterprises. We found the major form of ownership under *thattumadi*, gill net and *thoondil* units to be family ownership. As argued earlier, preference for job was given to relatives who did not own any instruments. Secondly, territoriality in labour absorption was strictly practiced by all communities not only to make the production unit economically viable but also to avoid unnecessary 'groupism' and inter-community conflicts. In short, family ownership, kinship, territoriality in labour absorption and membership of the church acted as preventing the growth of class antagonism in the community.

Apart from these checks, the existence of a *thalaivar* system in *Karamadi* enabled the owners to foresee the evaluation of antagonistic relations. Consequently it was possible for them to remove the potentially troublesome labourers from fishing operations. The core group had been always loyal to the masters due to its peculiar composition of relatives and/or family members. The consumption and contingency expenses of the core group were fully met by the owner by paying them more from the produce, helping them in times jobs in the cargo loading activities during the lean seasons. Above all the economic and political power of the owners and the community feeling diffused the growth of class antagonism in the economy.

Moreover, the *karamadi* owners regularly resort to physical violence to control the militant coolie workers.

Other Economic Relations

Apart from these social arrangements for the diffusion of the socio economic crisis, the communities had evolved their own internal mechanisms to prevent the total breakdown of the system completely. In order to overcome the impact of seasonality and other ecological destabilising factors, the communities depended/evolved three important survival mechanisms like extensive borrowing from the *elakarans*/money lenders/merchants for replacing instruments and for meeting the daily consumption needs in the lean season and through a voluntary cooperative system known as 'kootal' system which helped the fishermen endowed with insufficient gears and nets to combine their resources and fish throughout the year.

Elakaran System and Availability of Credit/Loans in Colachel

We have already pointed out that the church had to legitimise the *elakaran* system in order to collect money from production units. An important function performed by the *elakaran* system was the supply of small amounts of money to the middle and poor fishermen, mainly for replacing the torn/damaged nets. The amount varied from Rs.100 to Rs.300. All the production units had borrowed money from one or the other *elakarans*. Many *elakarans* combined the auctioning activity with money lending and trading. Consequently, different types of advancing existed in Colachel. For example money advanced for getting auction rights did not carry any interest. If the owner of the net had borrowed money, the *elakaran* deducted five per cent of the catch value as his commission. In case the net owner did not borrow, the commission was only three per cent. Two per cent went back to the owner of net. Secondly, the middle and poor fishermen also had borrowed money for meeting consumption needs and for expenses connected to some social functions like marriage, baptism, and deaths. For this type of advances, the *elakarans*/traders/merchants charged an interest of 36 per cent to 60 per cent according to the informal relations he had with the debtor. Many households in the village borrowed money for giving bride wealth, for constructing houses, and for other expenses. The point to be emphasised is that, despite the exploitative nature of such advances, fishermen did borrow money from these people for meeting their subsistence needs.[17]

'Kootaly' System

'Kootaly' system was a particular system of group formation popular among the poor gill fishermen household who did not have sufficient resources to purchase all the fishing nets needed to organise fishing round the year. Such households used to avoid borrowing from and evolve a cooperative arrangement which facilitates fishing possible round the year. The mechanism works as follows. Consider a *Thattumadi* owner. he can fish with a *Thattumadi* for six months. Once the season is over, he searches for another partner who did not own a catamaram but owns a *nethili valai* or a *sala valai* or any such net and makes him the 'kootaly'. While sharing the produce, he was given a proper reward for owning the net. As soon as the *nethili* season is over, the *nethil valai* owner becomes the 'kootaly' with the catamaram owner. This process is continued until the entire season is over. This system enabled many households to earn a livelihood.

---

17. The available secondary information also confirms this point. Govindan (1916:134) has reported that in Bhimarpalm village, (east coast) the 'jonkers' advanced money to the actual seagoing castes called the 'pattapus' and secured their fish at a pre-arranged rate. In Cannaore, for example, Govindan (1916: 53) again found: "A couple of boats with a full complement of various kinds of nets and advances made for the crew, costs Rs.1500 to 3000. An owner after investing so much may, owing to the failure of season, have to borrow money from the capitalist. For every 200 rupees thus borrowed, they give to the lender a sum equal to the earnings of one crew. Though no interest was charged, if the season is not good, the amount borrowed will double in a couple of years". In Quilandy, "As a rule, fishermen are indebted to Mappila merchant curers who advance money on condition of getting fish at 10 to 20 per cent less than the prevailing rates" (Govindan 1916: 57). In Tellichery, most of the boats were controlled by merchants (Govindan 1916: 54). In Adirampattinam, the producers borrowed money from the merchants, were forced to sell the product at a rate of 25 per cent lower than the current market rates" (Govindan 1916: 137). The nature of exploitation through such loans in Tanur was made clear when he wrote: "During the monsoon months, when they can not go out fishing, they purchase from the Mapila merchants rice and other provisions on credit at 50 per cent or more, over and above the market rate. They execute a document giving their boats and dwelling houses as security and agree to liquidate the debt within six months; they must pay the amount and interest thereon in a lump sum and no installment will be received. If the amount is not paid in time, they are liable to an enhanced rate of interest as penalty. The fishermen can never get together the amount in a lump sum so that the original amount multiplies itself very quickly and repayment becomes more and more difficult till at last they are dragged into court and their property sold" (*ibid.*: 58-59).

Conclusion

In this chapter we attempted to explain the nature of traditional ecological knowledge systems, property relations and the consequent modes of distribution of social product of the *mukkuva* fisherfolk of Colachel in Southern Tamil Nadu. We argued that *mukkuva* fishermen possessed a high degree of ecological knowledge which was used by them for evolving various labour processes. The presence of a high degree of fish species diversity in this eco-region necessitated in the evolution of a variety of craft gear combinations for trapping these different varieties of fish. Seasonal variations in the availability of individual species have also led to different ways of catching them. Fishing was organised within the limits of the local bio/ecological specificities which ensured the necessary biological diversity and sustainability.

We also noted that community was a pre-condition for sustainable fishing. There were (and still are) six communities in the village. Individual fishermen had access to the resource only as members of any one of these communities. Village communities had well defined social norms for sharing the communal property among them. This included, keeping the finishing instruments in front of the respective shore boundaries, fishing on the grounds, territories opposite to their shore, waiting until one fishing team vacates the ground, casting nets without entangling nets already launched and by sharing the knowledge related to the day to day fishing operations. These social norms were normally respected by all the members of the community. Violation of these rules was an offence to the authority and was checked immediately.

Apart from sharing the property within the members of the village communities, permission was normally given to 'outsiders' to use domestic fishing grounds during the rough season of the fishing cycle. This permission was given without charging any rent for using their property, and to be seen as a social responsibility of the domestic communities to the uncertainties caused by the specific features of the eco-region. This clearly shows that fishing grounds were not accessible freely to any potential outsider. Property rights were respected by local and 'outsider' communities and whenever necessary these rights were enforced by the local communities.

Membership of an individual in any one of the communities gave only a moral sanction for appropriating resources. The real access, however, was linked to the nature of ownership of necessary fishing equipments. We have shown in the text that the cost of acquiring an appropriate labour process combination differs and the community is divided into various classes. Therefore, community is a structured production collective and consists of various classes.

While discussing the distribution of the social product, we pointed out that the produce was shared by the *elakaran*, the church, the owners of fishing equipments and the coolie labourers. The role of *elakaran* as a cushion against risks and uncertainties in individual transactions was highlighted. The church claimed a portion of the social product by legitimising the *elakaran* system. However, it was noted that part of this surplus was invested by the local church for the creation of common goods and services on behalf of the village communities as a whole.

Discussion about that distribution of the social product reveals that excluding a limited number of rich *karamadi* owners and a few diddle fishermen households, the rest of the population in the village were at a subsistence level. In additions to this, roughness of the sea and the seasonality of the fishing cycle brought weaker moments into the system. However, the system did not break down due to the existence of some inbuilt mechanisms (non-fishing and fishery related jobs, subsistence credits and local usury markets organised by the *elakarans* and *kootaly* system) of survival specific to the socio-economics organisation fishing in this eco-region.

4

Housing—Public Policy Priorities

AROMAR REVI[1]

Introduction

The housing problem in India has been viewed as a matter of producing enough units, of a certain standard, to fulfil the need for housing. The basis of calculations of the housing 'gap', and basing policies thereon, has been founded on the norm that there must be at least one housing unit per household (Planning Commission, 1996). While this may be a simple enough starting point, housing is a more pervasive process for households and communities i.e. the (majority) producers and the 'consumers'. Since their conception of housing is not restricted to erection of a roof on four walls but around which life and habitat are woven, it is no surprise that programmes based on conventional wisdom of building construction is greeted more with failures than success. The process of housing is not a mere matching of supply with need for a housing unit but the process of development and regeneration of the 'built environment', and plays a central role in the sociocultural, political and economic life of the households, communities, social groupings and indeed, the country as a whole.

---

1. With Somnath Sen, Ranjan B. Verma, G.K. Bhat, Rupa Mukerji and Rajiv K.R. The authors would like to thank the Planning Commission, Ministry of Rural Development, BMTPC, Ministry of Urban Development of the Government of India, various state Governments for support in the series of research and consultancy reports that this article has drawn from especially the Rural Housing Technology Action Plan (1993) and the National Rural Housing Action Plan (1997). The authors would also like to thank the large number of professionals, researchers and respondents who have participated in the research across 17 states that lead to the development of these documents.

Box 4.1

The Built Environment is More Than Just Four Walls and a Roof

- It is (among many things):
  - shelter,
  - security,
  - locus of family and community life,
  - cultural continuity,
  - expression of identity and solidarity, and
  - home: sense of place and time.
- Knowledge generation, transmission and conservation around the built environment must be viewed in this holistic perspective.

Rural housing mirrors the continuing struggle in India today, for access to and control over basic resources that are necessary to live in security and dignity. The preparation of a National Action Plan for Rural Housing has to be predicated with the recognition that housing, especially in rural areas of the country, is more than just a roof on four walls; the local social processes are primal in housing; and that the organised private and public sectors will have, if anything, a limited role to play. The National Housing Policy (1994) adopted in the Parliament echoes a part of this spirit. However, the spirit of the above factors is yet to be really internalised in development of plans and policies. The contention of this article are that if constraints to the supply of building resources, materials, skills and technologies are removed, rural house building activity will become to that extent more affordable, closer to what households desire and productive to the national economy by virtue of its employment linkages.

Understanding the underlying building technologies and subsistence processes, development and promotion of appropriate materials and technologies and packaging these into manageable housing assistance programmes will be the key elements in this strategy. Development and implementation of rural housing plans in the country have not been able to reflect an organised framework in the past. A few preliminary steps have been attempted in the Eighth Plan and need to be strengthened in the Ninth Plan period. In order to put together an effective national action plan for rural housing, it is necessary to begin with the existing systems of rural building production rather than attempt unrealistic replacement of the stock with 'conventional' technologies which may be more suited for urban or organised housing endeavours. Evidence from housing programmes in the past have shown that efforts to supplant existing systems of building with these normative systems, have and will continue to fail in the widely dispersed, partly monetised, low investment and self and artisan dependent rural market for housing.

As enunciated in the National Housing Policy (1994) the most effective approach will be to support desirable and robust processes in rural housing. This will imply concentration of resources to not only provide for direct housing to the vulnerable groups but also planned interventions which enable the maximisation of employment opportunities and enabling in respect of increased availability of materials and appropriate technologies.

I. CURRENT SITUATION

Some Basic Problems

The failure of many building technologies and construction innovations developed by formal institutions in the past, have been traced to limited demand identification, inadequate programme design, product innovation and a complete lack of marketing (Revi, 1987). These factors have played a major role in the limited impact of government programmes in the rural sector. The primary failure of our 'unstated' housing policy however has been in the limited priority and resources allocated to rural housing (Revi, 1990; MoUD, 1990). The lack of understanding of the dynamics of rural housing has further led to the inefficient use of these limited resources and suboptimal programme implementation. The use of traditional building technologies and decentralised labour intensive and biomass based housing production and maintenance processes have been dismissed as undesirable *kutcha* or substandard. This has been contested since both in terms of technical efficiency of resources and their use these technologies perform considerably better than understood commonly (Baker, 1987).

Most of the housing programmes in the country have been centred on production of new housing units, i.e., building new houses. This may have been brought in part by the non-reportage of non-stock building activities and also the norm that one household must have one housing unit. Many studies and critiques have pointed out that the replacement of the house; addition, upgradation, repairs, and maintenance form a substantial part of housing activity in rural areas. Since most of these processes are incremental in nature, the housing programmes have not been able to assist the maintenance and upgradation of a large base of houses in preference to building new units, which are intensive on resources and inadequate in terms of their social and cultural appropriateness. On the supply side, a number of processes have instead reduced access of households and artisans to local building materials and government promotion of subsidised industrial products have displaced a number of artisan communities (Kumar, 1989).

Since the liberalisation of the economy in early 1990s, there have been a wide variety of changes in economic and social relations and these have considerably affected the expenditure and investment patterns in the country. While clear comparative data is not available to measure the impact of increased monetisation and liberalisation on rural housing, there are indications that rural livelihoods have been impacted in a variety of ways. It is unclear, however, whether these changes have brought more prosperity and improved investments in rural housing activities. In any case, the high flux in the economy has not adequately been reflected in the policies and programmes which continue to strive for better availability and production of housing units. The primary assumption in the past has been that the quality of living conditions has slowly but significantly improved.

An examination of access and control over public resources and commons indicates evidence to the contrary. The natural resource base for rural housing has been reducing. Instances of deforestation, reduced availability of clay, scarcity of biomass fuels and deskilling of artisans have been reported in the media more frequently than ever in this decade. Apart from absolute reduction or diversion of material resources for rural housing, the erstwhile structure of traditional and economic claims on community resources have been negated by forces of privatisation and market development. The traditional socioeconomic relations, which protected the address of rural artisans, have also broken down.

The customary response to rural housing problems is to define them in such a way as 'bridging the housing gaps', increasing investments or as has been espoused more recently, change in the role of the government from provider to facilitator. The resultant package of solutions tends to be increased in the budgetary allocation or repackaging of old programmes; increased coverage and unravelling of new schemes and parcelling out of different components of the programme to different government, ministries, and agencies. The outcome predictively is an indifferent performance of the public programmes while living conditions deteriorate in rural areas.

Living Conditions in Rural India

In the 1980s, the living conditions of the lower three deciles of the rural population declined in most regions of the country. An overall growth rate of 4 per cent in the GDP has had limited and even undesirable impacts on the security of homestead rights, augmentation and redistribution of housing assets and social mobility of the poor as expressed in their improved living conditions. Small and marginal farmers (57 million) in 1982 (74 per cent of all farmers) held less than 27 per cent of the land, while large farmers (2 million and 2.4 per cent of total farmers) held 23 per cent of all the holdings. This skew in holdings has had a direct impact on housing. The limited surplus available to subsistence farmers has led to a drop in housing investment.

About 85 per cent of the rural population in the country live in settlements less than 5000 persons. More than two-thirds live in settlements between 500 and 5000 population size. About a third of the rural population lived in small settlements of less than 1000 persons. More than half of the population lived in villages of less than 2000 persons. Hence, the nature of programme management and information collection in these dispersed settlements are immense and considerably different from those in the urban areas. In fact, the dispersed and the decentralised nature of rural housing has been a major difficulty in formulation and implementation of formal programmes. While the institutional structure cannot allow for too much of variety, technologies and management techniques to assist housing processes have not been evolved specifically for programme delivery in rural areas.

The state-wise break-up of housing shortage (NBO, 1996) indicates that the states of Bihar, Assam, Andhra Pradesh and the Northeastern states of the country seem to have special problems in rural housing. One of the most disturbing trends has been the stagnation of the total house construction rate in rural areas. According to the 1991 data, there is a minor reduction in the rate of growth of *kutcha* houses; a moderate 15 per cent growth in semi-*pukka* dwellings whereas *pukka* dwellings have grown by more than three-fourths. This indicates an abnormal growth in the *pukka* segment, which is the stock of the relatively better-off farmers and cultivators.

The availability of safe drinking water and adequate sanitation are necessary conditions for the improvement in the quality of rural life. Considerable progress has been made over the last decade in certain provisions of drinking water. The proportion of rural households receiving water from taps, hand pumps and tube wells has increased.

There has been no change in the sanitation situation in rural areas over the years with more than 90 per cent of the households without access. This is a major constraint to the improvement in public health in the villages as water sources are often contaminated. In water scarce regions with the increase in population pressure this is an acute problem. The major proportion of respondents in primary studies reported that toilets were not available. Those that reported access to toilets, complained of unhygienic conditions and the lack of privacy. Considerable regional variation exists in the type of latrines. Sanitation technologies need to be adapted to the local water availability, soil types and the depth of the water table, apart from personal preferences.

The major source of lighting in rural India still continues to be kerosene which is highly subsidised for this purpose, In spite of major rural electrification programmes, the rate of electrification has been very gradual. Fuel and fodder availability have strong links with the quality of living conditions in rural areas. The direct links relate to domestic energy, but the indirect competition of fodder demand with biomass for rural housing i.e. thatch, grasses and bamboo is proving to be the most serious constraint to the supply of building materials to the rural poor.

The access and distance to basic services is an indication of the state of living conditions in rural areas. Less than 40 per cent of the villages had provision for street drainage and 60 per cent to street lighting. The drop off in availability of water supply drainage and sewerage facilities with increasing distance away from the village is very sharp.

The natural resources base for rural housing is depleting rapidly. The traditional economic and social relationship that protected the village poor and artisans in the past, has broken down since the 1970s. The living conditions of the lower three deciles of the rural population has declined in most regions of the country over the last two decades. The annual rate of growth housing construction, increased from 1.7 per cent over the 1971-1981 period to 1.9 per cent over the 1985-1991 period. This however, was lower than the rate of new household formation. The root cause of this gap can be traced to the limited asset holdings, surplus and investment capability of rural households. This situation can only be changed by increasing the security of rural homestead rights, enhancing household asset holdings, reducing the negative impact of formal industrial and developmental interventions and facilitating the access of low income households to adequate finance, skills, building materials and technologies.

The deterioration of rural living conditions and dehousing (decline in the quality of housing stock) has been observed in many locations of the country under the combined impact of the impoverishment of the peasantry, and recurrent natural disasters (annual floods and cyclones). This will have serious implications on the quality of housing stock as the rate of new construction is approximately 50 per cent of the total construction activity. Net degradation or dehousing therefore, becomes a significant fraction of house building activity in many parts of the country. In some states, this is considerably larger than the size of public housing programmes.

The low levels of rural household expenditure, on housing have unfortunately been used as a basis to neglect public investment in this area. The claim that rural housing is not a priority, is not borne out by field data. Landless labourers and women are among two of the major groups in rural areas that perceive that, housing is a primary area in which government intervention is necessary. Environment, health, water supply and sanitation are housing related needs that are also, high on the priority list of people living in rural areas.

Improvement in Rural Environmental Services

A major change in the source of housing related environmental services, has been observed over the 80s. A shift in the major sources of water supply has taken place towards piped supply, and hand pumps and tube wells. At one level, this is a positive indicator of the improved provision of drinking water. The access of backward communities, on the other hand has not necessarily improved, because of the shift from low-investment sources to formally managed and centralised system of water supply. There has been no change in the sanitation situation in rural areas over the last decade, with over 90 per cent of the households having no access to sanitation. A number of groups (especially women, artisans and landless labourers) have expressed the need for improved sanitation facilities in villages. The major lighting source in rural India continues to be kerosene, which is used by 86 per cent of the households as the bulk of the houses have no access to electricity.

Housing Upgradation: The First Priority

One of the myths of public housing programmes, is that the first priority of rural households, is the construction of a new house. This is contrary to empirical evidence: upgradation constitutes 50 per cent of all rural construction. A restructuring of current priorities is necessary in the recast National Rural Housing Programme: maintenance, upgradation of existing housing stock and the construction of core units to meet the need of new household formation. It is only after these priorities have been met, that new construction of 'pukka' buildings should receive programme support.

Artisan Built Housing: The Dominant Mode of Production

The predominant agency of rural house construction are artisans who build houses with (or without) household contribution of labour. Contractors built only two per cent of rural housing in 1989. Public programmes, have unfortunately been focused on a contractor based approach for the dissemination of improved technologies. It is clear, that the engineer-architect-contractor linkage has failed to improve the quality of rural housing stock in the past, and new institutional arrangements are required.

The linkage of technology choice and promotion with housing production and financing processes has not been undertaken in an organised manner in the past. This has led to failure of many building technologies developed by formal institutions. This can be traced to lacunae in demand identification, programme design, product development and a complete lack of marketing support.

It will therefore be essential, to build upon existing systems of rural construction and building production rather than attempting to replace them with technologies and building systems that have been developed for large-scale industrialised urban housing markets. These 'industrial' technologies, have and will eventually fail in the provision of decentralised low-overhead, artisanal housing in rural areas. The magnitude and decentralised nature of the rural housing problem has been the major stumbling block to the effective implementation of existing formal programmes, which have used technologies, and management techniques that have been evolved to serve the urban markets.

House Stock and Material of Construction

In spite of the rapid growth of population and new household formation, the growth in the rate of house construction and transformation of housing stock has been slow and often negative in some areas. The inadequate condition, age and crowding in rural houses reflects the low level of investible surplus of the rural poor. There are, therefore, three major policy constraints in rural housing:

- the growth in housing stock has not kept pace with the growth in new household formation;
- the levels of crowding are increasing steadily as the average unit area of houses remain roughly constant; and
- the rate of upgradation of houses has fallen over the last two decades in many states.

An analysis of the changes on an all India basis over the 1981-1991 decade shows that there has been a significant increase in the share of tile roofs from about 37 per cent to 40 per cent of the total rural stock accounting now for the largest share. The popularity of biomass materials reduced from nearly half in the last decade to 38 per cent in 1991. While the usage of industrial materials increase in absolute terms, their overall significance remains low owing to their small base stock size.

While the overall direction of change indicates a good proportion of upgradation taking place in the roofing materials used, the deceleration of usage of biomass materials is also indicative of the lack of availability of these resources locally. Some of the lack of change in housing stock with biomass roots can also be explained by economic constraints of poor households, which prevent them from upgrading their wall and roof.

The increased use of tiles and burnt bricks in rural housing is indicative of transformation of many houses with country tiles into Mangalore and other types of tiles. These are the most important changes in the rural housing stock and can be considered as the outcome of market availability and continual upgradation, which is being undertaken by households themselves. This is in contrast with public housing programmes, which attempt to transform the stock from the biomass-earth segment directly to the *pukka* RBC/RCC burnt brick segment.

An examination of the building systems followed for building roofs and walls, reveals that with an exception of a few methods of building, restricted mostly to conventional structures, the technology systems and sub-systems are complex as they have evolved through tradition and been adopted to local requirements and availability of materials.

Biomass roofs are built in a number of ways: grass, thatch on bamboo purlins; biomass materials supported on bamboo purlins and pole timber rafters; thatch on mat, on purlins and rafters; etc. Similar types of variations are also found in usage of tiles, shingles and slates whereas there are fewer variations in the usage of ACC/GI sheets and RBC/RCC construction. Similarly, walling systems are designed and constructed in a number of complex ways.

Space Utilisation and Crowding

The average area of new construction as reported by the NSS in 1989 is 40 sq.m. for rural houses. *Pukka* houses were reported at 49 sq.m., 'semi-pukka' at 40 sq.m. and 'kutcha' at 30 sq.m. The average area of addition of space to rural houses was 25 sq.m.: the addition of roughly one room i.e. 10 sq.m. were added to 'kutcha' buildings, 25 sq.m. to 'pukka' buildings and 28 sq.m. to 'semi-pukka' buildings.

A wide variation in the materials of construction, built form and functions characterise rural housing in India. The diversity of house form is not only an expression of the range of site elevations, climate zones and local building materials but also human skills and the functional and cultural identity of communities. This diversity reflects the process of integration of rural communities with the local climate and resource base.

The core function of a house is to provide shelter against the climate and natural forces. Given the low asset levels and impoverishment of the bulk of the rural population, rural houses do this very efficiently, e.g. roof types and slopes vary consistently across climate zones with decreasing rainfall. A wide variety of traditional passive cooling and heating techniques used in rural housing have been identified in the document. With small amounts of technical input and better use of modern materials, considerable gains can be made in thermal comfort within traditional buildings.

Rural Housing and Employment

The rate of growth of employment in the rural housing sector has been 3 to 11 times the national average over the 1978 to 1988 period. This is partially due to the impact of rural development and employment programmes over the Sixth and Seventh Plan, and the growth in demand for new houses as rural household formation increases.

The housing and construction sector has shown rapid growth in rural areas, where its share in total employment has doubled over the 1983-1988 period from 1.7 per cent to 3.4 per cent of the total employment. The proportion of rural construction workers to main workers rose from 0.7 per cent in 1971, through 0.9 per cent in 1981 to 3.4 per cent in 1988. The growth rate of employment in this sector was above 5 per cent per annum.

The 1988 figures show that 8.5 million people are directly employed onsite in construction and housing activities. It may, therefore, be concluded that a large proportion of the shift of employment out of the agricultural sector in this period, was absorbed in the housing and construction sector.

This has additional significance as field studies show that the majority of rural artisans and building workers live below the poverty line. They would therefore be a primary target group for support to employment-guarantee-cum-housing programme.

Employment for Rural Building Artisans

The economic and social status of rural building artisans has been declining ever since Independence. This has accelerated during the 1970s and 1980s with the impact of modernisation. Reducing access to raw materials, improved technology, markets, declining skill levels and displacement have all contributed to the decrepit living conditions of rural building artisans. This is unfortunate, since the construction of bulk of the new rural houses and maintenance will still continue to be undertaken by them.

Government support would be necessary to building artisans, in terms of access to raw materials, market and assured demand from public housing programmes. The assets produced by these artisans, after adequate skill upgradation would lead to more durable houses.

The Planning Commission has seen considerable potential in the expansion of employment in housing and construction sector. A housing-linked-employment programme has three major types of benefits:

1. Sustainable employment for large numbers of building artisans and workers, many of who live below the poverty line.
2. Additional income in terms of induced employment of workers from the backward linkages generated by increased housing activity.
3. Improvement in the living conditions of not only the above group, but also large numbers of the rural poor because of better housing conditions.

Investment in Rural Housing in the 1980s

The high risk, which the non-cultivator households are exposed to by adopting innovative building technologies, could explain the slow pace of diffusion of most low-cost building technologies when targeted exclusively at the poor rather than across all income/asset groups. Investment in housing and land, is a capital investment whose dynamics are different from items of daily consumption. It is not possible, for households to utilise and retain a high value asset like a house and land in the face of marginal or negative surplus value. This also indicates, the critical link between housing programmes and decentralised tenure, land reform, employment and agricultural development programmes as necessary.

Given an average area of 40 sq.m. the indicative unit cost of construction of the bottom 24 per cent of the households was less than Rs. 485 per sq.m. and the bottom 57 per cent less than Rs. 136 per sq.m. in 1981. This is the root cause, of the large proportion of thatch and earth houses in rural areas and the strength of dependence on local materials, for rural housing people cannot afford anything better.

Nearly 40 per cent of rural households reported expenditure on repairs and maintenance in 1981. However, the average household expenditure was very small at Rs. 65. Only 37 per cent of households made cash investments in their houses. The average amount of cash investment was Rs. 242 in 1981. This points to the considerable flexibility, that will be required in housing finance arrangements across states as the investment level and price variations are large. The average amount spent on construction per house in 1989 was Rs. 8,296. The bulk of the finance came from households (74 per cent), followed by borrowing from individuals (11 per cent), money lenders (8 per cent) and formal agencies (5 per cent).

The technology promotion strategy that emerges from this analysis is to push towards the upgradation of all houses in the low-asset value segment (usually thatch or earth roofs on thatch or earth wall) to an 'intermediate' segment of tile or stone roofs (or alternative roof cladding) on improved earth, brick or stone walls. This will be in consonance with the asset holdings and affordability of low income households. It is not possible to rebuild the bulk of the existing housing stock, with RCC roofs and brick walls over the Eight and Ninth Plan period, given the annual 4 to 6 per cent real growth rate of assets and faster rise in building material prices than current inflation rates.

Box 4.2

Key Building Materials in India

- Natural
  - Biomass (Thatch, Timber, Bamboo, etc.) and Earth
  - Stone
- Fired Clay based
  - Brick
  - Tile
- Industrial
  - Steel
  - Cement
  - Other industrial products (sheets, blocks, etc.)

The average fixed capital formation in housing by rural households is estimated at just over Rs. 8000 crores. Of this, 82 per cent comes from cultivator households, which make up 76 per cent of the total population. The non-cultivator households contribute 12 per cent of the total investment with 24 per cent of the total population. Government and formal institutions are estimated to contribute only 6 per cent of the total investment. New construction and additions make up 78 per cent of the total investment, while repairs and alterations make up 22 per cent.

It is clear that the share of government and formal institutions in rural housing investment is small as compared to the overall household investment. Formal agencies can, therefore, at best play a catalytic role even with a doubling of investment as envisaged in the VIII Plan.

Rural Building Materials and Technology Choice

The bulk of rural houses are built with only six clusters of materials: biomass, earth, stone, brick, lime and sometimes cement. Traditional rural building materials have been used to meet the varying structural, functional and aesthetic requirements indifferent parts of the country. Each building zone has evolved its typical patterns of built form, building systems and construction practice. There are, however, a few common factors in the use of these materials across the country: a high level of skill and labour component of cost; high levels of local control, adaptability and maintainability and low level of energy utilisation and costs of construction. These materials are, however, limited in their low resistance to extreme natural forces and lower durability. As a result, the level and frequency of maintenance and the lower service life of traditional materials have emerged as a major constraint to their continued use.

Construction with conventional material has been increasingly undertaken across the country with the expansion of rural development programmes and market forces. It has, unfortunately, worked in a negative fashion because of the low quality of contractor built houses and the changed aspirations of the people to live in *pukka* buildings and hence become even more dependent on government subsidies.

Biomass

Biomass materials from various sources are used in rural housing. The most common sources of biomass are: timber and wood, thatch from grasses, palmyra, agricultural residues and bamboo that are used in roof substructure, roof cladding material and timber framework for walls and as a binder in massive earth walls and plasters. Close to 10 per cent of the rural housing stock would be built almost completely out of biomass in 2001. Thatch roofs are expected to be 43 per cent of the total stock, while biomass based walls are expected to support 37 per cent of the roofs.

The extensive use of biomass materials in rural houses is largely because of their low cost, ease of availability, replacability and high degree of the local control. Even though the comparative performance of biomass are lower than industrial building materials, the average life of biomass structures is between 5 and 25 years.

The estimated total requirements of biomass for rural housing is just less than 30 million tonnes per annum, averaged over the coming decade. The bulk of this, would be consumed by roofing (89 per cent), the rest by walls, given no change in the present technology mix. The major source materials by mass would be thatch (82 per cent), timber (16 per cent) and bamboo (20 per cent). This would be equivalent to 5.7 million cubic metres of timber per annum which is less than 25 per cent of the recorded annual timber production and less than 0.7 million tonnes of bamboo, which is a fraction of the total bamboo extraction by industrial users.

The bulk of the projected requirement of biomass is for biomass clad roofs (71 per cent), followed by tiled roofs (18 per cent), and biomass walls (11 per cent). The major technological breakthrough to increase the durability of thatch, would therefore to make a major impact on the requirement of biomass within the grass and agro-residues segment. The bulk of biomass demand over the 1991-2001 period would used for the maintenance of existing stock while only 5 per cent will be used for new construction.

Timber has been a major structural material for rural housing. Its use, however, has declined rapidly with the spiralling increase in costs of primary species. Increasing deforestation is a matter of great concern in rural India.

The total estimated quantity of grass and agricultural residues used as roof cladding material is over 50 million tonnes. It is likely that at least one-fifth of this stock needs to be renewed each year. The demand for thatch would be of the order of 10 million tonnes.

Bamboo is extensively used in both roofing and walling systems of rural houses as it has high tensile strength to weight ratio and is flexible in use. The estimated requirement of bamboo for rural housing over 1991-2001 period is approximately 1 million tonnes. This demand could be met over the decade by a total area of one lakh hectares under intensive plantation or 3 to 4 lakh hectares under regeneration.

The efficiency of biomass utilisation in rural housing, is high. The shortage of these materials, is not only due to the rapid growth of demand in the rural housing sector, but due to the exhaustion of existing biomass stock by urban and industrial demand.

The order of magnitude of biomass demand for rural housing is so small in comparison with the area of wasteland, degraded common land and forests that it is surprising that organised interventions to meet this have not been made before. The major obstacle to this process are legal and institutional constraints and the vested interests of forest contractors and industries that have prevailed over the basic needs of local people.

The major areas of material research on biomass are: treatment to the extend of life of thatch and structural biomass members; efficient use of small span bamboo and secondary timber elements for roof sub-structure; conversion of cellulosic biomass into roofing and wall cladding sheets; regeneration and propagation of bamboo and propagation of rapidly growing secondary timber species.

Earth

Earth is a most widely used building material for rural construction in India and is used both for roofs and walls. The major types of earth construction for walling are: cob, rammed earth, wattle and daub and adobe. The major advantages of earth is its easy availability, simplicity of processing and handling, high labour intensity and relatively high durability. Its major limitations, are low resistance to driving rains and floods, abrasion and pest attack and low tensile stress handling capability. A number of improved earth construction techniques have been introduced in the country since Independence ranging from compaction with hand rammers, soil block presses, and soil stabilisation.

The promotion of use of earth for construction and, specially, an expansion of brick and tile industry in an area, would need prior regional environmental impact assessment because of the large area of the country with low depth of soil cover. The bulk of the estimated requirement of earth over the next decade will go towards the maintenance of earth walls. Therefore, a technological intervention to improve the durability of earth wall will result in a major saving of earth for rural construction.

Earth will continue to be the dominant material for wall construction, therefore, improvements have to be made in soil selection, stabilisation, plasters, building details for cob and adobe walls, and through the propagation of compressed soil block technology in appropriate areas. Black cotton and expansive clays have emerged as an important area for intervention for both earth, and brick and tile production. The doubling of the current life of earth walls would reduce the requirement of earth for rural construction by 40 per cent over the decade. Major technological innovation will be required to upgrade the quality of existing walls and the life of new earth buildings.

Bricks and Tiles

Burnt brick is now being increasingly used by affluent households in rural areas and in government programme and is perceived to be of high status material. The supply of bricks have not kept up with the demand and their costs have gone up by an order of magnitude over the last two decades. This is largely because of the constraints in the supply of earth and scarcity of coal and other fuels. In addition, the thermal efficiency of most current brick kilns types is inadequate. A number of techniques have been developed to produce acceptable quality bricks from low grade soils. This would, however, have to be investigated and propagated at a large scale. The bulk of the demand for burnt bricks over the decade, is expected to come from the construction of new rural houses and a smaller amount for the maintenance of existing housing stock. The bulk of the demand for tiles, however, will be for the maintenance of existing buildings. This is indicative of the relatively low durability of country tiles, which implies that a technological intervention is required to improve the quality of tiles and supporting substructure.

The fired brick and tile industry is facing a wide range of problems including constraints on the supply of quality raw material and fuel and low technological efficiency of firing. Material and fuel constraints will have to be addressed extra-sectorally, however, technological innovation and dissemination will be required in the clay blending, forming, firing, and quality control processes. In addition, the product range of traditional artisans has to be extended to cater to local demand. Tiled roofing will emerge as the most important segment over the decade, considerable technical support infrastructure, will be required to be established immediately to upgrade current production processes and provide financial support. Energy conservation has to be promoted on a war footing, in this industry.

Stone and Sand

Stone is the most durable material used in rural construction. A wide range of stone types is available across the country. Stone is however being slowly discarded as a rural building material largely because of outdated extraction techniques and problems of quarrying.

Sand is a critical raw material for lime and cement mortars, plaster and concrete. The availability of coarse sands is proving to be a constraint in many locations of the country leading to an escalation rise in its cost. Scientific prospecting needs to be increased in rural areas to identify good sites for the extraction of sand for buildings.

Stone use has been declining in rural houses over the last two decades. This has to be corrected and supported, with the introduction of 'intermediate' mechanised stone extraction technologies and the promotion of the use of stone pattis, slabs and blocks in appropriate areas across the country. Laterites, will also have to be handled in a much more organised manner than in the past. The availability of good sand is projected to emerge as major constraint as the volume of construction increases. The identification and the grading of sand deposits have to be undertaken in a scientific manner in coordination with agencies such as GSI.

Lime

The bulk of the lime production in the country is in the unorganised sector and hence has not received much technological support for upgradation and marketing.

Lime, even though it is declining in popularity has considerable potential for use in a rural housing programme. Promotion of medium and small scale lime kilns and hydration units is necessary along with the production of lime-pozzalona cements to replace Portland cement in mortar and plaster use. This will require careful techno-economic appraisals and marketing interventions to re-popularise the use of this excellent binding material. Cement consumption should be reduced as much as possible substituted by low-energy substitutes. The production of low-strength cements for masonry mortars and plasters as has been undertaken in China, should be encouraged.

Cement

The production of cement provides the largest share employment within the formal building material industry. In spite of the massive annual production of this building material, there are continual shortages in rural areas and costs have risen beyond reasonable measure. The use of cement for rural housing, took hold in the late 70s and early 80s. This has often been wastefully used both as a mortar and plaster, when it could have been substituted by lime or even mud. Cement however, has an important role to play in RCC and RBC slabs, precast concrete elements, micro-concrete roofing and ferrocement elements.

Steel

Steel has been traditionally used in rural buildings for special applications. It is now entering into extensive use, as a reinforcement material in RCC and RBC slabs and window and door frames. The most important use of steel for rural housing, however has been in CGI sheets, which have been widely used in hill areas of the country.

Steel utilisation should be curtailed to catalytic uses as in CGI sheets for hill regions, reinforcement and critical hardware. Wherever possible, small-scale fabrication units should be promoted.

Agricultural Residues and Industrial Wastes

Agricultural residues and industrial wastes, have considerable potential to be used in rural building applications. The most important of these are rice and wheat straw; bagasse; jute stalk and banana waste for roofing and partitioning of boards; rice husk as a pozzalonic material; coir and saw mill waste as fibre intrusion in panel and roofing materials; red mud as a filler material for roofing and fly ash blocks as a possible walling material close to thermal power plants.

II. AN ACTION PLAN FOR RURAL HOUSING

An Action Plan for Rural Housing would have to be developed within the context of the role of the state of a 'facilitator' as stated in the National Housing Policy (1994). Based on the analysis above, eight major clusters of public intervention emerge:

Assuring Homestead Tenurial Rights

An intervention that enables the regularisation and registration of homestead land, especially of poor and backward communities, will be an important positive step in addressing this crucial problem. Provision will also have to be made for future homestead plots and de-densification of high-density village settlements.

Halting 'De-housing' and Promoting Housing Upgradation

The process of 'de-housing' by natural disasters, degrading environmental conditions affecting essential building resources and economic impoverishment is endemic to many less developed regions of the country. The first charge of public investment in the rural housing sector, should go towards halting 'de-housing' processes by vulnerability reduction, hazard modification, and intervention to ensure the access of the poor and backward communities to essential building resources. This is an immense challenge as a large fraction of the housing stock in the country is vulnerable to natural disasters, especially flood, cyclone, fire, and earthquake.

Promoting the upgradation of housing from traditional technologies to appropriate intermediate technologies will have to become an explicit objective of public rural housing programme. This will imply a curtailment of expenditure on high cost *pukka* structures for a few, in favour of a much larger coverage with intermediate materials (e.g. tile and brick). Efforts to channel credit and cost-effective technology and management expertise to units producing these building materials will have to be seriously undertaken. This implies that the District Housing Plan will have to be closely tied in with the District Credit Plan.

Access and Control of Essential Building Resources by Local Communities

The predominance of earth, stone and biomass based materials in rural housing implies a series of extra-sectoral interventions to ensure community and local access to these common property or open access resources. Where competing demands exist from industries, restrictions may be required to be placed on them as appropriate.

Access to Traditional and Improved Building Materials and Technology

With changing aspirations and lifestyle, a slow shift to upgraded materials like tile for roofs and brick for walls is a trend across much of the country. Within these building materials and technologies, however, some are more resource and cost-effective than others. The active promotion and dissemination of field tested improved building materials and technologies will play an important part in the success of rural housing programmes. Energy is a critical constraint to building materials manufacture. Energy efficiency in both production and transport has to become a major thrust area of technology development, management and promotion.

Access to Skilled Workers and Guaranteeing their Employment

Housing activity in rural areas is skill and labour intensive. Skill often substitutes for capital in most 'viable' rural housing production systems. In spite of projections to the contrary, the building construction sector is the most rapidly expanding source of rural employment with a very high investment elasticity. The lack of access to 'appropriate' technical support institutions and public employment schemes, which enable skilled building work to be undertaken, are important institutional constraints in this sector. A pilot employment guarantee programme for building artisans, including those involved in building materials production, which is tied to both public building works and rural housing, can be an important new initiative.

Access to Appropriate Civic, Social and Energy Infrastructure and Services

The access to basic civic services (e.g. water supply, sanitation and lighting), social infrastructure, and energy services are integral to the improvement of living conditions in rural areas. Health and economic benefits of improved housing are rarely achieved without the effective provision of these services. A systematic effort will have to be made especially for poor and backward communities to integrate new housing development with existing village infrastructure or enable the provision of separate service infrastructure. Integrated into this will have to be the provision for either public or community based operations and maintenance systems, with a referral process to deal with complex technical problems. The participation of communities in priority setting, design and the management of these services will be essential for their success.

Access to Affordable Credit and Finance

The major modes of rural housing finance in order of importance are personal savings, sales of assets, loans from relatives and moneylenders. Formal institutions in spite of their much touted lending programmes for rural housing, provide less than six per cent of the total funds in this sector (NSS, 1989). The role of micro-credit and material and technical assistance will have to be emphasised much more than current large scale institutional finance, where the cost of recovery may often be more than the loans given. An extension infrastructure that integrates the lessons of micro-credit for housing from neighbouring countries like Sri Lanka and Bangladesh, with a scale similar to the agricultural extension infrastructure will have to be built to address the needs in this sector, especially if displacing moneylenders and other high interest sources of credit, is a policy objective.

Promoting Community Mobilisation and Community based Housing Organisations

The lack of effective local institutions within and outside the *panchayat* system in many states is the most intransigent constraint to the operationalisation of an innovative and effective rural housing programme based on cost effective materials, local skills and social control. The lack of contact between conventional educational, S&T and housing institutions with building artisans, is one of the most important causes of the negligible impact of the formal sector innovations on rural building. The establishment and promotion of local institutional capacity to mobilise communities to address problems of land tenure, material access and skill buildings and technology choice will be important to counter balance the conventional inertia of public institutions in this area. In this context, both *panchayat* institutions and NGOs may play an important role, along with associations of artisans and building material producers.

5

Neglected Sources of Irrigation[1]

NIRMAL SENGUPTA

Introduction

This is an account of the little-known irrigation and water harvesting systems of India. There is nothing startlingly new here, since these systems have been in existence for a long time. Yet, it becomes necessary to write about them as they are often ignored and misunderstood. These systems have withstood the test of time. Their history of survival could have been regarded as proof of their eco-viability and efficiency. Instead, once they are labelled 'traditional', modern engineers tend to despise them, and development experts reject them. Which are traditional and which are modern techniques? In the Indian context, this question necessitates a rather peculiar answer. Some of the old water appropriation systems were understood and adopted by the engineers and came to be known as 'modern' techniques. The rest, which did not attract them, were rejected as 'traditional'. This is an account of only some neglected water harvesting systems which have performed well since the past.

There are indeed some systems in the world which truly qualify for the term 'traditional'. The rediscovery of such a system in the long-desolate Negev desert of Israel is an example. A similar occurrence is unlikely in India. Here, the techniques which survived the test of time continue even today. The task is to revitalise them, improve them and extend them. In India, the appreciation of their practical significance needs to be established with arguments because of the deadweight of traditional-modern dichotomy. Not many countries make such a distinction. For them, 'traditional' systems are those that are long-forgotten, like the Negevian one. All those which

1. Excerpts from *User-Friendly Irrigation Designs,* Sage publishers, New Delhi, 1993.

withstood the test of time were improved and modernised. In India, the same process occurred in only a few instances. The traditional techniques of irrigation through the Kaveri or the Doab canals had inspired the British engineers who renovated the systems, learnt the techniques, improved and extended them. Had this not happened, even these canal systems would have been termed 'traditional'.

There is a reason why only among the indigenous techniques canals were adopted by modern engineers while others were not. Canal irrigation allows centralised management which goes well with bureaucratic control. For the highly decentralised ones, which most traditional water harvesting systems are, bureaucratic management is not efficient or even viable in terms of cost considerations and personnel requirements. The only feasible system of management is at local levels through users' participation. This, however, had never been attempted sincerely either by the colonial or by the national governments. Several systems were, therefore, deprived of bureaucratic patronage even though their irrigation efficiency was unquestionable. The failure on the part of irrigation experts has been legitimised through the labelling of techniques as 'traditional' and outdated. This has had a disturbing consequence. Modern techniques like canals and tube wells cannot serve even one-fifth of the Indian subcontinent. The terrain structures, to a large extent, are hostile to these techniques. The only feasible techniques are the highly scattered traditional ones. Without rejuvenating them, improving and extending them, even a partial balance in the irrigation situation cannot be attained. Instead, these appropriate and useful water harvesting systems await their doomed destiny. The beneficiaries hope that in future some 'modern' techniques will replace them, and while they do so, history takes its own toll. With the passage of time these neglected works deteriorate and some units collapse without any substitute. The adverse consequence on the local economy is passively watched by the supposedly concerned bureaucracy.

If they had received due attention, modern engineering knowledge would certainly have improved the 'traditional' techniques, in which case there would not have been any cause left to call them traditional. The real distinction, therefore, is not between 'traditional/indigenous' and 'modern', or even between 'minor' and 'major'. The actual distinction is that some systems demand extensive people's participation while some others are amenable to centralised bureaucratic management. This is why we term the former 'user-friendly' systems, a characteristic they all share and which led to the deprivation of their due status. Modern engineering knowledge could have appropriated and improved these varieties of traditional techniques if only the engineers had learnt to facilitate people's participation.

What are the current tasks with respect to these surviving but neglected techniques? It has to be the same programme that was adopted for the Indian canal systems: to appreciate their importance, to study the techniques, improve and extend them. The task is not an easy one. Many of the existing systems await rediscovery by modern engineers and development experts. There are many which are known of only vaguely. One could end up preparing a long list of traditional techniques, a list replete with local names. It might create a flattering picture of the country with its immensely rich variety of traditional techniques, but this will defeat the purpose. Unless they are compared and categorised according to their basic similarities, modern knowledge cannot make much headway. Improvement and extension will, therefore, remain only a distant dream. At the same time, it is also important to study the differences, and the local adaptations of the basic designs. It will be dangerous to homogenise them all. The comparisons must be extended to a wider scope, with other techniques and with techniques in other countries. The first task is to scientifically document this wide variety of techniques.

Extent of User-friendly Irrigation

What are the different methods of irrigation in the country? Everyone knows of canals and dams, wells and tube wells. Even sprinkler and drip irrigation methods are not unheard of. But these are not the only ones. There are other methods of irrigation which appear in official papers under such titles as 'tanks', 'other sources' and 'private canals'. Not many have heard of them, or of all of them. Even the experts know very little about them.

How important are these sources today? More than a hundred years have passed since the first modern irrigation system was commissioned under the aegis of the British. The colonial government had made huge investments in this area, extending canal irrigation facilities to several million hectares. Much heavier investments have been made on irrigation activities since independence. Most of these have gone towards canals, tube wells and wells, the three favourite sources of irrigation of the concerned departments. What would be the current importance of those 'traditional systems'? Not much, one would expect. But on closer scrutiny the facts are quite different. Table 5.1 shows the area served by different sources. In 1987-88, the latest year for which data is available, the sources under inquiry had served an area of 6.24 million hectares. Although it might have reduced to about 6 million hectares over the last few years, an extent as large as 6 million hectares itself is a lot—there are not many countries in the world with a total irrigated area of this magnitude.

Table 5.1

Progress of Irrigation Since Independence

Year	*Net Area Irrigated (in Million Hectares)*		
	All Sources	*Sources Other than Govt. Canals, Wells and Tube Wells*	*Col. 3 as per cent of Col. 2*
(1)	(2)	(3)	(4)
1950-51	20.85	7.72	37.0
1960-61	24.66	8.20	33.3
1970-71	31.10 (29.1)	7.20 (6.2)	23.2 (21.3)
1980-81	38.81	6.61	17.1
1987-88	43.05	6.24	14.5

Source: Land Utilisation Statistics.

Note: Figures in parentheses for 1970-71 are of the 1970-71 Agricultural Census.

Considering the fact that these systems account for only 14 per cent of net area sown, their extent appears to be insignificant in comparative terms. Indeed, this low percentage, coupled with a decreasing hectarage over the years, has led to the popular belief that these systems will be ultimately replaced by modern ones. Far from that, there are no proper substitutes for them in their areas of incidence. Thoughtless extension programmes since independence did not help their furtherance while government canals and tube well technology were pampered. It is only as a consequence of this lop-sided policy that their share has come down in the total irrigated area. Now that large canal extension has come in for heavy criticism by running out of suitable terrain, and tube well overextension has already begun to show ecological problems, these sources must receive the attention which has long been overdue.

These systems would have called for greater attention had the regional specifics not been marred by the countrywide gross figures. It is true that the country has nearly 40 million hectares irrigated by modern sources. But irrigation facilities are unevenly distributed. Punjab, Haryana and Uttar Pradesh,[2] which account for less than 13 per cent of the total geographical area and 18 per cent of the net sown area in the country, have 38 per cent of the net irrigated area. Most of these areas are served by canals and tube wells. Indeed, these three states account for a very large share of the area irrigated by modern sources—37.7 and 74.2 per cent of net area irrigated by government canals, wells and tube wells, respectively. In the rest of the country the irrigation scenario is considerably different. Categories like 'private canals', 'tanks' and 'other sources' now become equally important by accounting for 21.6 per cent of the total net irrigated area and 38.1 per cent of net area irrigated by surface-water sources. A further disaggregated picture (Table 5.2) shows that these are practically the only sources of irrigation in the Himalayan states of Himachal Pradesh, Sikkim, Assam, Arunachal Pradesh, Nagaland, Mizoram, Meghalaya, Tripura, and Manipur. In states with special geographical features, like Kerala and Jammu and Kashmir, they account for over one half of the total net irrigated area. In the three other southern states (Tamil Nadu, Karnataka and Andhra Pradesh) and the eastern states of Bihar and West Bengal, they account for 20 to 30 per cent of net irrigation by all sources. Considerable parts of the net irrigated areas are served by these sources in the states of Maharashtra, Orissa and Madhya Pradesh. In the case of these states there are serious under-recordings which will be discussed later.

2. Throughout this article states are referred as they were in 1991, before Uttaranchal, Jharkhand and Chhattisgarh states were created.

Table 5.2

Area Served by Private Canals, Tanks and Other Sources (1987-88)

State	*Actual ('000 Hectares)*	*As Per Cent of Net Irrigated Area*
Assam	501	87.59
Jammu and Kashmir	172	56.03
Other Himalayan States	313	85.99
Kerala	153	50.00
Bihar	894	27.99
Karnataka	512	27.63
Tamil Nadu	626	25.68
West Bengal	482	25.22
Andhra Pradesh	785	23.30
Maharashtra	488	14.65
Madhya Pradesh	432	22.97
Orissa	234	13.99
Uttar Pradesh	423	4.21
Rajasthan	119	3.58
Rest of the States and UTs	107	1.26
All India	6241	14.50

Source: Land Utilisation Statistics.

Further disaggregation down the state level shows pockets of influence of these sources even in states with extensive modern irrigation facilities. In a state like Uttar Pradesh these systems serve just above 4 per cent of the net irrigated area which, however, is nearly 4 lakh hectare. Most of this is located in the hilly northern districts of UP[3] where other irrigation facilities are scant. There were 25 districts in the country for which the net area irrigated by surface-water sources other than government canals was above 20 per cent of the net sown area in the district. The great majority of the states have certain regions where one or the other of the systems under inquiry constitute important sources of irrigation. Yet, this is not the exact picture. There are some other systems of water conservation, for example in the central Indian highlands, which are not recognised as irrigation methods and the areas served by them were not included in the official statistics for areas under irrigation.

3. Mostly Uttaranchal now.

Data Sources

Irrigation statistics are collected by two agencies: the Land Revenue Department of the Agriculture Ministry and the Irrigation and Public Works Department of the Irrigation and Power Ministry. The first source is a component of the land utilisation statistics and is published in the form of the *Season and Crop Report*. The latter source is published in the *Annual Report of the Irrigation Ministry*. Both sets of statistics are collected at the village level. The statistics of the Revenue Department cover both public and private works. They are collected by village *patwaris* and entered into the basic village forms whose formats are prescribed by the land records manuals of the states. These are then aggregated. In Kerala, Orissa and West Bengal, land use statistics used to be collected through sample surveys; in the other states, a method of complete enumeration was in use. The Irrigation Department statistics are compiled by its field staff in the course of collection of water rates. Hence, the data may be excellent when it concerns the public works but cannot be relied upon to describe private works. Most of the sources under inquiry are in the private domain. It is therefore, best to rely on the Revenue Department for the present study. This data too is not without limitations.

The Ministry of Agriculture had in the past made some efforts to improve it but with little effect. After independence and the unification of the Federal State it was found that the existing land records manuals of the different states—which had been constituted from different provinces and princely states administered by divergent systems during the colonial days—were not uniform. The formats and concepts varied widely and seriously affected inter-state comparability. A Technical Committee on the Coordination of Agricultural Statistics was set up in 1949, which suggested the use of a standard proforma. With regard to sources of irrigation, the proforma suggested continuing the same set of heads as existed during the colonial period: canals, tanks, tube wells, wells, and others, along with the classification of the first four items according to ownership by government or private persons. In addition, the proforma had asked for:

(a) capacity of the irrigation sources—for a canal, mileage, for a tank, whether the *ayacut* was above or below 100 acres (40 hectares): and, for a well, whether it had (an) independent *ayacut* (service area) or it supplemented other sources of irrigation.

(b) Method of taking water: lift or flow, lift by electric pump or oil engine or traditional devices.

Although the states had accepted this format in principle, rarely does one collect information under all the heads. In certain other cases additional categories have been retained by them on the grounds that those are necessary for the revenue collection procedures followed by the concerned state. These include, for example, *kuhls* in the data of Himachal Pradesh and *diggis/guls* in the data of Uttar Pradesh (hill region). The data for Nagaland also shows the categorisation of 'minor irrigation channels' and 'springs', and that of the union territory of Dadra and Nagar Haveli shows 'lift irrigation'. In the southern region, for the Nilgiris district of Tamil Nadu, two categories, 'jungle streams' and 'checkdams' have been listed. However, 'springs' and 'jungle streams', 'checkdams' and 'lift irrigation' are practised elsewhere as well, not only in the few districts for which data is available. It is amusing to find a very small area in Karnataka shown under a special category of 'irrigation from rivers'.

The only categories which are of interest for this study and which have been followed by all the states are 'tanks' and 'other sources'. Besides, most of the states show the division into government and private canals. Therefore, these three heads alone promise some consistency and uniformity and offer the scope for interregional comparability. Yet, it will be unwise to accept their consistency unquestioningly. There remain such queries as whether storages of a particular kind have always been identified as 'tanks'; whether channels comparable to *kuhls* in other regions have always been included under 'private canals'. It is notable that in the absence of a rigorous identification process such cases may be included in 'other sources' or simply overlooked. Government records show ample evidence of such confusion and omissions.

The early publications (e.g., GoI, 1924) of the *Agricultural Statistics of India* used to record clearly that (with reference to Madras Province, column 4) "The term 'tanks' refers to a particular kind of dammed reservoir. These reservoirs are formed by enclosing depressions or throwing dams across the valleys of small rivulets and streams to intercept water during rains." In course of time this footnote was omitted and the distinction was eventually forgotten. Its consequence has been serious. For example, a Committee constituted in 1961 specifically for the Improvement of Agricultural Statistics had no hesitation in referring to *jhil* and *talab* as 'tanks' while making recommendations for the improvement of interstate comparability of agricultural statistics:

> The term *abi* (lift irrigation) in the State [Punjab] should be split up into (i) *jhil* or *talab* (tank) and (ii) other sources, *jhil* or tank being defined as any storage of water which is constructed for purposes of irrigation and from which water is led to fields directly either by lift or flow without the help of canals (GoI, 1962).

Several techniques of irrigation have been clubbed together under the head 'other sources' of irrigation without any further effort to study and classify them. When practically nothing is known about the nature of these irrigation systems no development measures can be adopted. This is so even in those states where they occupy extremely important positions.

The Committee on the Improvement of Agricultural Statistics, mentioned earlier, constituted by the Ministry of Food and Agriculture in 1961, provides the only available description of the kinds of techniques included in the category of 'other sources', of irrigation.

(a) 'other sources' may include, *inter alia*,

(i) weirs (*bunds, thungals*, regulators, anicuts, *bandharas*, etc.),

(ii) irrigation channels (*kuhls, dongs, lowkhongs, pynes*, etc.) which aim at providing gravity flow irrigation by mere diversion of stream water supplies without providing any means of storage, and

(iii) lift irrigation from rivers and streams in which water has to be lifted into irrigation channels, as the topography might not permit direct flow irrigation (GoI, 1962).

These are only recommendations, one does not know whether these definitions were later followed. Still, this is the only piece in official documents which provides any idea of the rich varieties of techniques included under the miscellaneous category of 'other sources' of irrigation.

The 1961 Committee had also addressed the problems that arose in identification. Many storage works are primarily meant for the supply of drinking water or some other non-irrigational purpose. They may provide irrigation facilities as secondary benefits. While addressing this kind of problem the 1961 Committee opined that:

> Ponds or *johars* not constructed especially for irrigation purposes but used as such, in a particular year, should be included as 'other sources' along with streams, etc. (GoI, 1962).

However, one can never be sure that this kind of entry has been made consistently in all the states every year.

While including weirs, irrigation channels and lifts from streams, the 1961 Committee had excluded the so-called submergence tanks or internal catchment storages. The Committee did advise against the inclusion of this system under any source of irrigation. It was noted that *sailabi* areas in Punjab were such areas, which had not been irrigated from any other source but got the benefits of retention of moisture in the soil due to floods, or what was called 'submerged irrigation'. This often used to be treated as 'irrigated' in Punjab, to which the Committee raised objections. A similar system of water conservation through field embankments (*bundhies*) was quite common in the northern districts of Madhya Pradesh, the Jhansi district of Uttar Pradesh and the Kotah district of Rajasthan. In the Vindhya Pradesh region[4] (western Madhya Pradesh) bunds used to be raised along one or more sides of a depression to accumulate water for submerged irrigation. The area of such bunds used to be included in 'barren and uncultivable land' while the committee recommended their inclusion in 'land put to non-agricultural uses'.

One would expect, from the confident tone of the Report, that the area served by *bundhies* were never included in the category 'land under irrigation'. At the most there could be confusion between their inclusion in the categories 'barren and unculturable land' and 'land put to non-agricultural uses', but not in the matter of irrigation. Yet, five years after this Committee, the All India Review of Minor Irrigation Works based on State-wise Field Studies by the Irrigation Team of the Planning Commission declared (GoI, 1966: 1) that the area served by 'submergence tanks including bundies (*bundhies*) providing irrigation through inundation' were included in the

4. Mostly Chhattisgarh now.

'irrigation statistics'. No one knows which of these complex and contradictory characterisations were honoured by each state, indeed, by each data collector, in subsequent years. None of these systems is of limited significance. Some of them serve areas of the order of one lakh hectares. While using the land use statistics, which are by far the best that are available, one must also remember their very serious limitations.

There is another serious flaw in the land use statistics. Its definitions and categories are not appropriate for development programmes. The categories of land use statistics were developed for administrative and revenue contingencies and not out of any technological considerations. Since the British government had undertaken the construction of canals and could thus enhance land revenue, there was a felt need to separately indicate the areas served by government and private canals. In south India, tank restoration was an important activity of the government, again for the purpose of revenue collection. Hence, 'tank' became a distinct category as well. All the rest were included in a miscellaneous category, 'other sources', without any technological description. Thereafter, revenue considerations determined the accuracy of the identification process. Many such systems which would qualify as 'tanks' or 'private canal' could be conveniently pushed into 'other sources' if the government had nothing to gain for its exchequer by conducting further inquiry into the techniques. Neither the term 'private canal' nor 'other sources' gives any idea of the techniques they comprise to help promote technological improvement. This drawback of the lack of technical understanding has restrained improvement schemes in this area. Only very recently the Minor Irrigation Census has introduced a different set of classifications: tank, diversion, and lift. This is the first taxonomy based on the technological considerations of the system. While appreciating this as an effort in the right direction, one still finds some limitations. The term 'tank' is used in the country to describe a specific kind of storage. That led us to prefer the category 'storage' over 'tank' used by the Minor Irrigation Census. Further, every diversion and storage work is based on some principle of lifting. This fact restrained us from using 'lift' as a distinct category. Instead, we subclassified the diversion and storage works on the basis of their lifting principles. The chapters 2-5 in my book *User-Friendly Irrigation*

Designs include a scheme of classification along with the introduction of the varieties of user-friendly systems.

Current Trends and Decay

It would not be correct to believe that the bureaucracy has always and everywhere failed miserably in the upkeep of these irrigation works. Even extension programmes have been successful. Since the government can more easily collate information about these rare success stories, there is no point in wasting effort on this here. Yet, without belittling the sincere and successful efforts, it would be better to undertake a study of the deterioration alone, as a warning today would be timely and vital. For those who are not complacent but are always eager to learn, the alarming rate of deterioration in the more recent years, in spite of all the development activities, will be the appropriate impetus for action.

There is a general belief that these indigenous works had suffered badly during the colonial period. This is not always true. For some reason, even the colonial government had made effective extension efforts in certain areas. In order to settle the Mewar tribe and to put a stop to their banditry, Colonel Dixon had constructed many tanks in the Ajmer and Marwar regions around 1835 (Wilson, 1903:200). Even the princely states were not always remiss. The Nizam of Hyderabad had been instrumental in extending tank irrigation to Telengana (von Oppen and Subba Rao, 1980), and Holkar did the same for the *pat* system in Nimar (GoI, 1908).

At the policy level the Famine Commission had first drawn attention to the protective role of these works. Thereafter the Irrigation Commission of 1901-1903 had introduced the concept of major and minor irrigation, thus calling attention to both kinds. Following the Second World War, the 'Grow More Food' campaign had promoted minor irrigation enthusiastically. In the first decade of the post-independence era, when the emphasis was on agricultural development, the first Five-Year Plan and the Community Development Programmes aided these systems considerably. Soon, however, the focus began to shift. The Second Five-Year Plan placed greater emphasis on industrialisation. The multipurpose river valley projects, hailed by Nehru as the temples of modern India, took over. In the minor irrigation areas tube well technology sprang up. Rural electrification made groundwater exploitation easier. From then on the deterioration of these works began.

The data available from the Agriculture and the Irrigation Ministries show two different kinds of trends during the post-Independence period (Table 5.3). The land use statistics show that there has occurred a steady decline after a peak period in the 1960s. The statistics of the Irrigation Ministry show a continuous increase over these years, being much higher than the land use data in the more recent years. Although the data of the Ministry of Water Resources relates to gross irrigated area, this discrepancy cannot be explained by this fact. In that case, the Ministerial data should have been higher than that of the land use statistics consistently for all years, which is evidently not the case with the data available for the earlier years. Even the data on gross area irrigated from the land use statistics does not give comparable figures.

Table 5.3

Decadal Changes Given by Two Sources: Disagreement in Trends (Million Hectares)

Year	* *'Tank' and 'Other Sources' as per Land Use Statistics*	@ *'Surface Water Development' (Minor Sources) as per Ministry of Water Resources*
1950-51	6.58	6.40
1960-61	7.00	6.45
1968-69	6.31	6.51
1979-80	5.89	8.00
1984-85	5.49	9.01
1989-90	n.a.	10.11 (provisional)

Notes: * 'Private canals' have not been included to retain comparability with the other source of data.

@ Ministry of Water Resources data for 'potential utilised'.

Source: *Land Use Statistics* of the Agriculture Ministry and *Statistics of Minor Irrigation*, Central Board of Irrigation and Power, 1989.

Information on the net area irrigated by each source is available in the land use statistics of the Season and Crop Reports published every year. We collected all-India time series data from 1950-51 to 1987-88. Table 5.4 shows the trend coefficients for the time series data of net area irrigated by different sources. The net area irrigated by the combined category of 'private canals', 'tanks', and 'other sources', by all user-friendly systems, shows a negative value for the linear trend coefficient but with a low R^2. The form that improves the fit is a discontinuous trend somewhere around the early 1960s. Regressions were run with different years as the point of discontinuity. Amongst all the forms the one with discontinuity in the year 1960-61 gives the best fit. This result has been presented in Table 5.4. A value of $R^2=0.86$ is a reasonably good fit.

Table 5.4

Time Series Analysis of Net Area Irrigated (in '000 hectares)

Source of Irrigation		*Trend Coefficient*			R^2	*Degrees of Freedom*
		Whole Series	*Before 1960-61*	*After 1960-61*		
Private Canals Tanks and Other Sources	a)	-47.05			0.53	36
	b)		+122.52 (18.982)	-85.95 (5.892)	0.86	35
Government Canals	a)	248.80			0.98	36
	b)		+177.02 (21.822)	265.27 (6.773)	0.99	35
Wells and Tube Wells	a)	454.47			0.94	36
	b)		-27.30 (29.899)	564.96 (9.280)	0.99	35

Note: Figures within parentheses are standard errors.

The regression results show a significant difference (at 99 per cent confidence level) in the trends before and after 1960-61. While in the previous period the net area irrigated by these sources increased at the rate of 123000 hectares every year, in the period after 1960-61 it declined at the rate of 86000 hectares a year. However, caution must be exercised while acknowledging this result. One does not know how much of the 86000 hectares actually became non-irrigated and how much was replaced by better modes of irrigation. During this period, the net area irrigated by both modern canals and groundwater sources increased. Some of these sources must have replaced the older and less efficient methods in specific localities. It is, however, unlikely that

Figure 5.1

Net Irrigated Area by Sources

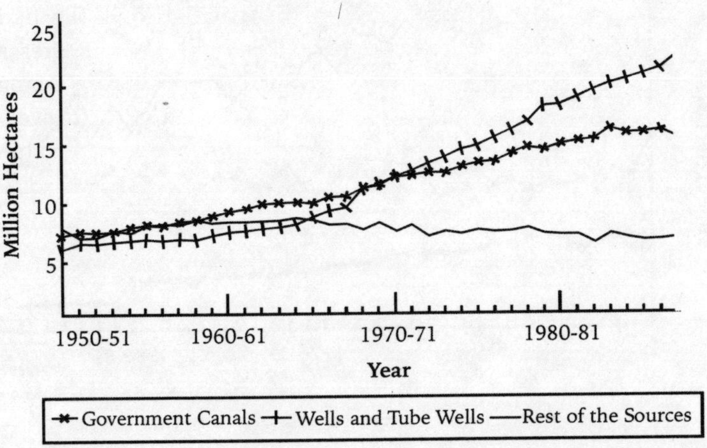

Figure 5.2

Net Area Irrigated by Private Canals, Tanks and Other Sources

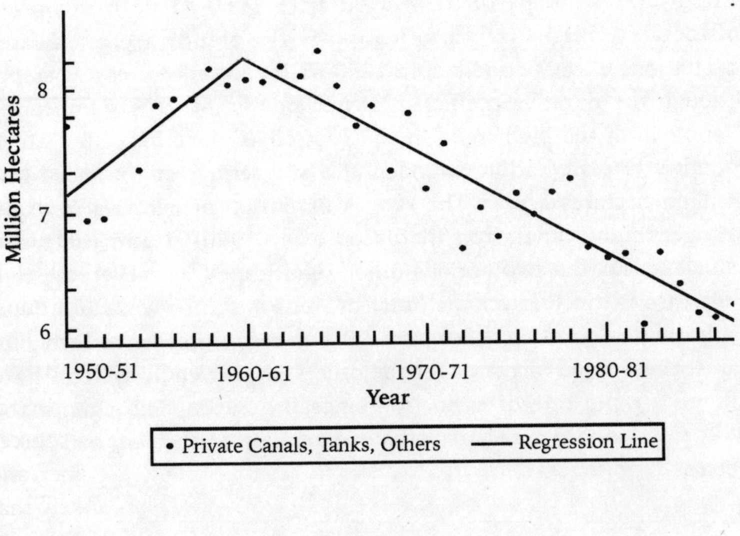

Figure 5.3

Net Area Irrigated by Each Source

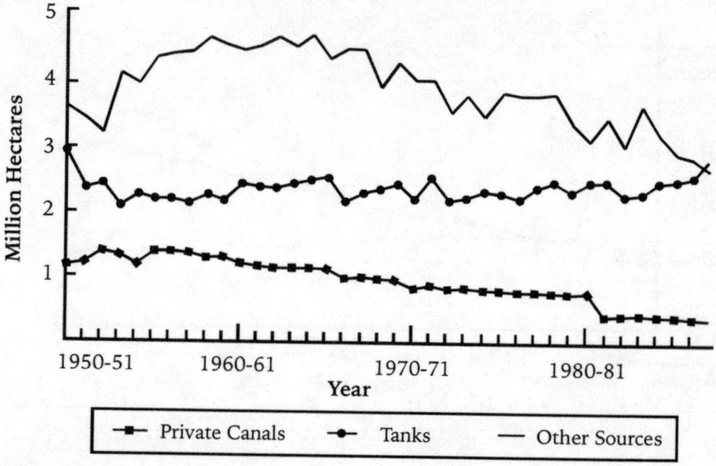

this was the case everywhere—some absolute deterioration in the irrigation situation has occurred.

During the later period, irrigation in general was not neglected. Instead, in a way, a discriminatory approach was pursued. Table 5.4 also shows the trends in net area irrigated by government canals and groundwater sources. In the period after 1960-61 both increased considerably. Particularly interesting is the trend in groundwater exploitation. In the period before 1960-61 it showed decreasing trend. Although the negative coefficient is not significant, it is significantly different from the high trend in the post 1960-61 period, after which groundwater exploitation extended at a staggering rate of above half a million hectares a year. The rate of extension of net area irrigated by government canals too increased after 1960-61 and the trend coefficients for the two periods differ significantly. However, the rate of increase is much lower than that of wells and tube wells. All these results were found significant at 99 per cent confidence level. As against these rapid increases for the others, user-friendly systems have suffered a rapid rate of extinction since the 1960s. Throughout the 1950s their service area was actually extending at the rate of 122000 hectares.

Table 5.5

Time Series Analysis of Net Area Irrigated by Sources (in '000 Hectares)

Source of Irrigation	*Trend Coefficient*		R^2	*Degrees of Freedom*
	Before 1960-61	*After 1960-61*		
Tanks	138.43 (16.18)	-68.82 (5.02)	0.84	35
Private Canals	0.15 (5.47)	-29.65 (1.70)	0.93	35
Other Sources	-16.06 (11.80)	12.53 (3.66)	0.26	35
Other Sources*	-201.09* (41.57)	12.19* (2.27)	0.52	35

Note: * Assuming the break in trend occurred in 1953-54 instead of 1960-61.

It would be interesting to know whether all types of user-friendly systems share the same fate. Although there is a lot of confusion in the classification of these sources, the available data for separate categories still needs to be analysed. The source-wise analysis of the trends during the same period has been shown in Table 5.5. Both tanks and private canals showed rapid deterioration during the period after 1960-61. In the case of private canals, development was stagnant to a certain extent before 1960-61, but the net area irrigated by tanks extended at the rate of 1.4 lakh hectares a year. This certainly indicates the success of the programmes undertaken during the First Five Year Plan. But after 1960-61 the net area irrigated by tanks began to decrease at the rate of nearly 70000 hectares each year.

The data for other sources does not give a good fit (R^2=0.26) when the change in trends is presumed at the year 1960-61. The fit improves considerably (R^2=0.52) if the discontinuity is introduced in an earlier year, 1953-54. Interestingly, the net area irrigated by other sources showed a reverse pattern, a negative trend before 1953-54 and a minor but significant increasing trend after 1953-54. Since this is a miscellaneous category the exact source of the increasing trend cannot be identified.

While analysing the land use statistics, one automatically assumes that the indicator of the output and performance of these systems is net area irrigated. Only when there is any decrease in the net area irrigated is the situation explained as deterioration. In their characteristic way of functioning these farmer-managed systems, however, meet many different objectives—groundwater conservation, flood control, drinking water supply, soil conservation, flexible crop choice and cropping practice, and even equitable benefit distribution. The worsening performance that occurred in one or the other of these aspects must also be considered as deterioration of the system. Unfortunately, such details are not available. At the most one can be alerted of the incomplete and the inappropriate analytical method used above.

Scope of Extension

Water Balance Estimates

The first attempt to assess the water resources of India was made by the first Irrigation Commission in 1901-1903. Since then several improvements have been made in the method of estimation. The procedure begins with a statistical analysis and an aggregation of rainfall data from all over the country. (Recently, estimates of the contribution of snow-melt have also been made.) Thereafter, hydrological relations are used to obtain the division of this aggregate into different forms in the water cycle. For some of these forms it is possible to get a second estimate from actual observation. These are then used either to cross-check or improve the calculated estimates. In this way the run-off flowing through rivers is monitored in several observatories. The Central Groundwater Board had made a district-wise assessment of availability and an estimate of draft in 1983-84.

These estimates show that the country receives about 4000 billion cubic metres (bcm) of total precipitation every year which results in 1850 bcm of run-off in the rivers and 400 bcm of percolation into groundwater strata. Figure 5.4 shows the currently accepted water-balance situation for the whole country. An estimated 1050 bcm of water is available annually for different forms of consumption. Some of the utilisable water resources are used for drinking and industrial purposes. The balance, 510 and 260 bcm of surface and groundwater, respectively, are considered quantities available for irrigation.

While the basic data for estimates of precipitation, run-off or infiltration is obtained from concrete observations, there is no reliable

Figure 5.4

Water-Balance on Full Exploitation (Billion Cubic Metres-BCM)

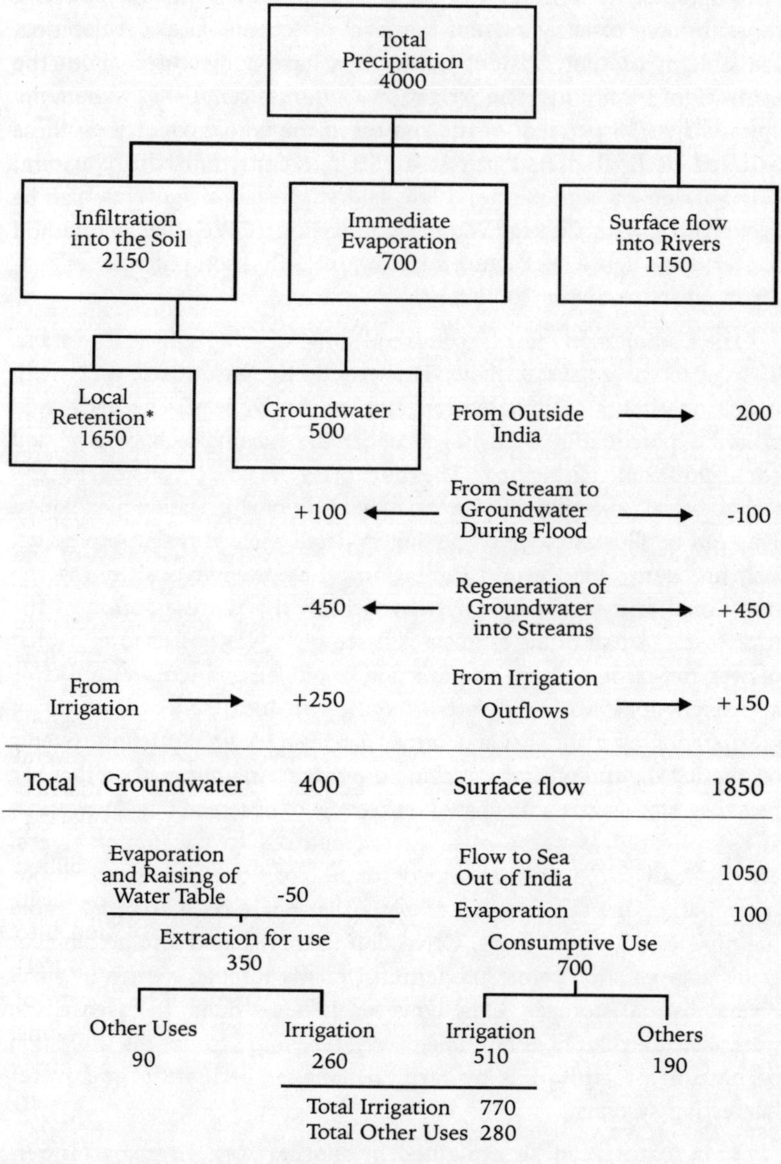

Note: * The Central Water Commission (CWC) described it as 'soil moisture'.

Source: CGB, 1983-84.

means of predicting what proportion of water can be used. The whole of the run-off flowing through rivers cannot be used because of physiographic conditions, the socio-political environment, legal and constitutional constraints, and the level of technological development available at present. Various authorities have conjectured about the utilisation possibility. The Irrigation Commission, 1972, was of the opinion that 35 per cent of the run-off in the whole country could be utilised. K.L. Rao had put it at 50 per cent, and the National Commission on Agriculture, 1976, had suggested a figure as high as 56 per cent. The Central Water Commission (CWC) has accepted a conservative figure suggesting a maximum utilisation potential of run-off in rivers at about 700 bcm.

The Commission must be commended for showing sufficient restraint in order to ensure sustainability. However, in the area of safe utilisation, it has no claims to imagination and innovativeness. The estimated utilisable potential is as envisaged under the existing technological and socio-political conditions. The authority has not considered the technological possibilities of the existing traditional irrigation techniques. This can be illustrated by discussing in detail the estimation procedure. The procedure has certain limitations that prevent positioning the traditional farmer-managed systems within the representation of the water cycle. A part of the estimate is based on A.N. Khosla's formula that derives run-off into rivers as a function of rainfall and temperature. This approach does not take into account the localised utilisation of precipitation by traditional and farmer-managed water harvesting systems preventing the run-off from reaching the rivers. Another method that has been used for estimation is based on records of observed flow at terminal sites collected at some observation centres in the major rivers. Theoretically, this estimate needs to be corrected for extra evapo-transpiration due to utilisation of water that might have occurred before the observations were made. Correction factors should also account for water appropriation before the terminal points through numerous small diversions and storages. This, however, is never done. In essence, the water-balance chart does not, in any way, take into account the utilisation of natural precipitation by farmer-managed irrigation and water harvesting systems.

This feature can be explained in another way. In many farmer-managed systems water is appropriated between the occurrence of precipitation and the resulting run-off in rivers. However, the system of hydrological balance, as in Figure 5.4, does not admit any utilisation possibility at that part of the water cycle. The water-balancing system locates utilisation possibility only at the stage when precipitation has already taken the form of run-off in rivers and thereby derecognises those surface-water appropriation systems which are based on a different principle, that of preventing the run-off from reaching the rivers. Many farmer-managed systems are designed to use the latter principle.

The other serious weakness of the water-balance calculation is in not considering the head 'local retention' as utilisable in any way, including irrigation. The souvenir issued by the Indian Water Resources Society on Water Resources Day, 1990, had termed this 'soil moisture' instead of 'local retention'. It was described as follows: "The whole of this (1650 billion cubic metres included under head 'soil moisture') goes back to the atmosphere as transpiration and evaporation.' This is, however, true of all parts of the water cycle: Both run-off in rivers and extracted groundwater meet with the same fate. Yet, if, in the process, they are diverted by artificial means to help agricultural production, it is known as irrigation. Should not one use the same standard for the other form, for 'local retention', as well? The official term 'soil moisture' is misleading. All the retained precipitation that does not percolate or meet rivers is not retained as soil moisture. Part of it is stored by farmers in various kinds of tanks and *in situ* storages. These, then, provide irrigation. Theoretically, utilisation is defined as the additional evaporation/evapo-transpiration, caused by human beings, of the natural water through its diversionary uses. It includes every sources, including that part of the locally retained precipitation which is put to economic use. Although this is the scientific concept it is difficult to operationalise. Hydrologists, therefore, are conveniently concerned only with the quantum of water withdrawn from places of major natural occurrence such as rivers or groundwater. The CWC uses this approach. Its estimation procedure conveniently takes into consideration the major and medium projects alone, since the quantum of withdrawal can be easily obtained for such projects. The quantum of potential withdrawal through numerous minor farmer-managed surface-water systems is ignored because it is difficult to estimate. It would have been appropriate to acknowledge the limitations instead of declaring the same source 'unutilisable', as the official water-balance chart shows.

An Appropriate Strategy

The 1650 billion cubic metres (bcm) share of annual precipitation, an average 500 millimetres of precipitation over the whole country, is 'locally retained' only in the sense that the amount does not reach the rivers. This water is, however, not always retained exactly at the same spot where the precipitation occurs. Surface depressions and vegetative covers attract and retain a substantial part from their vicinity. Thus, the locally retained precipitation also creates surface run-off although this remains within a small region and is unable to reach the rivers. Human beings alter the terrain characteristics in such a manner that localised run-off too is regulated and redistributed so as to facilitate the best utilisation of water resources. All these physiographic alterations, if used for agriculture, should be termed 'irrigation' systems. All water conservation and water management structures are indeed candidates for irrigation systems and need to be regarded as such, particularly in water-deficient countries like India.

A line of distinction, however, is always drawn for organisational convenience. The simpler structures are called 'water harvesting' systems which can be constructed, maintained and managed by the farmers. The more complex structures requiring specialised construction alone are called 'irrigation' techniques. Indeed, in strict technical parlance, tank irrigation is a dryland or rainfed cultivation method (Barrow, 1987; FAO, 1987); *dongs* are drainage works. However, in most countries, including India, this terminology is not strictly followed. Acknowledging the water-deficient condition of the country, 'tanks' and a few other sources are classified here as irrigation structures. However, that has not influenced the irrigation development strategy to the extent that it should. Although recognised, tanks and *kuhls* are not considered at par with the canals and tube wells as irrigation techniques.

This is further reinforced by additionally qualifying the latter, as 'assured' and 'complete' irrigation, qualifications, which are suspect. The irrigation departments then pamper 'assured' irrigation to such an extent that the recognition given to other sources like tanks remains mostly on paper. In consequence, technocratic preference prevails over an appropriate, balanced and scientific approach to extension. This is evident in the CWC's estimates of irrigation potential and the current strategy of irrigation development. The question is, how assured are the canal irrigation works when the delivery system is unable to meet the needs of the farmers in time? When the availability of power is so uncertain, how can groundwater lifting be considered assured irrigation? And, in the context of increasing waterlogging, salinity, and depletion of aquifers, how could these sources be called complete irrigation? These are, however, regarded by technocrats as organisational and environmental problems rather than technological ones. The appropriateness of a technology being validated outside the contexts of organisation, environment and sustainability is questionable.

Geographically, India is a country of great diversity. Within this diversity there are some locations, which have been favourable for the extension of modern irrigation facilities—the major canals and dams. However, when these become almost exhausted, it would be unwise to tread the same path. It would be reasonable to adopt a broader definition of irrigation, embracing at least a few more structures if not all those, which would functionally qualify for the categorisation.

The different types of user-friendly systems can be brought under five broad strategic heads:

1. When precipitation is low the terrain should be modified so as to increase the run-off on to cropped areas. This needs to be combined with fallowing for water conservation and the use of drought-tolerant crops with suitable management practices.
2. When the precipitation is moderate, the appropriate strategy is local conservation of precipitation, maximisation of storage within the soil profile and storage of excess run-off for subsequent use.
3. When precipitation is sufficiently high, attention needs to be paid to reducing rainfall erosion and to draining the surplus run-off. The surplus can be stored for subsequent use at a later date or at a distance from the storage.
4. When precipitation is very high, the primary task is drainage and flood control. The necessary quantities of water can be

drawn from the physical structures if supplementary irrigation is needed.

5. Areas with special features need to be tackled with imagination, like snow-melt appropriation at high altitudes or reclamation in coastal areas.

These are only the principles, not the descriptions of appropriate technologies by region. Since precipitation is mostly erratic within the same area and from year to year, the most successful policy would be to follow different principles for different years, and for different periods even within a single season. Exercising flexibility is a challenge to the extension and management services. With increased emphasis on participatory development, the ways to achieve this goal could be learnt by the extension services in the near future.

Irrigation Potential within the Alternatives

If, indeed, a functional definition of 'irrigation' is adopted, and if all the techniques that would then qualify are extended with determination and improved assiduously, a very large area can be brought under the irrigation systems. In 1988, that net sown area in the country was around 141 million hectare. In the next 35 years it might increase by another 10 to 15 million hectares. One hundred million hectares of this is regarded as rainfed agricultural land. This whole area may benefit from irrigation.

Table 5.6

Land Use Pattern, 1988 (Million Hectares)

1.	Net Area Irrigated	43.05
2.	Rainfed Agriculture	97.67
3.	Barren, Fallow and Uncultivable Waste	60.72
4	Land under Forests, Tree Crops and Permanent Pastures	82.48
Subtotal		240.87
5.	Land Put to Non-Agricultural Uses	20.41
6.	Area not Reporting	24.41
Total Geographical Area		**328.73**

Source: Land Utilisation Statistics.

It, however, should not be misconstrued that the 100 million hectares can be actually irrigated. The land use concepts appropriate for studying water utilisation in so-called 'rainfed' agriculture are not the same as those for irrigation through modern canals or wells. In the former kind, the run-off is usually multiplied by utilising a part of the surrounding area as catchment. Some of them require storage arrangements some others do not. Sometimes the storage areas are not nominal in comparison to the command areas. The net effect is that every bit of land in a locality cannot be irrigated but every bit of precipitation over a large area can be utilised in a planned manner. Understandably, the right units for water resource planning for these systems are not net sown area or net irrigated area but also those which must play the roles of catchment and storage areas. In the land use pattern data shown in Table 5.6, the subtotal of 240.87 million hectares is, therefore, more relevant as a potential land utilisation figure as against 97.67 million hectares. The barren and uncultivable lands are not irrelevant to the irrigation systems under consideration, but are likely to function as catchment and storage areas for them. After excluding a rough estimate for the interior forests which would not contribute towards this end, a conservative 200 million hectares may be regarded as the supporting and utilisable area for rainfed farming. Around 25 million hectares[5] of this land have farmer-managed water conservation systems which provide irrigation facilities to 3.6 million hectares through storage works. The unaccounted contour bunding and many other systems may have added another 10 million hectares. The works which are classified as 'private canals' and 'other sources' provide irrigation to 2.94 million hectares. These 2.94 million hectares may have another approximately 2 million hectares of catchment added to them. Thus, on a rough approximation, altogether 40 million hectares of the 200 million hectares of supporting and utilisable area in rainfed farming are currently in use by the existing traditional systems of irrigation. This is only about 20 per cent of the deserving area. It is necessary to plan for their extension over the rest—nearly 160 million hectares. The vegetative growth of this whole area will be facilitated under good water management, although the intensity of water application will vary even within the micro regions. The actual irrigated area, of course,

5. For the estimation see the original (Sengupta, 1993) pp. 55-56.

will depend on the definition adopted, for only a certain intensity of water application would be termed 'irrigation' to make it an operationally meaningful distinction.

In addition, the areas already under one or the other kind of irrigation can also benefit from this alternative strategy. Several such possibilities exist.[6] To summarise, the two possibilities are:

1. Improvement of existing traditional irrigation systems by taking help from modern science and technology.
2. Making existing modern systems user-friendly and sustainable. Certain design modifications would be needed to make them user-friendly. For sustainability, new structures in the command areas of the salinity-prone modern systems would be needed for the maximum use of rainwater.

This strategy may then be combined with currently accepted programmes like the Interbasin Diversion Programmes. Such gigantic programmes would find their water utilisation more efficient and have their economic viability established if they function as feeders to the user-friendly systems.

6. See the original (Sengupta, 1993).

6

Arsenic Catastrophe and a Safer Tradition[1]

MEERA M. HIRA SMITH

Introduction

In 1995, an International Conference was organised in Kolkata by the School of Environmental Studies of Jadavpur University to portray the severity of the effects of arsenic in drinking water. The overwhelming picture was of a vast number of people being exposed to high levels of arsenic in drinking water obtained from shallow tube wells. In 1996, the number of victims who were suffering from diseases caused by arsenic in drinking water was estimated to be 220000 (*British Medical Journal,* 1996). In the same year it was estimated that more than one million people in 8 districts out of the 16 districts of West Bengal, including 560 villages had arsenic-contaminated water (*Current Science,* 1996). Since then numerous studies have been done on the source of arsenic, examination of hydro-geological and chemical hypotheses concerning the entry of arsenic into aqueous solution, and assessment of health effects.

International research studies have established that long term exposure to arsenic causes the following diseases:[2]

- skin lesions and skin cancer;
- internal cancers—bladder, lung, kidney;
- neurological effects;

---

1. Revised version of an article "An Assessment of Alternative Methods of Providing Arsenic Free Water in Villages of North 24 Parganas, West Bengal, India" published in the Proceedings of the International Seminar of *Changing Environmental Scenario of India and Adjacent Countries since Independence* and XII Annual Conference of Indian Institute of Geomorphologists (IGI), 2000.
2. Smith H. Allan, Lingus O. Elena, Rahman Mahfuzar (2000). "Contamination of Drinking Water by Arsenic in Bangladesh: A Public Health Emergency", *Bulletin of World Health Organization,* 78(9): 1093-1103.

- hypertension and cardiovascular diseases;
- pulmonary disease;
- liver disease;
- peripheral vascular disease; and
- diabetes mellitus.

Numerous hypotheses have been formulated concerning the origin of arsenic in the shallow tube wells that were installed to stop morbidity and mortality caused by gastroenteritis that resulted from drinking surface water. One such theory is that there is fluctuation in the levels of underground water tables due to variations in rainfall and the extent of water mining in different parts of the state of West Bengal for use in agriculture. As a result there could be constant leaching of arsenic into different layers at different depths throughout the arsenic prone region.

To provide arsenic free water, different methods need to be considered depending on local conditions. Various mitigation plans and methods of providing arsenic-free water to the people have been proposed but with little consensus on strategies or plans of action, nor on decision criteria to be applied in specific local circumstances. When trying to decide how to proceed with plans for providing arsenic-free water, no comparative information could be found which would assist in making local decisions. The purpose of this chapter is to present the results of investigations conducted in the hope that the information may be of value to other groups and communities making decisions in their particular circumstances about the best method for obtaining arsenic-free water.

Objective

To assess some of the methods to provide arsenic free drinking water and their advantages and limitations for particular villages of North 24 Parganas.

Method

A comparative study of different methods of providing arsenic free water was undertaken. To do so various observations were made by visiting selected villages of North 24 Parganas where there are cases of arsenic caused diseases among the villagers. The different methods to provide arsenic free water are discussed below along with their advantages and limitations, and a comparative study of the costs of each method.

Deep Tube Wells

The investigation was started with deep tube wells because it has long been known that the lower aquifers, below 500 feet in many places of the alluvial Indo-Gangetic Plain, have low concentrations of arsenic. However contaminated deep tube wells that are more than 500 feet deep have been reported including those in the village called Ambikanagar of North 24 Parganas. These findings suggest caution in proceeding with deep tube well plans.

The contamination is probably caused by cross contamination between aquifers that may result from improper installation of the tube wells. Geologist Dr. Asit Kumar Roy has reported a mechanism for the flow of underground water within the Gangetic alluvium.[3] Concerning deep tube wells, he notes that when a deep tube well is being installed, it should penetrate the non-contaminated impervious aquifer 'fully' and the mouth of the pipe should touch the non-contaminated aquifer fully. He also stated that if any sort of partial penetration were done, there would be transmission of contaminated water both horizontally and vertically between the aquifers. In addition, as noted by Dr. Timir Hore[4] of New Jersey, USA, deep tube wells should be sunk by the 'proper method', with casing and sealing.

The main reasons for disqualifying deep tube well for installation in the selected villages for this study in West Bengal were:

1. Non-availability of detailed local geological maps to identify the arsenic contaminated aquifer.
2. Lack of experience in the 'casing and sealing' method and difficulty of supervision of the proper installation of deep tube wells.

In order to make drinking water readily accessible, numerous deep wells would be required. Probably one for every 10 households, which would be very expensive.

---

3. Roy Asit K. (1997). "The Past and the Future of the Effects of arsenic Poisoning". The article was published in Bengali in the science section of the journal *Desh* on 26 July, pp. 113-119.
4. Timir Hore, newspaper article in Bengali Newspaper, *Bartaman*, published on 11th June, 1999.

Low Cost River Water Treatment Plant at Gaighata

In Gaighata, another village of North 24 Parganas, a proposal to construct a low-cost-river-water-treatment plant on the river Yamuna/Ichamati was considered. Apart from the large installation cost, the most important reasons for disqualifying the plan are:

1. The river Yamuna/Ichamati is highly polluted.
2. A separate chemical treatment plant would be required to remove the pollutants. This would increase the cost of installation and maintenance.
3. The volume of water in the summer season is not sufficient.
4. The cost of maintenance would be high.

Tanks Filled from Natural Ponds

One of the ideal sources of arsenic free water is harvesting of rainwater. Rainwater can be harvested in many different methods one of which is natural ponds or *pukur*. The water of natural ponds does not contain any arsenic due to their shallow depth.

Pond water is contaminated by pathogens. To remove these pathogenic bacteria the water:

(a) needs to be treated either by storing the water in a tank or reservoir for chemical treatment or by using roughing filter also known as pond sand filter. The method of building tanks from natural pond is expensive and to maintain it people would have to contribute Rs. 25 per month (Table 6.1). The roughing filter system is more economic. Treating the natural pond water by the roughing filter would yield 1000 litres of potable water for Rs. 1.25.

(b) The other alternative is boiling water but this is expensive and inconvenient, and not likely to be fully complied with.

Disadvantages of the Natural Pond Method

The natural pond method has some serious disadvantages. Villages like Simuliapara, Chikonpara and Amkhola of Gaighata Block and Kamdebkathi of Deganga Block of North 24 Parganas were visited to get the opinion of the people about the natural pond.

Table 6.1

Comparison of Various Methods of Providing Arsenic-free Water

Source of Arsenic-free Water	*Population Benefited*	*Capital Cost (in Rupees)*	*Maintenance Cost (in Rs.) per Annum*	*Capital Cost Per Family (in Rs.)*	*Maintenance Cost Per Family Per Month (in Rs.)*
Deep Tube Well	1,000	92,400	Negligible	370	Negligible
Low-Cost-River-Water Treatment Plant	10,000	7,60,000 + Chemical Treatment Plant	2,00,000	304 + Chemical Treatment Plant	10
Tank from Natural Pond	1,600	6,50,000	60,640	1625	25
Household Filters	Not Evaluated Due to Difficulty in Properly Disposing the Sludge from Individual Homes				
Community Filter (Mullickpur)	400	65,000	5000	650	15
Concrete Dug Wells, 'Indara'	150	10,000	2000	266	10

Source: Local NGOs of North 24 Parganas, West Bengal.

1. The main reason for disqualifying the natural pond method is that in spite of being offered a rental contract, no pond owner was willing to have his pond used for this purpose because fish is a vital source of income as well as it is consumed.
2. Another equally important problem that was realised during investigative field trips was that the larger the number of beneficiary members the harder it would become to maintain the pond and water purification system. From one natural pond 400 families would benefit. To collect money for maintenance could become difficult which might lead to closure of the system and a total failure. In West Bengal many community-based ponds, operating for other joint ventures such as fishing, have failed. Community organisation in rural village settings works better when sustainability depends on smaller groups.

Community Filter

On another field trip, the use of two arsenic removal filters was assessed. In Amkhola, the filtering device was attached on top of the existing contaminated shallow tube well. After being chemically treated the residue or the sludge was getting discharged and collected in an open concrete tank of about three-sq. ft. (Ultimately the sludge that was to be discarded would contaminate the surface soil and water bodies unless it is properly removed from the collecting pit). Another filter at Mullickpur that was filtering the arsenic containing water had the sludge collected in a closed concrete tank of about four sq. ft.

Disadvantages of the Community Filter

1. Proper disposal of sludge is a big problem for community filter systems. Some reports state that the spent medium can be disposed of easily as a non-hazardous material for land fill, road construction and asphalt industry. The problem is the maintenance of the filters, collection of the arsenic-rich sludge from the respective villages without causing any human, water or agricultural exposure. Proper systematic methods of collecting the sludge from individual villages should be designed and implemented with caution to avoid any sort of pollution in the future.
2. In contrast to the indigenous methods like ponds or dug wells, the use of some community filters require bringing outside technology into the community that creates problems of sustainability.

From the Table 6.1 it is clear that the capital cost per family (Rs. 1625) is highest in case of the natural pond and reservoir or tank system. Also the maintenance cost is high at Rs. 25 per month per family. The capital cost per family for the community filter system assessed is Rs. 650. The maintenance cost is low, but the problem in the long run would be in the safe disposal of the arsenic-rich sludge. The capital cost per family for the river water treatment plant would be higher than Rs. 304 when unknown cost of the chemical plant would be added in. The maintenance cost is considerable. The domestic filters used to remove arsenic from the tube well water would be risky in the long run for they would add to polluting the environment in different ways.

Thus from this assessment of the different methods, it has been concluded that concrete dug wells, locally known as 'Indara', would be the cheapest form of providing arsenic free water to the community of North 24 Parganas. The capital cost per family is Rs. 266 and the maintenance cost estimate is Rs.10 per family per month. However this method requires care to make sure the wells do not develop bacteriological contamination.

Dugwells or Indara (Concrete) or Kua (Earthen)

The specifications for concrete dug wells for North 24 Parganas, West Bengal, are:

Table 6.2

Dimensions for Concrete Dugwells for North 24 Parganas

Depth	8 m-10 m or 26.4 ft-33 ft
Maximum Depth	18 m or 59.4 ft
Height above Ground	1.2 m or 4 ft
Minimum Diameter	1 m or 3.3 ft
Thickness of Wall	25 mm or 1 inch
Apron Width Minimum	1 m or 3.3 ft
Ring	Made by RCC
Number of families	Maximum 20
Population	80 to 100
Construction Period	April/May when water table is low

The depth of each dugwell should not exceed 18 metres. In fact, in North 24 Parganas the depth of a dugwell can be around 10 metres because the water table is high and at places it can be reached at 4 metres. The diameter of the well should be a minimum one metre and the height above the ground should also be minimum one metre to avoid any kind of drainage of water or dirt into the well especially during the monsoon season. A concrete boundary wall around the well should be built to stop people from tampering with it. A hand pump that will be located outside this boundary can be connected to the dugwell to draw out the water, rather than inserting buckets which are touched by human hands. In this manner, regular human contact with the well water can be totally avoided thereby reducing the risk of contamination.

Specifications for selecting the site:

1. The *indara* or concrete dugwell should be on higher ground than the surrounding area so that water does not drain into it.

2. It is ideal to build the dugwell at least 100 feet away from the cultivated fields to avoid leaching of pesticides and fertilisers used in the field.
3. To avoid any fecal contamination it is very important to make sure that there are no latrines within 100 feet of the well.

Figure 6.1

A Rough Sketch of Indara or Concrete Dugwell

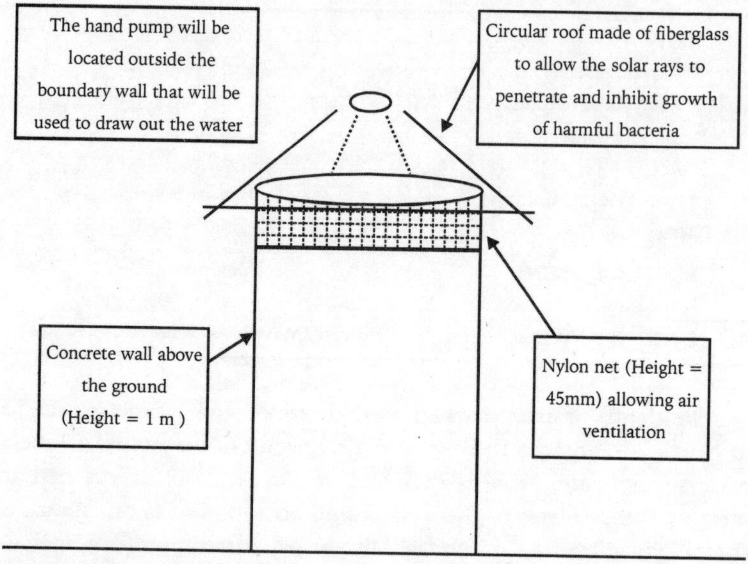

Source: Primitive method modified by Meera M. Hira Smith.

The coliform counts of almost similar dugwells used during pilot project in Bangladesh are shown on the Table 6.3.

The coliform test [Table 6.3(a)] shows that out of 11 water samples with coliform levels higher than 100. In fact 2 samples show very high levels of coliform.

Another study in a different area of Bangladesh showed [refer to Table 6.3(b)] 1 out of 14 samples with total coliform count per 100 ml as high as 2200. The other 13 (93 per cent) of the total samples were zero.

Table 6.3
Caliform Tests

(a)

Sl. No.	*Subject*	*Address*	*Coliform Counts*
1	ZM	Noyabari	50
2	MAH	Aminpur	83
3	JA	Tang Bari	6
4	SP	Tang Bari	29
5	MM	Shinduri	115
6	HU	Amninpur	105
7	LR	Tang Bari	62
8	AM	Madhapara	1360
9	RM	Natia Bari	55
10	SH	Noya Bari	3000
11	AR	Tang Bari	40

Source: Dhaka Community Hospital, recent report of Bera Option Water.

(b)

Sl. No.	*Lab #*	*Total Coliform/100ml*
1	951	0
2	952	0
3	953	0
4	954	0
5	955	0
6	956	0
7	957	0
8	958	0
9	959	0
10	960	0
11	961	0
12	962	0
13	963	0
14	964	2200

Source: Dhaka Community Hospital Report dated 5.7.2000.

Maintenance

(a) To take care of the quality of water and its proper distribution, the consumers of water from each dugwell will form a beneficiary committee comprised of a president, a treasurer and a secretary. The beneficiary committee will be responsible for the welfare of the dugwell.

(b) To maintain potable quality of the water, it will be tested periodically by a reliable laboratory in the nearby city.

(c) The bacteriological tests are expensive, and to cover the expense Rs.10 per month from each beneficiary family will need to be collected, including well cleaning and water disinfection.

(d) The report of the water analysis will be posted on a board together with a pie-graph denoting the quality of the water. The pie-graph will have the following information: Green-Safe to drink; Orange-Caution; Red-Unsafe; and White-Dry.

(e) An arrow will be fixed on the circle that will be rotated according to the quality of water. The position of the arrow on green will denote that the water is safe to drink and when it is on orange it would signify caution. That means the water after collection should be either boiled or treated with some chemical at individual's home or filtered to remove bacteria. The red colour denotes the water is unsafe for drinking and the well should be cleaned and disinfected. White means the well is dry. At these times, expected to be between 0 and 2 months per year, people should go to the nearest non-contaminated source of water.

Figure 6.2

Water Hazard Figure

(f) The above figure will be posted at every dugwell site. It will be drawn on a metallic sheet and nailed to the wall of the dugwell. To avoid any tampering, the figure will be protected by a net and kept locked all the time. Only the president and the secretary of the beneficiary committee will have access to it.

Some of the advantages and specifications for the use of dug-wells which are being installed are:

1. *Availability of Local Skilled Labour:* The design and skill for digging such 'dugwells' is easily available locally. No scientific technology is required, and there is no toxic waste to dispose of. The advantage of concrete dugwells over earthen ones is that chances of pathogenic infections are lower, but local material, skills and labour are available to make concrete dug wells.

2. *Primitive Method that is Easily Adaptable:* Dugwell, *indara* or *kua* is a traditional method that existed 30 years ago. This conventional method should not be hard to be adopted by the villagers.

3. *Type and Method:* The dugwells should be made out of concrete rings. A roof made of fiberglass rectangular sheets, that would permit solar radiation and prevent external contamination such as bird's droppings and dirt particles, can cover them. A nylon net of about one and half foot height should be placed on the mouth of the well to allow aeration. It is important not to cover the well totally with concrete or any opaque body.

4. *Hand Pump:* To draw out the water a hand pump needs to be connected to the dugwell. This method of withdrawal of water will prevent contamination caused by the bucket or/and the rope. Hand pump technology is available since that was the method used for shallow tube wells that the dugwells will replace.

5. *Beneficiary Community:* One dugwell can be shared by as many as 20 families of four members each (80-100 persons). The water will be strictly used for drinking and cooking purpose. Supervision will be done by respective beneficiary committees.

6. *Individual Preventive Water Treatments:* Cleaning and disinfecting the dugwells will be done annually or bi-annually by trained labourers to remove pathogenic bacteria. The collected water should be treated at individual's home when the arrow is in orange position, by any of the three following methods:

a) boiling for more than 10 minutes;

b) adding zeoline tablets or a pinch of alum ('phitkiri' or *kopur*); or

c) using domestic filter that removes harmful bacteria.

Conclusion

While local circumstances may lead to different conclusions in different areas, it was concluded that the best solution for the particular villages in this investigation was to insert concrete dugwells, locally known as *Indara*.

Additional Note

It would be helpful if a detailed report of the entire arsenic prone region is made available by the State Arsenic Board. The reports of all the work that have been done by governmental and non-governmental organisations so far in all the districts including the water test results, the methods provided in particular villages to supply arsenic free water, need to be combined. This would save a lot of time wasted during the process of gathering information from different departments. The State Arsenic Board should keep track of the extent of the arsenic work going on throughout the state. It should be made compulsory to send a report to the State Arsenic Board on the work or projects that each organisation, governmental or non-governmental, have done, are doing or are planning to do. With the help of such reports, perhaps made available on the Internet, it would be easier for future planners to select the next village to adopt in a drinking water programme. It is a waste of time to find later that the village in the plan has already been approached by other concerned organisations.

Updated 2003[5] by Meera M. Hira Smith

The dugwell on the exterior has been modified during the construction of wells in 2001 and in 2002. As you may see in the Picture 6.1 that a tin sheet cover is used on the top of the square boundary wall of height of approximately 1 foot to 2 feet that is sloping in one

5. Hira Smith M.M, Hore T. P. Chakraborty, D.K. Chakraborty, X. Savarimuthu and A.H. Smith (2003). "A Dugwell Program to Provide Arsenic-Safe Water in West Bengal, India: Preliminary Results", *Environmental Science and Health, Part A* (Toxic/Hazardous *Substances and Environmental* Engineering), Jan., 38(1):289-99.

Picture 6.1

Dugwell #PW10 at Kamdebkathi

Picture 6.2

Dugwell#PW44 at Kharoo

direction. A padlock is used to avoid any tempering. Inside the tin cover a second nylon net cover is used to prevent any debris like leaves, frog or snake, to drop into the well. This is to avoid any kind of organic material to be in the water that may lead to the release of arsenic into the water on decomposition. Arsenic is present in the soil.

Please also note that the diagram of the indicator board (Picture 6.3) is also modified but the objective is the same. Future developments will appear in website *www.projectwellusa.org*.

Picture 6.3

Indicator Board at Dugwell

7

The Economy of Homestead Garden[1]

MOUCHUMI K. BORGOHAIN

Introduction

By definition homestead gardens are the gardens adjacent to the house dwelt in by people. In the rural households of Assam, land was not a scarce factor till the recent past. At the time when transport links were not developed properly, the geophysical location of the state amidst the surrounding hills of The Himalayas in the north and northeast, and the Patkai range of mountains in the south gave a characteristic of inaccessibility of the region to the outsiders. The state bears following ecological characteristics that are conducive for plant growth:

(1) An average annual rainfall of around 2275.3 mm. and a humid climate with annual average of relative humidity around 80.8 per cent

(2) For the state, the average annual maximum temperature (July-August) lies between 30 degree Celsius to 33 degree Celsius and the minimum temperature (Dec.-Jan.) lies between 6 degree Celsius to 12 degree Celsius.

(3) Average sunshine hours for the state is 4-6 hours/day during summer and 8-10 hours/day during winter.

These ecological characteristics give a wide range of plant varieties although inadequate sunshine hours and temporary waterlogged conditions have checked the productivity level. This spontaneous growth of wide varieties of plants is one main reason for the growth of homestead garden in Assam, which appears as one unique character especially pertaining to rural economic structure of Assam.

1. Paper presented in the Third Biennial Conference of The Indian Society of Ecological Economics, December 2003, and is a part of the author's Ph. D. research work, Dibrugarh University.

Assam, which is lagging behind the other states of India in many developmental indicators, has created concern and awe among many conscious policy makers and development planners. Situated in the farther part of north eastern region with relatively weak transportation link, be it railway, roadway or airway, the state at the present juncture is facing numerous socioeconomic and political problems. All these relate to the failure of the state to develop at par with the other well-off states of the country; rich in exhaustible natural resources like mineral oil and coal, the state and its inhabitants fear the problem of resource crunch in the near future as these resources are extracted out and put to different industrial uses within the country. The industrialisation drive is not equally fared by the people of Assam, which is one important reason for the growing dissatisfaction among the young generation who feel endangered of their rights on one hand and inability to play meaningful role in the region's development on the other hand. Agriculture is the predominant sector for the state yet agricultural productivity lags behind the national average. Rural economic structure forms the backbone of the economy but its developmental aspect is neither adequately nor effectively focused at different policy levels. Villagers living in the rural areas when asked about their income, economic conditions, etc. give replies to confirm their low income level, poor economic conditions hardship in living, etc, which are not at all encouraging. Yet some unsolved queries still prickle one's mind in the sense that rural people of Assam never sought to migrate to cities and other areas in search of jobs and alternative source of income. If the answer is sought by assuming that the opportunity cost of getting employed or engaged elsewhere is not up to their expectation, then one may put here a vital point to ponder and thorough probe; it is that the income and means of livelihood generated as farmers and cultivators are supplemented by some other source of real income generation. Keeping aside home based weaving and handloom activities to which the women of this region are aptly attached and qualified, it is the practice of maintaining homestead garden in every household that provides supplementary benefit through generation of shadow income from the products produced in this garden.

Keeping in view these aspects of rural scenario of Assam, this chapter attempts to focus the covert economy of homestead garden of rural Assam. The historical linkage of this type of garden goes back to around 14th to 15th centuries AD. The region was at that time under the rule of Ahom dynasty, who had entered from the northeastern side of this land area in the 13th century AD.

> As the story goes, the king once visited the residence of his distinguished minister Mumai Tamuli Borborua one day and was highly impressed by the *Baari* (homestead garden) that the minister had developed with meticulous care surrounding his house. When asked, the minister put the logic for planting different types of trees in different areas of his garden so convincingly that king ordered his ministers to direct the people to set up similar types of garden surrounding their houses. The practice flourished and in due time became a tradition among the well-offs as well as among not so well-offs.

Methodology

Field study was carried out in three revenue villages that lie at the vicinity of Jorhat town. The villages are Komar Hazarika *gaon* (V1), Merdia *gaon* (V2) and Cheuni *gaon* (V3). Ten households from each village were taken as sample units. The selection of sample is done on the basis of judgment sampling so that in the choice of samples, household with big landholding as well as with small landholding are incorporated in the samples. Questions relating to land, homestead land and their uses are put to the sample households through questionnaires. In the questionnaires, the values of the useful plants grown in the homestead garden are calculated by putting questions on the following aspects to the heads of the sample households.

In construing the monetary values of useful trees and plants, different standards are adopted for different types of plants. For the fruit trees, values are construed on the basis of products of the trees and their market valuation. For the fuel-wood trees, the value is construed on the basis of the price that a mature tree can obtain in the market. In case of bamboo tree, value is construed on the basis of number of bamboo that a single tree bear and the price of a full length bamboo in the market. In case of banana tree, the value is on the basis of the price of a bunch of banana in the market.

The collected data/information of three villages are tabulated in three tables. The information pertaining to the samples are totalled and the mean, maximum and the minimum of relevant subjects are calculated and noted down.

On the basis of the data entered into three tables pertaining to the three villages, the following table is constructed with regards to village 1, village 2 and village 3.

Table 7.1

Indicators	*Village 1 (V1)*	*Village 2 (V2)*	*Village 3(V3)*
1. No. of Sample Households	10	10	10
2. Total Landholding of the Samples (Hectares)	19.19	13.34	11.47
3. Average Size of the Landholding (Hectares)	1.9	1.3	1.15
4. Largest Size of the Landholding (Hectares)	6.7	5.1	1.9
5. Smallest Size of the Landholding (Hectares)	0.32	0.53	0.26
6. Total of the Homestead Land (Hectares)	4.34	3.37	3.25
7. Mean of the Homestead Holding (Hectares)	0.43	0.34	0.33
8. Largest Homestead Holding (Hectares)	0.93	0.80	0.63
9. Smallest Homestead Holding (Hectares)	0.05	0.13	0.13
10. Total of Useful Plants and Trees in the Homestead Gardens	1220	597	775
11. Average Number of Useful Plants per Homestead (rounded up)	122	60 (rounded up)	78 (rounded up)
12. Total Varieties of Useful Plants in the Gardens	157	126	143
13. Average of the Varieties per Homestead	14	13	14
14. Total Monetary Values of the Useful Trees and Plants (Rupees)	55343.00	38440.00	32675.00
15. Total of the Varieties of Medicinal Plants in the Homestead Gardens	96	93	89
16. Average of the Varieties per Homestead	10	9	9
17. Total of the Varieties of Winter Vegetables in the Gardens, (Average)	100 (10)	100 (10)	93 (9)
18. Total of the Varieties of Summer Vegetables in the Gardens, (Average)	84 (8)	88 (9)	90 (9)

The Findings

Among the sample household, 95 per cent solely depends on agriculture. It indicates that source of livelihood comes from agriculture and allied services, agro-based crafts and farming. The data relating to income generation shows that average annual income of the sample households of village 1 lies above both estimated income poverty line (IPL) which is Rs. 3000 per capita per annum as well as expenditure poverty line which is Rs. 3802 per capita per annum. The average annual income incorporates income from-

(a) Agricultural cultivation (includes monetary valuation of paddy cultivation at the current market prices and other cultivations like oil seeds, spices, etc. which are carried out in the agricultural fields);

(b) Livestock

(c) Water resources

(d) House craft (including weaving and handloom activities which is solely carried out by the women folk of each household)

(e) Income from salaries and wages, if any;

(f) Other businesses, if any.

For village 1, the average annual income from these sources, comes out around Rs. 27000. The income per capita per annum comes around Rs. 4500.(It is arrived at by dividing income per household by the average number of family members which is 6.)

For village 2, the average annual income from the above sources comes out around Rs. 20000. The income per capita per annum becomes Rs. 3333.3 which is slightly above the income poverty line estimate of 1998-99 but below the expenditure poverty line estimate.

For village 3, the average income from these sources comes around Rs. 17500 and income per capita stands at Rs. 2917.66. This level is below the income poverty line estimate as well as the expenditure poverty line estimate.

The Role of Homestead Garden

The figures in table 7.1, relating to total of the landholding and the total of the land under homestead gardens for the sample households of the three villages give the following estimations—

1. In village 1, total land under homestead garden is 22.6 per cent of the total landholding. **2.** In village 2, total land under homestead is 25.26 per cent of the total landholding. **3.** In village 3, total land under homestead is 28.33 per cent of the total landholding.

Figure 7.1

Percentage of Land under Homestead Garden

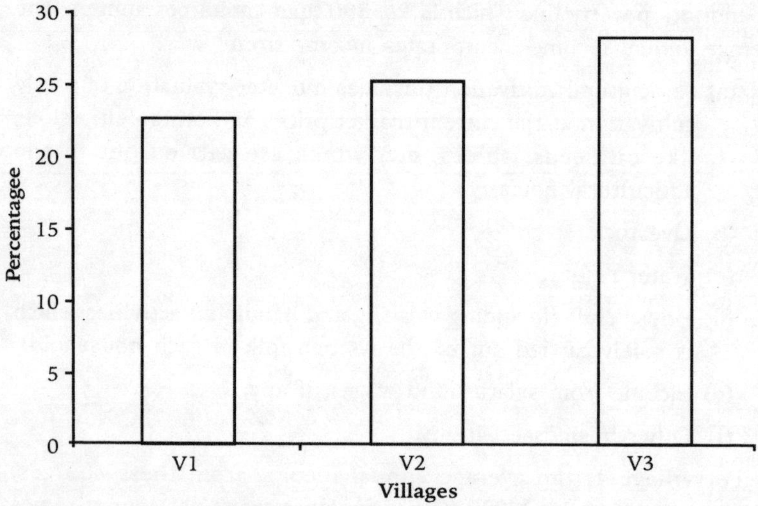

The mean size of the garden for village 1 is 0.43, for village 2 it is 0.34 and for village 3 the mean size is 0.33. The total values of the homestead gardens in three villages show the asset value of this natural wealth. This asset value plays positive role in determining the price of homestead land, which is in addition to the value of the plot of land itself, although there is lack of accuracy in exact calculation of such values. What is important is the use value of the product of homestead garden—their role in supplementing dietary intake, the shadow income generated through the use of these products in household and ultra-household economic activities, home-based crafts and cottage industries.

In the traditional village structure, one important role of homestead garden and its product pertains to the ecological dimension. The plantation of useful trees in the vicinity of the household is to a great extent influenced by what has to be and what has not to be. In following this tradition-bound obligation with regards to the plantation of trees in the homestead garden, the villagers unconsciously reveal in-depth knowledge regarding the surrounding eco-structure.

The Dietary Supplement

The nutritional standard of the three villages were calculated by taking into account the food items consumed by the sample households per month. Then the calories generated from the items consumed and the per capita calorie intake for each household member was computed. In the process of collecting data, it was noted down that the green leafy vegetables, a major part of other vegetables (excluding potato and onion) and the fruits consumed were attained from the homestead garden. Accordingly, in addition to the per capita calorie intake for three villages, the calorie intakes from green leafy vegetables, vegetables and fruits are separately calculated and put in the Table below.

Table 7.2

Sample Unit	*Per Capita Calorie Intake (kcal)*	*Per Capita Calorie Intake from Leafy Veg. (kcal)*	*Per Capita Calorie Intake from Veg. (kcal)*	*Per Capita Calorie Intake from Fruits (kcal)*	*Total of Columns (3,4 &5) (kcal)*	*Difference in Calories (Col.2-Col.6) (kcal)*
1	2	3	4	5	6	7
Village 1	2237.5	91.7	83.1	101.6	276.4	1961.1
Village 2	2219.5	100.8	73.3	152.5	326.6	1892.9
Village 3	1935	157.2	83.8	130	371	1564.0

In the Bar diagram furnished in Figure 7.2, Series1 is the per capita calorie intake. Series 2 is per capita calorie intake from leafy vegetables. Series 3 is per capita calorie intake from vegetables. Series 4 is per capita calorie intake from fruits. Series 5 is the total of the calorie from leafy vegetables, vegetables and fruits. Series 6 is the difference in the per capita calorie intake when calorie value from homestead product is subtracted.

Figure 7.2

Calorie Intake-V1, V2, V3

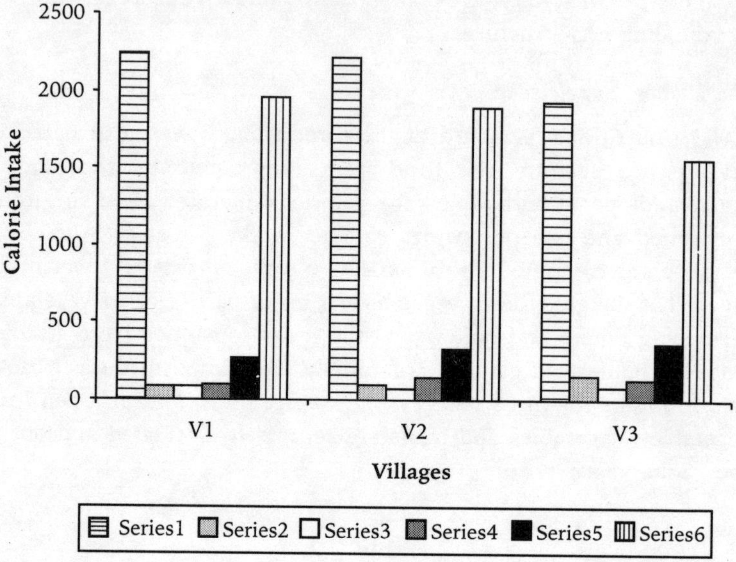

The information that can be obtained through the data contained in Table 7.2 relates directly to the role of the homestead gardens in the sample household. The dietary intake in terms of calorie value of the food confirms to the minimum average requirement of 2200 kcal for village 1 and village 2 but the dietary intake for village 3 sample units lags behind the minimum average requirement by a margin of 265 kcal. For village 1, the food supplemented by the vegetables and seasonal fruits grown on the homestead garden is about 276 kcal. In absence of these dietary supplements, the average dietary intake falls below the minimum dietary requirement (1961.1). For village 2, the dietary supplement from the products of homestead gardens is 326.6 and this amount also plays a significant role in keeping the nutritional standard above the minimum requirement. Village 3, that lags behind the other two with respect to total landholding and other indicators, remains below the minimum standard of 2200 kcal but without the dietary supplementation from the products of homestead garden it would have been far below the acquired amount (the per capita calorie is 1935, when the calorie value obtained from the homestead garden is subtracted, per capita calorie becomes 1564).

The above findings in terms calorie supplementation in the dietary intake shows that the gardens have been playing a vital role by keeping intact the daily energy requirement of the sample household.

The Medicinal Plants

The medicinal plants that grow in the gardens naturally in every household is another important dimension associated with the rural life and its sustainable character. As the Table 7.1 shows on average, number of medicinal plants grown per household is around 9 to 10. The plants grow in abundance almost all over the garden as well as any uncultivated area in the surrounding locality that does not require any specific allotment of area of its own. It is the reason for which the villagers did not answer the question on the area under medicinal plants.

The scientific names of the plants grown in the gardens are given below:

1. *Centella asiatica (manimuni)*
2. *Paederia foetida (vedai lata)*
3. *Houttuynia cordata (mosundari)*
4. *Alternanthera sessilis (matikanduri)*
5. *Oxalis corniculata (tengesi)*
6. *Leucas aspera (doron sak)*
7. *Ipomia aequetica (kalmou)*
8. *Enhydra fluctuans (helanci)*
9. *Bacopa monnieri(brahmi)*

Few other commonly found shrub type plants are–

Ocimum sanctum (Tulsi), *Azaderachta indica (Neem)* and *Murraya koenigii (Narasinha)*.

The use of these herbs in curing different health related issues and diseases is traditionally determined and appeared as time-tested herbal-medicines for the rural people in case of ailments like cold, tonsilitis, pharyngitis, dysentery, asthma, colic pain, pneumonia, piles, skin diseases, snake bite, rheumatism and likes. In fact, calculation of the shadow prices of these medicinal plants could emerge as an important area of research. Like so many non-monetary subjects in the rural livelihood, this has remained an unexplored domain so far. Establishing the corelation between the use of the medicinal herbs and infrequent visit of the villagers to the primary heath centre can show the utility of the medicinal plants. The practice of using medicinal herbs that grows in the nome garden is a traditionally transmitted culture among the rural people of the Northeast and its impact and influence in the development of the state's economy has not been properly assessed until now.

The Bamboo and Betelnut Plants

Among the trees invariably found in the gardens bamboo and betelnut come first. The role of these plants in the rural household had been surveyed while interviewing the sample households and the findings are put in a summarised form below.

The Bamboo Tree

In the study, it was found out that the average number of bamboo trees per household is around 5 to 7 plants in the three villages. Each plant bears 50 to 100 bamboos. In the village life, the bamboo plant is revered by each and every one and placed on a significant position due to the manifold uses to which the plant is subjected. A fully grown bamboo fetches 15 rupees to 20 rupees inside the villages and when these are brought to the adjacent town markets, the price of a full length bamboo goes up to Rs. 30 and more. Bamboos are in high demand in the town area as well as inside the village economy. Few of its manifold uses are-

(a) In the house construction, bamboo is used as for constructing walls, ceiling, etc.

(b) In constructing boundary fencing or any other type of fencing.

(c) In the household craft of making hand fans, baskets, indigenous handloom sets, furniture, etc. In recent times the demand for bamboo outside the state has increased for making diversified bamboo products which also includes ornamental craft work.

(d) Bamboo shoots are popular as a food item and used for making pickles and meat, fish and egg curry. These are uses associated with income supplementary functions of the bamboo trees.

Another important function associated with the existence of bamboo plants in the homestead garden is its role in the environmental and ecological aspects.

The villagers in general had put their justifications for planting the bamboo trees in the western boundary in the following ways: (a) They plant bamboo trees in that direction so that there can be no obstruction of the sun rays from falling on the garden products. (b) Bamboo trees act as wind barrier which otherwise may damage the useful plants and houses. (c) The plant has got various utilities but the root system of the plant does not allow other plants to grow near its vicinity. So planting the tree in the western boundary of the homestead land allows the other plants to grow well.

The Betelnut Tree

In case of betelnut tree, it was found that there is a traditional wisdom with regards to its plantation. These plants are planted in the boundaries of houses and adjacent homestead gardens to ensure a clear and straight outline of the boundaries. The tall, lean and straight body of the plant can automatically correct any ambiguity that is present in defining boundaries of the houses and adjoining garden.

The average number of this plant per household in the 3 villages is 20 and the average bearing of nuts per tree is around 500 in number; these numbers being born in 3-4 bunches of every fully grown betelnut tree. The price of a single betelnut is about 50 paise and a single betelnut tree generates an income of Rs. 250. So, the income that can be brought from 20 fully grown betelnut trees is around Rs. 5000. Betelnuts have good market demand and this part of income can be earned by every household by imparting minimum effort for the process.

Besides its significant role in income generation for the household, the plant also carries a great cultural and traditional value among the villagers. The fresh nut with the leaves of betel vine, little amount of lime and tobacco makes *tamul-paan,* a kind of *mukh-suddhi* offered to the guests and is taken by adult persons commonly after taking any meal. This *tamul-paan* is offered in religious offering, social functions, etc. and without it, the welcoming/offering/servicing activities remain incomplete. Although the nutritive value of *tamul-paan* is not significant, it generates calorie value and the villagers maintain that the hot and humid days of summer and cold chilly days of winter months become bearable with the chewing of *tamul-paan* at regular interval.

Along with these two varieties of plants, other plants and their role in income generation, garden culture, etc. were discussed with the heads of the sample household during interview. It was found that, on the average, they do not assess the trees from the angle of income generation; rather they make the assessment from the uses that these trees generate for them.

The Banana Plant

The banana plant that every household had in their gardens, is a plant put to diversified uses. The bearing of banana fruit takes its peak in all seasons except in the winter season, and when planted in a planned way, the tree provides fruit almost all round the year. The price that a bunch of banana can obtain when traded lies within the range of Rs. 80 to Rs. 150 at the wholesale rate depending on the variety of the banana. The stem and the leaves of the tree are put to use in religious ceremonies. The stem of the young plant, when cooked, is a delicious source of curry called *posala tarkari* and the banana trees planted in the home gardens raise the level of adjacent land area. Household's waste products are dumped near the plants and the stem and the roots of the plant can absorb sufficient amount of rainwater and other water to protect the surrounding land area from waterlogged condition.

In addition to these economically and ecologically viable trees in the garden, there are other trees of economic significance. These are fuel-wood trees that provide the poor household with fuel-woods for cooking. The burning of trees generate air pollution, but side by side there are the *neem* trees in every sample household that has air purifying quality. The flower trees that grow in the homestead do not generate any economically viable values but are good source of aesthetic satisfaction as a public good. Some of the flower plants also serve as medicinal plants for ailments like worm problem.

Conclusion

The above points made by the villagers with regards to the homestead garden relate to the ecological dimension of sustainability of the system to which they are accustomed. It was found that they have traditional wisdom with regards to planting of trees in the garden but they lack the vision of generating substantial amount of regular income from these sources. Because of the second aspect with regard to village dwellers' approach towards products of homestead garden, that plantation of trees and plants is carried out in the form of a traditional practice among the villagers. This has served the purpose of keeping the surrounding ecology and environment intact, but failed to recognise this significant micro-sector of every household as a prospective sector of income generation.

The study of homestead gardens in this chapter reveals that there is ample scope of developing the rural economy at the micro level by structuring the homestead gardens in a dynamic manner. The tradition bound heritage of nurturing home gardens gives the village people a sustainable system, may be at subsistence level for some people, but proper planning and policy intervention at the national, state and regional level will enable this sector to play a determining role in the state and regional level economic structure.

8

Intellectual Property Rights: Options Assessment[1]

APARNA BHAGIRATHY[2]

Intellectual Property Protection in Knowledge Goods

In today's knowledge-based economy, the debate surrounding intellectual property rights (IPR) has taken on new dimensions. The products of the core sectors of the knowledge-based economy, such as digitally distributed products, biotechnological processes and genetic sequences are widening the scope of what constitutes intellectual property and are also raising a specific set of issues in the design of IPR systems to cater to the requirements of intellectual property protection of these 'knowledge goods'. Digital technologies are expensive to produce but are easily copied at low costs. Biotechnology and genetic engineering have directed focus on ownership of biological and genetic resources, as they constitute the sources of raw material for these sectors. Thus, the delineation of rights over these resources and the rules governing their access and use assume tremendous significance. Innovations for protection under IPR systems cover a wide range that now includes, plant varieties, genetic sequences, life forms, digital codification of facts and software programmes and traditional or indigenous knowledge.

There are specific issues that arise in protection of intellectual property in knowledge goods, given their peculiar characteristics. In an age, where information technologies and knowledge-based services

1. This chapter is the result of a project funded by the South Asian Network for Development and Environmental Economics (SANDEE).

2. I am thankful to SANDEE for both financial support and research inputs received from the panel of reviewers during the biannual research meetings. I wish to thank Prof. Nirmal Sengupta, MIDS for several helpful discussions and comments in developing this chapter and for his guidance over the entire course of the project. All errors are, of course, my own.

are rapidly evolving and spreading their impact in the working of a number of sectors, the design of IPR systems must also change to cater to specific requirements of these knowledge goods. David (1993) describes the peculiar characteristics of knowledge when classified as a commodity and how it differs from other commodities for the purposes of intellectual property protection.

- Once a piece of knowledge/information has been obtained, there is no value to obtaining it a second or a third time. The information once obtained can be used repeatedly but the stock of knowledge does not get depleted with use.
- Knowledge can be possessed and enjoyed by several persons at a time. It is what is known as a non-rival good.
- There are private and social costs to creating and transmitting, filtering, interpreting and utilising information. For instance, in order to use technological knowledge contained in patents, scientific papers, etc. access to the information alone is not sufficient to implement the technology; complementary know-how is also required.
- What really sets knowledge apart from any other public good is that the complete attributes of the information good are not known beforehand. There is asymmetry in distribution of information about costs and benefits of innovations among the agents involved. Administrators and researchers do not have identical information about the potential social value of the inventions and the expected costs.
- Innovation is often cumulative and interactive in nature. Each advance builds on an earlier innovation or existing stock of knowledge. Knowledge evolves and acquires new utility through cumulation and interaction.

It is immediately apparent that the characteristics of knowledge listed above apply just as well to 'traditional' knowledge also.

The institutional arrangements discussed in relation to allocation and production of knowledge and information goods are similar to solutions to the problem of allocation of public goods. In the case of public goods there are three kinds of solutions—subsidies, governmental production and regulated monopoly. Similarly, in relation to knowledge commodities, there are three kinds of institutional arrangements, often classified as prizes, research contracts (including government procurement) and intellectual property rights. Each of these systems has particular advantages and shortcomings as incentives for R&D and specific conditions under which one may be chosen.

IPR systems for traditional knowledge are developed by adapting existing IPR laws for prevention of misappropriation of traditional knowledge and/or by developing new legislation for recognition and registration of rights and establishing a reward system for sharing of benefits with the holders of traditional knowledge. Adapting existing IPR systems involves amending legal provisions either by providing a wider interpretation of the subject matter for protection to cover traditional knowledge products and processes or by introducing new provisions specifically for protection of traditional knowledge. For example, trademarks and industrial designs are used to protect traditional names and designs. Countries like China and Vietnam have been taking efforts at amending their patent laws for protection of pharmaceutical products based on traditional knowledge. Recently, at the fifth WTO Ministerial Conference at Doha, it was mandated that Geographical Indications protection be extended to products other than wines and spirits. This, of course can be interpreted to include traditional knowledge products also, where such protection can be particularly suited to protect traditional knowledge products and processes.

Even before the Convention on Biological Diversity (CBD), pharmaceutical prospecting was touted as an incentive mechanism for conservation of medicinal plants. Widespread ethnobotanical research and high returns from trade in plant-based medicinal drugs led pharmaceutical companies to invest in bioprospecting in expectation of high revenues from drugs developed thereon. The debate on whether pharmaceutical prospecting generates sufficient revenues for conservation of medicinal plants has gone a full circle starting from the 'Magic Well' picture that changed drastically as studies[3] showed 'vanishingly small' values derived from prospecting of medicinal plants. Currently, the debate is again at a more optimistic lead, as studies indicate that traditional knowledge led searches for active

3. See for instance, Pearce and Moran, (1994) and Simpson *et al.*, (1996).

compounds in medicinal plants (as opposed to random searches) lead to result in higher 'hit rates' and lower search costs in drug discovery.[4] With the rapid development of biotechnology and bioinformatics, interest in bioprospecting and traditional medicine is high. As Mathur (2003) explains, with 40 per cent of the pharmaceutical patents due to expire by 2006 and with the advent of biotechnology and pharmacogenomics, biotech firms are trying to discover and develop new active ingredients from traditional medicine. The choice of an appropriate method for estimating the value of medicinal plants and the lack of empirical evidence are problems, which are as yet unresolved. There is another significant factor that has not received much attention in the literature on valuation of medicinal plants. Most valuation studies calculate the value of medicinal plants by focusing on the contribution of traditional knowledge as useful leads in reducing search costs of pharmaceutical prospecting. An important factor that is often overlooked is the growing market worldwide for traditional medicine and medicinal practices itself. The global market for traditional therapies stands at US$ 60 billion a year and is steadily growing. New models, based on the value of medicinal discoveries for alternative markets, will be particularly useful for developing policies and legislation governing access to and use of medicinal resources for traditional or complementary and alternative medicine.

The CBD suggests that benefit sharing arrangements can be used to implement provisions of prior informed consent and equitable sharing of benefits from use of biological resources. However, evidence from experiences of the benefit sharing models experimented with so far show that they have not been successful in fulfilling the CBD objectives. The reasons for the same are analysed below.

Over the last decade, several pharmaceutical companies involved in pharmaceutical prospecting also developed models for benefit sharing from drug development with the indigenous communities. Some of the well-known cases are the Costa Rican INBio-Merck & Co. case; the Shaman Pharmaceuticals model; benefit sharing arrangements developed by Government sponsored programmes like the International Cooperative Biodiversity Groups (ICBG) programmes

4. See recent studies by Rausser and Small, 2000; Pushpakumara *et al.*, 2002; Kumar, 2001.

of the US Government and research institutes like the Tropical Botanical Gardens Research Institute (TBGRI), India. Except for the case of TBGRI, commercial drugs are yet to be completely developed from any of the other initiatives, though several leads have been obtained. In fact, the extremely high costs, and the risk and time involved in clinical trials and R&D in drug development resulted in the bankruptcy and closure of Shaman Pharmaceuticals. In the one successful case of the early nineties, the Kani-TBGRI case in Kerala, India, there were several problems after the drug Jeevani was developed. There were problems in terms of access to the plant resource, market establishment, in balancing competing claims of representation for benefit sharing and calculation of shares in distributing the benefits from royalties and licence fees. Some of these issues are yet to be resolved.

A common result that these cases show is that using leads from traditional knowledge reduce search costs related to identifying potential samples. However, there are also very high transaction costs in obtaining consent and collection of samples from indigenous peoples and in further clinical trials for R&D. Though the government-sponsored programmes are in a better position in terms of availability of funds, they face other problems regarding valuation of the monetary benefits after drug development and in identifying and compensating the beneficiaries. One of the most important issues in the implementation of the benefit sharing models is the identification of the beneficiaries. This is a problem faced while awarding IPR rights also. There is seldom a single beneficiary. As the rights over the resources and knowledge are held collectively, questions revolve around how the communities are defined (for instance, geographically, ethnically or politically, etc.) for the purpose of sharing the benefits.

Each of these incentive systems has specific advantages and shortcomings. According to the suitability to and requirement of the situation in different countries, one or usually, a combination of the above systems is used for protection and promotion of traditional knowledge. However, there is very little economic analysis on the choice of the incentive systems and their effectiveness in relation to the objectives of the CBD. This chapter attempts to review the IPR system as an incentive mechanism for protection and promotion of use of traditional knowledge in the context of commercialisation of the knowledge. The objective of this chapter is to draw up a framework for analysing the design of IPR systems for traditional knowledge. In the following sections such a framework is developed using relevant economic theories of IPR.

Economics of Intellectual Property Rights

The principal economic theory underlying analysis of intellectual property is grounded in utilitarianism—intellectual property rights have historically been justified as incentives 'to promote the progress of science and useful arts' through the creation of exclusive rights of limited duration so as to balance the social welfare loss due to monopoly exploitation (Menell, 2000); North *et al.*, 1973; North, 1981) attributes the rapid pace of technological development and innovations during the Industrial Revolution to the existence of a systematic protection of rights over intellectual property. However, there were also opposing views (Plant, 1934) regarding the usefulness if IPR as it was argued that innovative activity is largely spontaneous and there was no need for IPR to stimulate such activity. This issue was resolved in the seminal analysis of the markets for information. Arrow (1962) describes that any information, for e.g. on a new method of production, available free of charge ensures optimal utilisation of the information, but provides no incentive for investment in research. IPR, through the creation of property rights, thus basically serve as incentives to direct investment into innovative activity, rather than innovation *per se*. Patents provide a means of bringing the private rate of return closer to the social rate of return, thereby encouraging investment in innovation and its spread.

Economic analysis of patents primarily focuses on the tradeoff between the benefits accruing from increased innovation against the deadweight loss imposed due to granting temporary exclusive rights to innovators over their innovations. Nordhaus (1969) formally analyses this trade-off by providing a framework for designing the optimal IPR policy. In the classic Nordhaus model, only one policy instrument was considered in the design of the optimal policy—the duration of the patent. He argues that the patent life can be adjusted to provide optimal duration of protection such that it balances the incentives provided for innovation against the deadweight loss due to monopoly exploitation. However, there are several problems with this. In the first place, only if the patent life can reflect the R&D costs and benefits, is it possible to choose the efficient research firm and grant a patent long enough to cover the costs. If so, the optimal patent duration would be the shortest one that gives the inventor enough incentive to invest. Secondly, there is usually, asymmetry of information about the costs and benefits of R&D. The patent authority does not have the same information about the costs and potential benefits of an invention, as does the researcher or an innovating firm. Thirdly, there is an *ex ante* uncertainty about costs and benefits. Making patent length depend on R&D costs would lead innovators to overstate their costs, while a system that rewards only successful innovations would reduce the incentives for investment in research. This problem could again be addressed under the patent system if the patent life could reflect R&D costs and benefits or alternatively, the authorities use some mechanism by which, agents reveal private information about their strategies and costs.

Subsequent studies have focused on another policy instrument; the patent breadth or the scope of the protection as a variable affecting per-period profit of the patent. Broadening a patent will result in higher per-period profit. Then the patent life can be made shorter so that the loss due to monopoly exploitation is reduced, without discouraging R&D. So, what is patent breadth? Gilbert and Shapiro (1990) take the flow rate of profit available to the inventor (determined by the patentee's ability to raise the price of the patented product) as a proxy for patent breadth, while Klemperer (1990) in an alternative approach defines it as the product space covered by a patent. This difference in interpreting patent breath correspondingly produces different results in designing the patent policy. Gilbert and Shapiro, in their model, argue for narrow patents of infinite duration, because broad patents, as per their definition are more costly in terms of deadweight loss. In Klemperer's model, the source of deadweight loss arises due to substitution to alternative products. Increasing the breadth in this case would mean that non-infringing substitutes are made less attractive to the customers and thus, the patent life could be shortened without discouraging R&D.

With the analysis of patent breadth as an alternative instrument to address the Nordhaus trade-off, theories of IPR started incorporating the dynamic aspects of innovation, not considered earlier in the models. Inventive activity is rarely undertaken in isolation. There are usually, several inventors or research firms working simultaneously, often towards the same patent, but with different research strategies and expectations of the costs and benefits involved. Under such dynamic models of innovation, Green and Scotchmer (1995) interpret patent breadth as the minimum improvement required to avoid infringing a prior patent.

While, patent length or patent breadth can be used as instruments for patent policy, there are some additional issues that have to be dealt with in designing an optimal policy. David (1993) explains that in order to secure benefits from the increasing stock of knowledge, it is desirable to promote full and prompt disclosure of new findings, so that they may be disseminated, verified by replication and put to use by others engaged in intellectual pursuits. This in turn implies that rewards are based on some criterion of priority, such as, the first to invent or first to register for a patent. This gives rise to patent races and inefficiencies due to duplication of inventive effort. Excessive inventive effort could be avoided under a contract system if all the agents are fully aware of the potential costs and social value of the findings of all the innovators.

An important feature of innovative activity that until recently was not incorporated in the economic theories of IPR is the cumulativeness of innovations. The design of IPR incentives takes on new dimensions when we consider that the social value of an invention is compounded by the fact that it facilitates future innovations. Given this, the incremental value accruing from such future discoveries must also be incorporated into the social value created by the initial invention (Scotchmer, 1991). Cumulativeness in innovations implies that inventions of one inventor become a foundation for subsequent innovations by other inventors. These could largely be of four types—improvements over earlier products; cost reductions for producing earlier products; applications of basic technologies and enabling technologies, such as, research tools. The basic problem with cumulative innovations is the division of joint profits from the cumulative innovations between the original and subsequent innovators. In order to provide incentives for investment in innovation, the first inventor must be able to appropriate a share of the profits from subsequent innovations facilitated by his/her original invention. Simultaneously, it must be ensured that the incentives are designed so that this sharing of profits with the original inventor does not reduce incentives for the subsequent innovators to undertake R&D.

The CBD objective of equitable sharing of benefits is essentially the same issue as that of cumulative innovations—division of joint profits with subsequent innovators. Economic theories of IPR incorporating cumulative nature of innovations are germane to the analysis of the design of incentives for intellectual property protection of traditional knowledge. In order to provide incentives for the preservation and continuation of traditional knowledge and practices, the holders of traditional knowledge must be able to appropriate a share of the profits from the innovations facilitated by their existing knowledge and practices. In designing these incentives, it must be ensured that while providing a share in the rewards to the original holders of traditional knowledge, it doest not discourage R&D by the subsequent innovators. There are also divergences in the context of traditional knowledge as cumulative innovations. There does not usually exist a patent on the original invention nor is there a single innovator. Often, the original innovator(s) are not identifiable. Models of cumulative innovation sometimes assume that the original and subsequent innovations take place contemporaneously. Obviously, this assumption does not hold for traditional knowledge. These issues are studied in detail in the subsequent sections as a framework is developed using cumulative innovation theory for a formal analysis of IPR incentives in the context of traditional knowledge.

Cumulative Innovation Theories

The cumulative nature of innovation was incorporated into models of intellectual property protection with the policy debate on alternative instruments, such as, patent breadth in addressing the Nordhaus tradeoff. In the earlier models, innovation is often represented as a single, stand alone inventive effort that is seldom improved upon. However, in reality, this is rarely the case. There exist very few pioneering innovations, while most innovations build on earlier works. When there are positive externalities from innovations, there arise issues of contracting between the original and subsequent generations of innovators. The cumulativeness of innovations and the extent of the breadth of the patent have implications for incentives to innovators, both original and subsequent to invest in R&D to develop the innovation.

As seen earlier, Gilbert and Shapiro (1990) and Klemperer (1990) introduced the patent breadth dimension into the policy debate. Scotchmer (1991) extended it further to incorporate cumulativeness of innovation by providing for possibilities of *ex ante* agreements between innovators in designing optimal patent breadth. As explained earlier, the cumulative nature of innovations has implications for the social value of the innovation, which is compounded by the value of subsequent innovations facilitated by the original innovation. This therefore, brings up the possibilities of contractual arrangements between the innovators involved in the original and subsequent research. Innovations are essentially improvements over a stock of knowledge and the optimal patent must provide for claims over future research (Green and Scotchmer, 1995; Chang, 1995 and O'Donoghue *et al.*, 1998). These models interpret patent breadth as the minimum improvement required to avoid infringing a prior patent. A solution provided in these models to the problem of designing incentives is through *ex ante* contracting. However, there are positive transaction costs associated with such contracting and different alternative forms of governance structures in each case.

Another view of patent breadth in the context of cumulative innovation is provided from the legal approach—litigation in enforcing patents determine the boundaries of protection available to the firm. Merges and Nelson (1990) for instance, explain that judicial practices like reverse equivalence determine the effective patent breadth. In a further analysis, Llobet (2002), establishes that patent breadth is determined by litigation technology by relating the concept of breadth to the probability that the patent holder succeeds in court and the size of the future innovator.

The specific problems in the cumulative innovation models are briefly described below. An example of cumulative innovation is the case of 'basic' and 'applied' research. Transferring profits from the second-generation product to the first innovator, so as to provide the original inventor with sufficient incentive to undertake basic research is difficult. Denicolo (1996) explains that if the second product is made patentable, it transfers profits from the first innovator to the second, thereby reducing the incentive to invest in the first innovation but increasing incentive to invest in the second. Subsequent products, that are improvements over the original products or technology may displace the original products from the market. This reduces the incentive for the initial inventors to undertake research.

Establishing an optimal patent length or patent breadth or a combination of both provides a solution to this problem. Designing IPR policy for cumulative innovations first involves determining if the subsequent product developed from the original innovation infringes the patent on the original product; whether the second product is itself patentable; and if so, the lengths of the first and second patents. The other related factor is regarding patent breadth. Patent breadth can be construed to mean the minimum improvement required to avoid infringing the first patent. If the initial inventor is provided with a broad protection, he/she can earn profits through licensing. This might have an adverse impact though, on the second innovator's incentive to undertake further R&D on the basic research. For instance, if small improvements were patentable then firms might become too modest in their aspirations relative to the social value of improvements. When small improvements are not patentable, firms aspire to larger ones (O' Donoghue, 1998). *Ex ante* agreements to share both costs and profits can bring about a balance but the characteristics of these arrangements would depend on the bargaining positions of the two sets of innovators.

Recent models[5] of cumulative innovation also consider infinite sequences of improvement, where each inventor will both licence from the earlier innovator and licence to the next. In this scenario, the difference between original and subsequent innovators will fade eventually.

In the case of infinite sequence of quality improvements, the effective patent life largely depends on the patent breadth. The patent on the first product ends when a non-infringing better product is introduced in the market and replaces the original innovation. Thus, increasing the effective patent life by increasing the breadth will have a positive impact on the profits of the innovators. However, in that

5. Scotchmer, 1999; O'Donoghue, Scotchmer and Thisse, 1998.

case, just as an innovator may earn more profits through licence fees, similarly, he/she will also have to pay more in terms of licence fees to the preceding inventors.

Another important factor is the determination of the subject matter of patentability. Patent law establishes the conditions under which, the second-generation product infringes on the first patent and when the second-generation product itself is patentable. While, whether a product infringes a patent is determined by the breadth of the first patent, patentability is established by the novelty (inventive step) requirements. Scotchmer explains that if infringing applications of basic innovations are patentable, then, patentability is unnecessary to protect profits and an exclusive licence on the prior patent would be sufficient. Patentability of the subsequent product improves the second firm's bargaining power for an exclusive licence and undermines the profit of the initial innovation. When the second product is both infringing and patentable, then both the firm could end up with blocking patents *ex post*.

While there are several theoretical models in relation to cumulative innovation theory, there is as yet, very little empirical evidence in this area.

A Cumulative Innovation Model for Traditional Knowledge

Traditional knowledge and innovations developed from it are cumulative in nature. The social value of traditional knowledge is compounded by the value of future innovations facilitated by the existing stock of traditional knowledge. The theory of cumulative innovations (CI) provides a framework for analysing the central issues of the design of IPR protection (length and scope of protection) for traditional knowledge and an appropriate mechanism (licensing and contractual arrangements) for sharing with the holders of traditional knowledge, joint profits arising from traditional knowledge-based innovations developed. In designing incentive systems for traditional knowledge, it must be established if subsequent innovations based on traditional knowledge are in fact patentable (or qualify for any other form of IPR protection) and if so, the requirements for the same. There is no patent on the original traditional knowledge; the IPR provisions developed must therefore establish the level of quality improvements required for patenting of the second-generation traditional knowledge-based innovations or in other words, the breadth or scope of protection. Another important issue is the length of protection. The protection for the original innovation represents an infinite period of time. The length of protection for the subsequent innovations however, must be established.

The knowledge regarding the particular characteristics and specific uses of the medicinal plant species in an area, held over generations by the local communities or groups of individuals, is the original stock of knowledge. In CI theory, this is known as basic research. For pharmaceutical companies and biotechnological firms, this is an important resource base for future innovations. Leads obtained from traditional knowledge considerably reduce search costs involved in prospecting and result in higher 'hit rates' in identifying active compounds from plant species for drug discovery. The leads obtained from traditional knowledge are also useful in developing products that are applications of or improvements over the existing knowledge.

As already pointed out, there are some divergences in cumulative innovation in scientific and technological research from that in traditional knowledge. The holders of traditional knowledge do not own patent rights or any other form of intellectual property rights over their knowledge. There is rarely only a single inventor; the rights over the knowledge are held collectively, which raises issues in sharing of joint profits from subsequent innovations. Another problem is that of asymmetry of information about the value of traditional knowledge. However, these issues can be addressed through contractual and licensing arrangements. Further, the Traditional Knowledge Digital Library (TKDL), a database enabled with features of search and retrieval of traditional knowledge pertaining to medicinal plants addresses to an extent, the problem of asymmetry of information about value of traditional knowledge. Though, the TKDL has been prepared by the Government of India as non-patent literature database to prevent the incorrect grant of patents over traditional knowledge, it is also an important source of valuable traditional knowledge that will serve as the basic research for subsequently developing useful traditional knowledge-based innovations. Licensing arrangements developed for the database act as the vehicle to transfer profits from future innovations. This database is a means to both preserve and promote the use of valuable traditional knowledge. The need for developing a mechanism to resolve potential conflicts in intellectual property rights from use of the knowledge in the database is imminent, but guidelines for regulating access to and use of the database are yet to be established. CI theory provides guidelines for developing an appropriate mechanism for regulating the access to and use of TKDL. The application of the theory to TKDL is examined in detail in the final section.

There are two basic questions that arise on the commercial utilisation of traditional knowledge outside the context of the community that holds and preserves it. First, under what conditions, will there be an incentive to invest in R&D to develop traditional knowledge-based innovations? Second, what kind of a mechanism should be developed to ensure sharing of joint profits from commercial products derived from the basic traditional knowledge, with the holders of the knowledge? These issues are central to CI theory. The solutions to the above question basically lie in designing the optimal IPR policy by establishing the optimal length and scope of IPR protection, given the cumulative nature of traditional knowledge-based innovations. This in turn determines, how the rights of the different parties are defined and their bargaining positions in a licensing agreement.

The Model

A formal analysis of the design of IPR systems for cumulative innovations in traditional knowledge can be developed using a simple formulation of a cumulative innovation model provided in Scotchmer (1999).

As explained earlier, traditional knowledge is a form of basic research, which on its own commands no commercial value, but in turn, derives its value from the value of future innovations facilitated by it. There are two notions of value[6] in this context: market and non-market values. One is the value of traditional knowledge derived from the traditional use of the resource and associated knowledge within the local context of the community and the other is derived from its use outside the local context of the community. These may be broadly

6. I am thankful to Prof. Kanchan Chopra for a very useful discussion on this section.

classified as the non-market and market use of the traditional knowledge relating to biological resources. The market value of traditional knowledge is determined when members outside the community that traditionally own the rights over traditional knowledge, use the knowledge to develop further products or cost-reducing processes. Commercialisation of the traditional knowledge, closely held within a community may involve a loss to the community in terms of changes in access to and the traditional use of the resources and knowledge. It no longer remains as traditional knowledge embedded within the social and cultural context of the community. However, given the declining use of traditional knowledge and practices in some cases, such commercialisation of traditional knowledge can also prove to be beneficial as it translates to the community the viability of preserving the tradition.

Let the initial period commercial value of the traditional knowledge be equal to zero.

$x(t)$ = per period market value of traditional knowledge, which at $x(0)=0$.

The time period just prior to commercialisation of traditional knowledge is referred to as $t=0$. The market value of traditional knowledge at this point is equal to zero. But traditional knowledge is also a form of basic research and it derives its market value from future innovations that are applications of the basic traditional knowledge. This is included in what is known as the social value of the basic innovation.

$\pi(x, T)$ = market value of the basic traditional knowledge innovation for a given number of years of protection, 'T'.

$\pi(x, T) = f(x, T, c_1, r)$

x = $x(t)$ per period market value of the traditional knowledge innovation

T = duration of protection

c_1 = costs undertaken in preserving and transferring traditional knowledge

r = rate of discount

The market value of the basic traditional knowledge innovation for a given period of time $\pi(x, T)$is a function of the value of the basic research (x); the duration of protection (T); the costs undertaken in developing the basic research (c_1) and the discount rate (r). As explained above, prior to commercialisation of traditional knowledge, the market value of the basic research is equal to zero.

The well-known Kani tribe-TBGRI[7] case can be used here, as an illustration. The anti-stress and immuno-stimulating properties of the fruit of the plant, *arogyapacha* (*Trichopus zeylanicus travancoricus*) was known only to the members of the Kani Tribe[8] of Kerala. This knowledge served as the basis to the TBGRI scientists for detailed scientific investigation and chemical screening to identify the active compounds and develop a restorative, immuno-enhancing, anti-stress and anti-fatigue drug, Jeevani. With the potential for development of a pharmaceutical drug, there emerged, a commercial value of the traditional knowledge for the tribe. Thus, 'x' represents the market value of the basic traditional knowledge, i.e. the knowledge about the medicinal use of a plant species or a method of production etc. This is the original traditional knowledge 'innovation' that facilitates future innovations. In this case, the basic traditional knowledge innovation is the knowledge about the medicinal properties of the fruit of the plant *arogyapaacha,* which was held only within the community. Within the Kani tribe, the rights of transfer and practice of certain traditional medicinal knowledge customarily rests with tribal healers (known as *Plathis*). The market value of the traditional knowledge innovation was initially zero till the potential for developing a pharmaceutical drug from the knowledge was discovered.

In case of a modern scientific or technological innovation protected by a patent, 'T' represents the length of the patent protection, which, as per the requirements of the TRIPS Agreement, is currently for 20 years. The market value of the innovation increases with an increasing T.A longer duration patent results in higher profits to the innovation, but also increases the dead weight loss to the consumers due to

7. The scientists of the Tropical Botanic Garden and Research Institute (TBGRI), Kerala learnt of the medicinal properties of the plant from the two Kani tribe members who were acting as guides to their team during an expedition in the forests. For details, see Anuradha, 1998 and Gupta, 2000.

8. The members of the Kani Tribe live in the forests of the Thiruvananthapuram district of Kerala, South India. Their current population is estimated to be around 18,000.

monopoly exploitation. In the case of traditional knowledge, of course there exists no such patent protection. Yet, the knowledge is preserved and transferred through customary systems by the holders of the knowledge for generations, as is done by the traditional healers of the Kani tribe. Hence, 'T', can be interpreted to represent an infinite term of protection, in the case of the traditional knowledge innovation.

The costs incurred in developing the basic research are given by c_1. The solution to the classical Nordhaus model is that the optimal duration of IPR protection should be such that it covers the costs of the innovation. In the case of cumulative innovations, as the basic innovation is of no commercial value, the first innovator must be able to appropriate a share from the profits of the future innovations, so as to recover the costs incurred in developing the basic research. Otherwise, there will be no incentive to invest in basic research. While traditional knowledge exists over generations, the communities or group of individuals involved continue to incur costs in preserving and transferring the knowledge. The objective of benefit sharing provisions envisaged in Article 8J of the CBD, 1992 is to reward the holders of traditional knowledge for incurring costs for their efforts in conservation and sustainable use of biological resources.

$\pi(x, T)$ is actually the present market value of the basic innovation for a given time period T. A suitable rate of discount 'r' has to be determined to calculate the present value of the traditional knowledge innovation.

Given the cumulative nature of traditional knowledge innovations, the value of traditional knowledge is compounded by the value of future innovations that are developed based on the initial stock. The traditional medicinal knowledge, once obtained by pharmaceutical companies becomes the base for developing further marketable drugs. The concept of social value of innovation captures this additional value generated from cumulative innovations. The social value of innovation is represented by $W(x, T)$.

$$W(x, T) = f(x, T, c_1, r, a)$$

where, c_1 refers to costs of both basic and applied research, where $i=1, 2$ (the original and subsequent innovators, i.e. the traditional knowledge holders and the pharmaceutical company, respectively).

a = per period market value of the application, which is the pharmaceutical drug developed.

Thus, in addition to the market value of the basic innovation, the social value of traditional knowledge includes the market value of the subsequent innovation (i.e. the pharmaceutical drug developed from application of the traditional knowledge innovation) and the costs involved in developing the application. Hence, c_i refers to the costs of both sets of innovators: the original innovators, i.e. holders of traditional knowledge and the subsequent innovator i.e. the pharmaceutical company that develops a marketable drug based on the traditional knowledge. Using the same earlier example, the social value of the traditional medicinal knowledge of the Kani tribe is compounded by the value of the drug Jeevani developed by the TBGRI based on the traditional knowledge associated with the *arogyapacha* plant. Thus the social value of the innovation W(x, T) increases with the market value of the application 'a' developed from the basic innovation.

In this case, we consider only one application developed from the traditional knowledge. In reality, there is usually a sequence of innovations based on the original innovation. The medicinal properties of the drug Jeevani could in turn serve as the basic knowledge for further improved drugs or cost reducing processes. This system of sequential innovations, which include several stages of innovation over the basic research, is common in the information technology and biotech industries. The computer chip and several software programmes that undergo regular successive improvements are examples of sequential innovation. Pharmaceutical and bioengineered products also undergo a series of improvements with time. This is described as a 'quality ladder', in which, the difference between the basic and applied research, or the first and second innovators fades eventually. Correspondingly, the social value of the original innovation will also reduce with time, as its contribution to future applications is also lower at the later stages of innovation.

W(x, T) for any basic innovation protected by a patent reduces with increased length of protection, as a longer patent implies a greater deadweight loss. In case of sequential innovations, the classic Nordhaus tradeoff appears as the effective length of the patent has to be long enough to cover the research costs but must also ensure that incentives for subsequent research are not reduced.

W(x, T) > π(x, T). The social value of the basic traditional knowledge innovation is greater than the private market value of the knowledge as it is compounded by the value of subsequent innovations also. The social value of traditional knowledge further includes any costs borne by the community due to its loss of traditional knowledge on commercialisation. Similarly, it also includes any gains to the community that accrue from sharing of the profits from subsequent innovations developed. Thus the social value of the innovation, can be represented as W(x, T) where, in case of a two stage innovation of basic and applied research, i=1,2. The first innovator is the entire community[9] or group of individuals holding the rights over the basic traditional knowledge and the second innovator is the pharmaceutical company interested in developing the drug. In case of a quality ladder, *i*=1,2,3....n, where there are n-1 stages of innovation and one company at each stage interested in developing the application.

This brings up the question, "Under what conditions will investment in subsequent R&D to develop applications based on traditional medicinal knowledge take place?" This question is directly addressed by the design of incentives to promote traditional knowledge based innovations. The design of a suitable IPR policy, determining the length, scope and subject matter of protection and the mechanism for sharing of joint profits will determine the incentives for traditional knowledge based innovations.

Let us first consider the case of a two-stage innovation of basic and applied research, where there is only one innovator interested in developing the application. The firm developing the application has an idea, (a, c_2) where,

a = per period market value of the application

c_2 = cost of developing the application

$\pi(a, T)$ = Market value of the application for a given T (length of protection)

$$\pi(a, T) = f(a, T, c_2, r)$$

Unlike the case of the basic traditional knowledge innovation, the

9. We assume that the value of TK is the same for all the holders of TK within one community, represented by x_1.

application developed based on the traditional knowledge innovation, has a market value that can be determined as it is sold in the market. 'a' is the market value of the pharmaceutical drug developed from application of the basic traditional knowledge innovation.

Likewise, the application can also be protected under a patent. With a longer patent life, the market value also increases. Simultaneously, the patent breadth must also be established. The subject matter of protection under the patent system must ensure that there is sufficient inventive step in the application of the original traditional knowledge and is not merely a repackaging of what is already known. This includes, determining whether the application is patentable at all in the first place, and if it is, the degree of novelty requirement in order to qualify for a patent and the specific conditions under which a patent is granted.

The IPR system must also ensure that the costs incurred by the firm in developing the application are covered. Else, there will be very little incentive for investing in subsequent R&D. As in the case of developing a pharmaceutical drug, there are huge costs involved in clinical trials, tests, standardisation and validation before the drug is developed. This often takes several years apart from requiring large amounts of investment. Unless the firm is able to recover the costs incurred through a patent or any other system, it will not have the incentive to invest in developing the drug at all.

In multiple stages of innovation based on traditional knowledge, W(a, T), the first application developed based on the original traditional knowledge innovation, is compounded by the value of further innovations facilitated by it. This raises the question of patent length and breadth for the subsequent innovations. O' Donoghue *et al.*, 1998 explain two types of solutions for determining the effective patent life in the case of a quality ladder. One solution is to provide a long statutory patent with limited breadth, while the other, is to provide patents of a finite length and unlimited breadth. In the first case, the longer the patent length is, the greater is the deadweight consumer loss due to consolidation of property rights. In the second case, where the patent breadth is very large, there might occur wastage of R&D resources; for it requires, subsequent innovations to be in the nature of large improvements. In the absence of an existing patent on traditional knowledge, suitable licensing arrangements can be designed so that holders of traditional knowledge can stake their claims over future innovations developed based on their traditional knowledge. In order to provide incentives for investing in subsequent R&D, the effective patent life awarded for the applications must be such that it covers the costs of the innovation and adds to the joint profits of both sets of innovators.

Returning to the original question, "Under what conditions will investment in subsequent R&D to develop applications based on traditional medicinal knowledge take place?" The result that is already obvious from the above discussion is that, there is incentive to invest in developing the application, whenever it adds to joint profits and the costs of the innovation can be recovered fully.

If $\pi(a, T)-c_2 > 0$ then, the investment in subsequent R&D to develop the application based on the original traditional knowledge innovation will take place.

If the market value of the application exceeds the costs involved in developing it, then, there is an incentive for the subsequent innovator in investing in R&D to develop the application. In order to ensure this, the effective patent life has to be determined so that the costs of developing the innovation 'c_2' are recovered. If $\pi(a, T)-c_2 < 0$, there is no incentive for investing in subsequent research as the market value of the application is lower than the costs involved in developing it. This could occur, if the costs of the innovation are too high or the effective length of the protection available does not cover the costs. For instance, a relatively minor improvement over traditional knowledge may require large amounts of investment. As in the case of pharmaceutical drugs developed from traditional medicinal knowledge, substantial resources are devoted to clinical tests, standardisation and R&D. The value of the drug developed eventually, may be relatively small in comparision to these costs incurred. Put in other words, if the IPR system for the protection of the application does not enable the innovator to recover the costs incurred, then, there is very little incentive to develop the application. Either, the length of the patent (T) should be long enough for the innovator to recover the costs or in the case of a finite patent life the patent breadth must be larger, so that returns can be earned through licensing.

However, it should be remembered that the application is developed from the existing stock of knowledge and though, there exists no patent, the traditional knowledge holders have a claim to the profits from the application. In the absence of a share of benefits from future innovations, there is no incentive for the community holding the traditional knowledge to share their knowledge with the pharmaceutical company or in some cases, where there is declining use of traditional knowledge and practices within the community itself, to continue its preservation. Licensing arrangements enable the profits from the marketing of the traditional knowledge-based application to be transferred to the traditional knowledge holders. The rights of the parties involved and their bargaining positions determine the terms of the licensing arrangement. The novelty requirements of the patents for the subsequent innovations can be determined if the applications are 'infringing' on the existing traditional knowledge. The cases of incorrect grant of patents over traditional knowledge essentially present this problem. There is no patent on traditional knowledge to prove that the subsequent innovations are infringing. Patent laws establish that patents cannot be granted over 'prior art', i.e. knowledge already known or in use. Thus, patent laws for subsequent traditional knowledge-based innovations can clearly define the novelty requirements so that the innovator demonstrates sufficient inventive step over traditional knowledge, in order for the application to qualify for a patent.

Now, if the entire surplus is transferred to the original inventor, there is very little incentive for the subsequent innovator to undertake investment in R&D. Even if the condition $\pi(a, T)-c_2 > 0$ is satisfied it might still be unprofitable for the pharmaceutical firm to invest in the innovation, for the surplus from the application is transferred to the traditional knowledge holders. Following are different types of licensing arrangements that determine relative shares of profits for the innovators and their incentives to invest in innovations.

Scheme 1: Ex post Licensing of Innovations

Licensing arrangements to share profits from cumulative innovations can be developed *ex post*, i.e. after the costs in developing the application are sunk. Given this situation, where the firm has already invested in R&D to develop traditional knowledge-based innovation, the bargaining surplus available to be shared between the innovators is the entire surplus from the application, which is otherwise, the market value of the application.

$\pi(a, T)$ = Bargaining surplus.

k and $1\text{-}k$ are the respective shares of the traditional knowledge holders and the pharmaceutical firm in dividing the bargaining surplus

The licensing arrangement divides the bargaining surplus $\pi(a, T)$ into non-negative shares of k and $1\text{-}k$ between the traditional knowledge holders who provide the basic research and the pharmaceutical firm that develops the drug based on traditional knowledge.

$\pi(a, T) - c_2 > 0$ is the condition for the pharmaceutical form to undertake the investment for developing the application. However, in an *ex post* licensing arrangement, we find that even if the above condition that the application is developed every time it adds to joint profits is satisfied, investment by the firm may not be profitable. The firm will expect to cover the costs of innovation with the profits it earns from marketing the application. This may not take place as explained with the help of the licensing arrangement described below,

$(k)\pi(a, T) - c_1$ = anticipated profit for the holders of traditional knowledge

$(1\text{-}k)\pi(a, T) - c_2$ = anticipated profit for the pharmaceutical firm

Thus, even if $\pi(a, T) - c_2 > 0$, it might still be unprofitable for the firm to invest in the application, as costs of innovation may not be covered fully. Only if $(1-k)\pi(a, T) - c_2 > 0$, will it be profitable for the firm to invest in the application. One way to ensure this is to increase the life of the patent available to the pharmaceutical firm, but as seen earlier, this increases the deadweight loss to the consumers. W(a, T) decreases with a longer T.

Under the scheme of *ex post* licensing, the condition that the application is developed every time it adds to joint profits does not hold. Even if the application adds to joint profits, the share of firm investing might not be sufficient to cover its costs and the entire costs sunk in developing the application is borne only by the firm. While profits are shared, the costs are not.

Scheme 2: Ex ante Contracting

Ex ante contracting i.e., before the costs c_2 are sunk, can ensure that the application is produced whenever it adds to joint profit. But it cannot ensure that the entire profit surplus is transferred to the original innovators as in the previous case.

$\pi(a, T)-c_2$ = Bargaining surplus

$k(\pi(a, T)-c_2)-c_1$ = Anticipated profit to the traditional knowledge holders

$(1-k)(\pi(a, T)-c_2)$ = Anticipated profit to the pharmaceutical company

Thus, the entire surplus $\pi(a, T)$ is not transferred to the holders of traditional knowledge. While, this ensures that investment in the application takes place whenever, $\pi(a, T)-c_1 > 0$, it also splits the costs of innovation between both sets of innovators. *Ex ante* contracting can help to increase social welfare as it ensures that the application is developed. Considering that the value of traditional knowledge is derived from future innovations, ensuring that applications are developed adds to the profit earned from commercialisation of traditional knowledge. However, the share in the bargaining surplus is reduced for the traditional knowledge holders as the costs of the application are also shared and the entire surplus from the application is not transferred. This problem can be addressed by providing a longer duration of protection. As it is, there is no fixed term of protection for traditional knowledge; T is interpreted to refer to an infinite time period. Licensing arrangements or *sui generis* systems developed for traditional knowledge can ensure that profits from subsequent innovations are transferred to traditional knowledge holders for a time period that rewards them for their efforts and compensates them for costs incurred. In other words, the condition $k(\pi(a, T)-c_2)-c_1 \geq 0$ must hold. This is a stronger condition and as explained above requires a longer term of protection.

Thus, *ex ante* contracting arrangements can be arranged in a manner such that it is beneficial to both sets of innovators and adds to joint profits. As opposed to *ex post* licensing, this ensures that the condition for investment in the application holds. The design of an appropriate licensing arrangement depends on the bargaining positions of the parties involved and the terms for sharing the joint profits. A coordinating agency such as the government, for instance, acting on behalf of and with the consent of the community holding traditional knowledge, can make available to a pharmaceutical firm, an exclusive licence over traditional knowledge. Through a system of *ex ante* contracting, terms of the licensing arrangement can be determined in advance so that corresponding shares in the joint profits for the holders of traditional knowledge and the firm with the licence to produce and market the traditional knowledge application are calculated and implemented.

Scheme 3: Ex ante contracting with several subsequent innovators

I have indicated earlier that there can be several stages of cumulative innovation over the basic stock of knowledge. However, there can also be several innovators interested in developing traditional knowledge applications at one stage. *Ex ante* contracting ensures that the application is developed whenever it adds to joint profits and provides a means for sharing of joint profits. However, there is rarely only a single firm interested in developing an application. Several firms can compete for an exclusive licence over TK to develop the application. In such a situation, problems arise from asymmetry of information between the original and subsequent innovators. The firms interested in developing the application all hold private information about their costs and benefits of innovation.

The condition for investment in the application is:

$\pi(a_i, T) - c_i > 0.$

There are several firms with the idea (a_i, c_i) where,

i = 1…n; the number of firms interested in developing the traditional knowledge application

a_i = per period market value of the traditional knowledge application to the ith firm

c_i = cost of developing the traditional knowledge application to the ith firm

$k(\pi(a_i, T) - c_1)$ = profit for the traditional knowledge holders

$(1-k)(\pi(a_i, T) - c_i)$ = profit to the ith firm that procures the *ex ante* licence

The problem is in assimilating the information on all (a_i, c_i). This problem may be addressed by a mechanism design. The government, any other agency or a representative of the community itself can act as the principal on behalf of the group of individuals holding the rights over traditional knowledge. The pharmaceutical companies are the multiple agents interested in developing traditional knowledge-based applications. These companies hold private information regarding the different (a_i, c_i).

Again, *ex ante* licensing arrangements can ensure the development of the application and a suitable system for the sharing of joint profits. As in the mechanism design game, the government, for example, as the principal chooses a mechanism based on the agent types. A system, such as a fee for the exclusive licence to use the traditional knowledge or the number of licences that will be auctioned to the companies has to be determined and announced. The pharmaceutical firms interested in developing the traditional knowledge based innovation can then choose to accept or reject the mechanism. Accordingly, the firms that accept the licence fee or the auction system play the game as specified by the mechanism and reveal their true types. Once this information is collected and the game played, the bargaining surplus can be divided as per the guidelines of the *ex ante* licensing agreements.

These forms of contractual arrangements already exist in case of traditional knowledge databases where, *ex ante* licensing arrangements are announced. The access to and the use of the database are regulated through these licences. Apart from licensing systems, certain types of IPR can be used to redefine the rights over traditional knowledge in the changed context of its commercial utilisation outside the community. These rights also help to better determine the bargaining position of the traditional knowledge holders in a licensing arrangement. *Sui generis* systems can be developed to define the rights of the communities over their knowledge. Some examples of countries that are developing *sui generis* systems have already been described earlier in this chapter. These systems enable the government and the communities holding traditional knowledge to regulate access to and use of biological resources and the associated traditional knowledge. While patents may not be a suitable mechanism, alternatively, forms of collective IPR may be developed and used. For instance, neighbourhood rights provide moral and remunerative rights to performing artists and record publishers in authorising copies of an artwork or a musical performance. A similar system that guarantees rights of the community over the traditional knowledge and establishes a mechanism for controlling access to and use by parties outside the community will determine the bargaining positions of both parties in a licensing or contractual agreement and help to develop an optimal policy for protection and use of traditional knowledge.

Conclusions

In this chapter, a framework for economic analysis of the design of IPR for traditional medicinal knowledge has been drawn up using a model of cumulative innovation. traditional knowledge is also a form of cumulative innovation; it serves as the basic stock of knowledge for developing future innovations that are improvements or applications of the existing knowledge. Given this framework, the question of equitable sharing of benefits is essentially that of division of joint profits arising from innovations based on traditional knowledge, between the communities that share their knowledge and the firms that develop innovations based on this knowledge.

This involves designing IPR incentives to encourage investment in innovation to develop an application based on traditional knowledge. For this, not only does the application developed have to add to joint profits, the firms developing it must also be able to recover their costs of innovation and the holders of traditional knowledge earn a share in the returns for their contribution in facilitating the innovation in the first place. *Ex ante* contracting provides a solution in addressing this tradeoff. *Ex ante* licensing arrangements ensure that applications are developed whenever it adds to joint profits and that both, costs and profits of innovation are shared between communities holding the basic traditional knowledge and the firms that invest in further traditional knowledge based innovations. This further involves determining the length, scope and subject matter of IPR protection for subsequent products developed from traditional knowledge. Simultaneously, existing IPR and/or *sui generis* systems have to be established for regulating access to and use of traditional knowledge and associated biological resources to ensure that the resources are not over exploited and are used in a sustainable manner. I have also briefly demonstrated in the last section, the application of the CI theory to develop incentive mechanisms in the cases of benefit sharing models and digital databases for traditional medicinal knowledge related to biodiversity.

As already indicated in the CI model, there can be several innovators interested in developing traditional knowledge based innovations at one stage. Also, innovation based on traditional knowledge is not restricted to a one time improvement or application; there are several stages of cumulative innovation that is possible and is also undertaken. Thus, the basic CI model can be developed to incorporate both of these aspects—expansion horizontally by including multiple innovators at the second stage and by building the model vertically by analysing the case of 'quality ladders' for traditional knowledge based innovations. Empirical estimation and evidence would go a long way in supporting these models and will be particularly useful for policy making by the government. There is in the existing IPR literature for scientific and technological innovations, empirical studies on the impact of patents and other IPR, but these are limited and mostly pertaining to the pharmaceutical industries. Another aspect relates to the methods for estimating the market and social values of traditional knowledge and innovations developed from it. The values can then be incorporated into the CI models.

As countries are developing national systems of legislation for protection and sustainable use of biological resources and related traditional knowledge, the guidelines from CI theory are particularly useful in addressing the issues involved and designing incentive systems. The objective of this chapter is to highlight the kind of economic analysis that is possible and required in the area. To conclude, I would like to emphasise that there is need to initiate further research along these lines and also to identify alternative approaches to address the central CBD issues of protection of collective rights over resources and knowledge and of equitable sharing of benefits arising from their use.

9

Economics of Bioprospecting[1]

PUSHPAM KUMAR AND
NORI TARUI

Introduction

Bioprospecting refers to the extraction and screening of chemical compounds from plants to develop useful leads for potentially new drugs. In its early stage, prospecting largely centred on plants from the forest ecosystem. Recently insects, algae, and microorganisms of different ecosystems (e.g. grassland and marine) have also been explored with considerable expectations and success. While scientists are trying to derive useful extracts from the biodiversity of different ecosystems, economists, ecologists and policy planners are debating over the benefits and its value in the bioprospecting processes. The economic value of plants or living organisms for pharmaceutical purposes is crucial not only to pharmaceutical firms but also for the host country or local people, who command exclusive ownership of the biological resources and expect adequate compensation for resource uses especially after the Convention on Biological Diversity (CBD) in 1992. The Convention clearly establishes the control and sovereignty of local agency over the biological resources and its diversity.

The phenomenon of bioprospecting faces a typical situation where crucial raw materials (genetic resources) are primarily owned by the poor tropical countries while the necessary biotechnology and R&D capacity are owned by the pharmaceutical firms of the developed world (US and Europe in particular). Whatever benefits arise from bioprospecting have to be shared in a way acceptable to both parties. This issue becomes the bone of contention when prospecting firms

1. An earlier version of this chapter was published as *Working Paper* No. E/234/2003 of the Institute of Economic Growth, Delhi.

claim the following: the process of bioprospecting involves elements of high risk and cost, and hence they deserve a greater share of benefits. Host countries and locals on the other hand, suspect foul play in this. In this context, this chapter tries to examine the following:

(i) Are there any benefits of bioprospecting (or value of medicinal plants)?

(ii) If yes, how much?

(iii) What are the major findings of some of the recent studies in this direction?

(iv) Do the empirical experiences of bioprospecting confirm that the contribution of indigenous knowledge and information enhance the value of biodiversity in the process of bioprospecting?

An attempt has been made to answer these questions by citing facts from real world events. We have selected two widely debated studies on valuation of biodiversity for pharmaceutical prospecting; one by Simpson *et al.* (1996) and the other by Rausser and Small (2000). These studies can be looked into as representative of diverse views on this issue. After reviewing recent medical discovery from wild plants in the rest of this section, in Section 2 we review these two studies that measured the bioprospecting values of ecological species in several resource-rich regions in the world. We will conclude that the different estimates by these studies are driven by different assumptions on the role of available ethno-botanical information in each region. In Section 3 we have put forth the arguments that the bioprospecting values of species will be higher than those predicted by the two studies if one takes into account local-specific information on the species—the information available from local people—in addition to the widely available ethno-botanical information considered by Rausser and Small (2000). We also propose a model to examine the contribution of indigenous knowledge to the bioprospecting value of diverse species. Section 4 concludes our discussion with the explication of the future agenda by providing recommendations for further research which follows from the directions we have developed in this chapter.

Medicinal plants found in nature have been in use for pharmaceutical purposes in different parts of the world for centuries. Also, active ingredients from flora and fauna are found to be dominant in a large number of drugs. In the past many of the known useful drugs have been derived from leads provided by these medicinal plants. In US alone, 57 per cent of the prescriptions filled from January through September in 1993 contained at least one major active compound 'now or once derived or patented after compounds derived from biological diversity' (Grifo and Downes, 1996). Examples of deriving drugs from plants are numerous and a common knowledge. Table 9.1 provides representative samples of medical products derived from wild plants.

Table 9.1

Medical Products from Wild Plants

Name of the Wild Plants	*Location*	*Derived Drugs*	*Use*
Pacific Yew	Pacific Northwest	Taxol	Ovarian Cancer
Rosy Periwinkle	Madagascar	Vinblastine Vincristine	Blood and Lymph Cancer
Foxglove	Europe, Africa, Asia	Digitalis	Cardiac Arrhythmias
Meadowsweet	Worldwide	Aspirin	Fever and Pains
Cinchona	Tropics	Quinine	Malaria
Snakeroot	India	Rauwolfia	Hypertension and Schizophrenia
Curare	Amazon	Tubercurarine	Muscle Relaxant

Source: Compiled by the authors.

Comprehensive list of all medicinal products coming directly or indirectly from wild biota could be an unending one. The perceptible contribution of biodiversity to human welfare is thus likely to be enormous.

Value of the Benefits from Bioprospecting: Review of Literature

Alternative Views on the Value of Bioprospecting

One of the enduring questions in the economic research on bioprospecting has been whether it provides private firms (such as pharmaceuticals) with an incentive for preservation of ecological habitats in resource-rich regions. If the value of biodiversity in an undisturbed habitat for pharmaceutical research exceeds the opportunity cost of conservation, it may result in market-based preservation of the habitat without external intervention on the land use. If this is the case, then the policy needed for ecosystem preservation will have to be considered differently. With this motivation as governing factors, a number of estimations of benefits of medicinal plants have been conducted. In one of the earlier estimates, Farnsworth and Soejarto (1985) in their pioneering effort calculated the value of medicinal plants that were expected to disappear by 2000 in the US. Based on several assumptions, they estimate the value of the whole plant in the US as $ 203 billion (1980 USD). Principe (1996) calculates the value of medicinal plants as a total figure of $ 6.2 billion for the US in 1985. Mendelsohn and Balick (1995) aggregated the potential social value for undiscovered tropical forest. They estimated the pharmaceutical value of the medicinal plants as $ 147 billion (1980 USD) yielding $ 48 per hectare of tropical forest. This estimate is of the social value of forest for medicinal plants, but the market value may be lower than this, which has been admitted and estimated to be $3 to $4 billion (1980 USD).

Recently, Simpson *et al.* (1996) estimated the value of biodiversity for bioprospecting. They advocate that the incentive for biodiversity conservation on the basis of benefits of bioprospecting is not tenable because the value of the benefits is very small. In another significant study, Rausser and Small (2000) present a contrasting finding and explain that if the search for a useful lead is based on scientific inputs and information, rather than being a process of brute testing, then the value of biodiversity can be significant. In the next subsection we examine these two seminal works to identify why they offer different recommendations on the value of the bioprospecting benefits from the same biological resources.[2] The study by Simpson *et al.* has generated a great deal of attention, and hence it becomes imperative to examine their findings in some detail.

---

2. See Kumar (2001) for a detailed review of the valuation studies on medicinal plants.

Simpson et al. versus Rausser and Small

Both studies begin by introducing a theoretical model as a basis for deriving a demand function for biodiversity by prospecting researchers and determine their willingness to pay for the species as an input into commercial products. The model by Simpson *et al.* (1996) characterises bioprospecting as a process of sequential search on species (or leads) for the discovery of a new product. Each species has the potential to provide genetic information useful for the new product, which earns a net revenue $R > 0$ gross of sampling cost $c \in (0, R)$. They assume that the probability of a discovery (p) is common to all the species under consideration. With these assumptions, each new sampling is treated as an independent Bernoulli trial with equal probability of success p. In valuing the contribution by an additional species, Simpson *et al.* (1996) emphasise that discoveries may be redundant; once a successful product is found, further discoveries of the same product become valueless. They made this point clear by explaining why genetic resources may be redundant in practice: the same species may be formed over a wide range; there are numerous instances in which identical drugs have been isolated from different species; and there may be non-organic substitutes for the leads discovered from biological resources (p.169).

Given such potential redundancy of discoveries and the same probability of discovery for all species, the value of the entire collection N of samples is given by

$$V(N; P) = \frac{p^{R-c}}{p}[1-(1-p)^N]$$

and the value of an additional species is

$$MV(N; p) = V(N+1; p) - V(N; p) = (p^{R-c})(1-p)^N$$

Here the marginal value MV is concave in p and there is a global maximum $p^*(N) \in (0, 1)$ under the assumption $R>c>0$. Simpson *et al.* claim that the maximum marginal value MV $(N; p^*(N))$ is modest at the best. One reason is obvious: as N increases, the value goes down. Simpson *et al.* (1996) also explain another insight: if all species are promising sources of leads (i.e. p is high), then most would be redundant and the marginal species would be valueless. Conversely, if p is low then it is unlikely that any species will prove to have value. On the other hand, a rise in the likelihood of success with any species (p) causes the expected payoff in the event that the species is tested to increase. At the same time, however, another equally valuable species may be discovered first so that the expected payoff of the species declines. This is the cost generated by redundancy.

As a numerical example, Simpson *et al.* goes on to estimate MV(N; p*(N)) using data on 18 ecologically distinctive ecosystems (the biological 'hot spots', Myers, 1988).[3] They demonstrated that the value of an additional unit of land in these ecosystems is modest even under optimistic assumptions on the profitability of discoveries (Table 9.2). This result implies that bioprospecting alone does not provide private pharmaceutical companies with sufficient incentives for habitat conservation.

As Simpson *et al.* (1996) admits, pharmaceutical researchers do not generally conduct random searches even though they assume random sampling for their model. Rather, a pharmaceutical firm begins testing with the most promising species first. Rausser and Small (2000) explicitly incorporate this aspect of pharmaceutical research into their model by assuming that the hit probability (p) may vary among species. With a model otherwise as identical to the one by Simpson *et al.* (1996), they claim that an optimal search programme involves testing a lead with the maximal hit probability among those not yet examined (Proposition 1, p.181). Letting $p_1 > ... > p_N$ be the hitting probabilities of samples 1, ..., N, the optimal order of samples to be searched is 1, 2, ..., N. Given this optimal sequence, the expected payoff to the search at its outset is given by

$$V_1\left(\{p_i\}_{i=1}^{N}, N\right) = \sum_{n=1}^{N} a_n (p_n R - c) \qquad ...(1)$$

where $a_n = \Pi_{i=1}^{n-1} (1 - p_n)$, the probability that the search is carried to the 'th' stage. Correspondingly, the *ex post* expected value of continuing the search after n–1 leads have been tested unsuccessfully is recursively given by

$$V_n\left(\{p_i\}_{i=1}^{N}, N\right) = p_n(R - c) + (1 - p_n)(V_{n+1} - c), \; n = 1,...N.$$

3. In fact, what they estimated is the value of an additional unit of land in each hot spot with the same species density in the corresponding ecosystem.

Then the incremental value of lead (the maximum a firm will be willing to pay at the start of a search project for a call option on lead n), denoted by v_n, is a function of the hitting probabilities of all leads $p_1,...,p_N$ as well R as and c :

$$v_n\left(\{p_i\}_{i=1}^{N}, N\right) = v_N\left(\{p_i\}_{i=1}^{N}, N\right) + \tilde{v}_n$$

where $v_N\left(\{p_i\}_{i=1}^{N}, N\right) = \prod_{i=1}^{N-1}(1-p_i)(p_N R - c)$ and

$$\tilde{v} = \frac{\prod_{i=1}^{N-1}(1-p_i)}{1-p_n}(p_n - p_N)^R + \left[\sum_{i=n+1}^{N-1} \frac{\prod_{j=1}^{i-1}(1-p_j)}{1-p_n}(p_n - p_i)\right]c$$

In contrast to the marginal value by Simpson *et al.* (1996), these incremental values are sample-specific and not necessarily the same across the samples 1, ..., N. Their point is that leads that are promising contribute more than the others to the chance of an eventually successful outcome for the project. Moreover, the addition of a higher probability lead to the existing leads reduces the expected total search cost by making the less promising leads more redundant. Thus, in addition to the scarcity rents (given by v_N), promising leads command 'information rents' (given by $\tilde{v}_n$) associated with its contribution to the chance of success and the avoidance of search costs. This information rent is zero if and only if all priors are equal (which is the assumption made in Simpson *et al.*, 1996). In fact, we have $v_N(\{P_i\}_{i=1}^{N}, N) = MV(n-1; p)$ if $p_i = p$ for all i=1,..., N; the marginal value by Simpson *et al.* and the marginal value (value of sample N) by Rausser and Small (2000) coincide if the researcher cannot differentiate the samples. Treating the hit probability as the same for all the species can be interpreted as a situation where researchers have no prior information as to which species has a higher likelihood of containing valuable genetic information. If prior information is available (i.e. if the success probability varies among the leads), then the value of certain species contain positive information rents and can be high enough to encourage private incentives for conserving that species (and possibly the habitat containing it).

Rausser and Small (2000) conducted a numerical simulation using the same data as Simpson *et al.* (1996). They argue that, under plausible conditions, the bioprospecting value of certain genetic resources could be large enough to support a market-based conservation of biodiversity. In their simulation, a lead is given by a unit of land in each of the 18 hot spots. The hit probability of a unit of land is assumed to be proportional to the density of endemic species in the area. They multiply the probability 1.20×10^{-5}, which is the value for p used in Simpson *et al.* (1996), by these density values to obtain the hit probability of each land area. Their result suggests that the bioprospecting information rents can be large enough to affect land use decisions (Table 9.2). For example, the bioprospecting value of a land area (1,000 square metres) in Western Ecuador (which is on the top of the list of the hot spots) is calculated to be $ 20 by Simpson *et al.* (1996) whereas it is $ 9,177 by Rausser and Small (2000).[4] As Rausser and Small (2000) emphasise, they agree with Simpson *et al.* (1996) about the value of marginal species (i.e. species N): it will be too small to promote private firms to preserve them. However, taking into account the prior information on the success probability of the species, the value of the most promising ones may be high enough to enhance market-based preservation of biodiversity. For the same set of area, the value of biodiversity estimated by Rausser and Small for each hot spot is larger than that by Simpson *et al.*

A Critical Evaluation

As far as the real life situation is concerned, Rausser and Small's model is more convincing than Simpson *et al.* Search for potentially useful plant and animal biota is in fact not random. It is often based on good taxonomic information and ethno-botanical knowledge. In this section we review evidence on bioprospecting supporting the

---

4. Although the numerical examples are based on the same original data by Myers (1988, 1997), the way the value of a unit of land is calculated is different in the two studies. In Simpson *et al.* (1996), the marginal value (value per unit area) is calculated as the value per species, which is constant across species, multiplied by the species-area coefficient assuming a log-linear relationship between species and area size. Rausser and Small (2000), on the other hand, incorporate the density of endemic species into the hit probability. Simpson *et al.* (1996) calculate the value per species using 250,000 as the number of species N in consideration, where 250,000 is the number of higher plant species that are considered to contain valuable genetic information for pharmaceutical firms. On the other hand, N in Rausser and Small (2000) is given by 74,640, the sum of the number of units of land in 18 hot spots. This difference partly explains the gap in the estimated marginal values in the two studies. However, the difference in numbers cannot be fully explained by this difference alone; even if the number 74,640 is used in Simpson *et al.* (1996)'s calculation, the value is still $ 100 per hectare at most (due to calculation by the authors).

Table 9.2

Bioprospecting Values in Several Ecosystems, As a Function of Density of Endemic Species

Biodiversity Hot Spots	*Forest Area (1,000 ha)*	*Density, Endemic Species/1,000 ha*	*Hit Probability (/1,000 ha)*	*Incremental Value ($/ha)*	*Simpson et al. Scarcity Rent ($/ha)*
Western Ecuador	250	8.75	1.05E-04	$9,177	$20.63
Southwestern Sri Lanka	70	7.14	8.57E-05	$7,463	$16.84
New Caledonia	150	5.27	6.32E-05	$5,473	$12.43
Madagscar	1,000	2.91	3.49 E-05	$2,961	$6.86
Western Ghats of India	800	2.03	2.44 E-05	$2,026	$4.77
Philippines	800	1.98	2.38 E-05	$1,973	$4.66
Atlantic Coast Brazil	2,000	1.88	2.26 E-05	$1,867	$4.42
Uplands of Western Amazonia	3,500	1.10	1.32 E-05	$1,043	$2.59
Tanzania	600	.88	1.06 E-05	$811	$2.07
Cape Floristic Province of South Africa	8,900	.71	8.52 E-06	$632	$1.66
Peninsular Malaysia	2,600	.62	7.44 E-06	$539	$1.47
Southwestern Australia	5,470	.52	6.24 E-06	$435	$1.22
Ivory Coast	400	.48	5.76 E-06	$394	$1.14
Northern Borneo	6,400	.42	5.04 E-06	$332	$0.99
Eastern Himalayas	5,300	.42	5.04 E-06	$332	$0.98
Colombian Choco	7,200	.32	3.84 E-06	$231	$0.75
Central Chile	4,600	.32	3.84 E-06	$231	$0.74
California Floristic Province	24,600	.09	1.08 E-06	$0	$0.20

Source: Small (1998) and Rausser and Small (2000)).

Note: Both studies by Simpson *et al.* and Rausser and Small assume 10 successes per year, revenues of $ 45,00,00,000 per success, a cost of $ 483 per test, hit rates based on 1.2E-05 per species, and a discount rate of 10 per cent.

aforesaid view. Further, in the first subsection, we also (i) identify a factor that is not considered in either of these studies—contribution of indigenous knowledge on biological resources, and (ii) claim that the bioprospecting value will be even higher than the estimate by Rausser and Small (2000) if the contribution of indigenous knowledge is considered. The next subsection introduces a model that provides a conceptual framework to incorporate the contribution of indigenous knowledge to the bioprospecting value of species in the hot spots. The final subsection discusses how the bioprospecting firms can obtain indigenous knowledge (i.e. under what conditions the local people are willing to share their knowledge with the firms).

Contribution of Indigenous Knowledge

The importance of ethno-botanical information in drug discovery is well acknowledged (Balick *et al.* 1996; King, 1996; Cox and Balick, 1994). These studies amply prove that search for new drug (or lead for it) is far more successful when it is based on the clue related to their use by local people. Drug-searching pharmaceutical firms such as Pfizer or Shaman Pharmaceuticals Inc. (now Monsanto) make use of traditional/indigenous knowledge about the medicinal feature of the plants or biota in general. They do it through field collection, literature or database searches. In order to use the local information in the search process, firms also approach the locals directly. In such cases, locals can claim for a higher royalty linked to the net sales revenue from developed successful drug (Smith and Kumar, 2002). Prevailing practices also confirm this argument. It is reported that crude extracts of plants used by a healer in Belize (Brazil) produces four times as many positive results in lab tests for anti-HIV activity than did specimens collected randomly (Cox and Balick, 1994). If a search for useful drugs is led by the knowledge of indigenous people who know possibly more about the characteristics of these plants, the probability of getting a 'hit' will considerably improve. Shaman Pharmaceuticals Inc. is an example of a company which collects plants for assaying and screening after discussions with the indigenous healers and observing them work. Shaman Pharmaceuticals has employed a plant targeting strategy where they choose a plant for testing as and when they find that two or more communities use the same plant for medicinal purposes. The success rate of drug discovery after following this rule of thumb has been more than 50 per cent

(Cox and Balick, 1994). This finding authenticates the importance of grassroot information in bioprospecting. In fact, much disillusionment about bioprospecting experienced by scientists in the recent past has been caused by the fact that their search process has been devoid of any ethno-botanical information. The experiences of National Cancer Institute (NCI), US are worth mentioning here. For NCI, one sample in 10,000 will show promising activity in the area the researcher is interested in. Out of this, 1/10 of these promising samples might go to clinical trial, and finally, 1/10 out of this might go to the market (Macilwain, 1998). This low probability is a typical example of a brute search where consultation and interaction with the locals before and during the search is entirely ignored and missing. During 1956-1975, NCI is reported to have screened around 35000 plants and animals, in searching for anticancer drugs. In fact, this process of search ended due to its failure in getting any clue in the right direction. An evaluation study for the US Congress (1993) concludes that the success by NCI could have been doubled, had they taken into account the knowledge of medicinal folk to target testable species. Therefore, successful search processes are based on some ground truth of finding a probability of favourable outcome. Otherwise, scientists of Novartis and Merck could not have travelled in the wilderness of the Amazon and Costa Rican forest in search of unique phytochemicals which cannot be imagined to synthesise in the laboratory of combinatorial chemistry. Therefore, one finds enough evidence that the value of benefits of bioprospecting may be quite significant and that local's information in the search process can significantly enhance the strike rate of a 'hit'.

In case studies on bioprospecting discussed above, we observe two reasons why bioprospecting is not a random process of choosing sites and species. First, bioprospecting firms choose a site of bioprospecting using scientific information that is widely available (e.g. species density in each site, geographical, climatological information and so on). Second, in a chosen site, the firms utilise local-specific knowledge (that only local people know) to select those plants or insects that are most promising for medical discovery. The difference between the values by Simpson *et al.* and Rausser and Small is explained by the first factor. In calculating the bioprospecting values, neither of these studies considers the second factor, i.e. the use of indigenous knowledge in their bioprospecting models. The reason why Rausser and Small came up with a different numerical result from Simpson's is because they consider heterogeneity among biological reserves (hot spots) in terms of species density. Knowledge on species density does not come from local people's knowledge; rather, it comes from more general scientific knowledge that is not local-specific. Their model tells us which site (amongst hot spots) we should choose as a place to conduct bioprospecting. However, it does not tell us which species a bioprospecting firm should look at given a biological reserve. For the latter question, local people's knowledge is crucial. In fact, as described in the above paragraphs, the existing bioprospecting contracts between local people and pharmaceuticals are about which species to choose in a given biological reserve. With indigenous knowledge, the value of some species will be higher; hence the firms, if they could, would be able to utilise efficiently such indigenous information. Consequently, the value of bioprospecting will be higher than what Simpson *et al.* and Rausser and Small have calculated This argument strengthens the point by Rausser and Small (2000) that the market-based conservation of ecosystem may be possible with bioprospecting. The next subsection introduces a framework to analyse this contribution of indigenous knowledge to the benefit of bioprospecting.

Modelling Indigenous Knowledge

To summarise the above arguments, a bioprospecting process can be decomposed into two stages:

Stage 1 (site selection): Choose a site where bioprospecting is conducted.

Stage 2 (species selection in a given site): Choose species for bioprospecting in the site selected in Stage 1.

Correspondingly, we can modify the framework used by Simpson *et al.* and Rausser and Small to incorporate into it the role of indigenous knowledge in the following manner.

A potential bioprospecting firm can make its bioprospecting decision by solving the above two-stage problems with backward induction. Suppose there are M sites for bioprospecting where there are N_j species in site j (j=1,...,M). (If we consider the hot spots by Myers 1988, M is given by 18.) At stage 1, the firm chooses a site based on the prior belief on the average hitting probability in each site. As in Rausser and Small (2000), the firm forms this prior belief by using globally available biological information such as species density in each site. Denote the firm's prior belief on the hitting probability of species in site j by $(p_j,\ldots,p_j)$, an N_j dimensional vector of probabilities. Prior over M sites $\{p_j\}_{j=1}^{M}$ corresponds to the hitting probability in different hot spots calculated by Rausser and Small (2000). Suppose site j is chosen at stage 1. Then, at stage 2, given site j, the firm chooses how much to pay to the local people in site j to maximise the expected profit from bioprospecting. We assume that, without indigenous knowledge, a firm cannot distinguish species with higher success probability from the less promising species. By obtaining indigenous knowledge, a firm can update its belief and identify a couple of species with relatively higher probability of success. By making a payment to local people, the firm can obtain such indigenous knowledge, i.e. local-specific ethno-botanical information. Assume that, with indigenous knowledge, the prior success rate of a species p_j is updated to $\pi(p_j)$ where $\pi:[0,1]\rightarrow[0,1]$ is an increasing function such that $1>\pi(p)>p$ for all $p\in(0,1), \pi(0)=0$ and $\pi(1)=1$.[5] Let m be the number of species with which the firm can update the prior. The number m depends on how much the firm pays to the local people, w. The more the firm pays to the local people, the larger the number of species with which the firm can update its prior; that is, $m(w)\geq m(w')$ for $w\geq w'\geq 0$. Without payment, the firm cannot update its belief: $m(0)=0$. If the firm pays to the local people, then the firm's belief and the expected payoff change in the following way. First, the prior belief $(\{p_j\}_{i=1}^{N})$ is updated to $(\{\{\pi(p_j)\}_{i=1}^{m(w)}, \{p_j\}_{i=m(w)+1}^{N_j}\})$. The updated belief is such that, out of N_j species, $m(w)$ have a hitting probability of $\pi(p_j)$ and the rest have probability p_j. Second, the firm's expected revenue from bioprospecting in site j, net of unit sampling cost, is given by $V(m(w), w; p_j, N_j)$ where

$$V(m(w), w; p_j, N_j) = V_1(\{\{\pi(p_j)\}_{i=1}^{m(w)}, \{p_j\}_{i=m(w)+1}^{N_j}\}, N_j)$$

and V_1 is as defined in equation (1). In words, $V(m(w), w; p_j, N_j)$ is the value of the total species in site j when the firm pays w to the

5. For example, $\pi(p)\geq 4p$ for small p according to Cox and Balick (1994) (section 3.1).

locals and obtain an updated belief on the hitting probabilities of the species. With this set-up, the stage-2 problem for the firm is to maximise this profit choosing how much to pay to the locals:

Stage-2 problem: $$V^*(p_j, N_j) = \max_{w \geq 0} V(m(w), w; p_j, N_j) - w \quad \text{for } J = 1, \ldots, M.$$

Now consider the stage-1 problem. Assume that, from widely available information, the firm knows that the fixed cost of establishing bioprospecting facility at site j is given by $F_j \geq 0$. Given $\{V^*(p_j, N_j)\}_{j=1}^{M}$ and $\{F_j\}_{J=1}^{M}$, the firm's stage-1 problem is simply to take the maximum over the net total values for M sites:

Stage-1 problem: $$\max_{1 \leq j \leq M} \{V^*(p_j, N_j) - F_j\}.$$

In this model, contribution by the local people on bioprospecting value at site J, denoted by LC_j, is given by the following formula (2):

$$LC_j = V^*(p_j, N_j) - V(m(0), 0; p_j, N_j) \quad \ldots(2)$$

The indigenous knowledge contributes to an increase the bioprospecting value by offering a pharmaceutical with differentiated probability of success of each species in a site. The values obtained by Rausser and Small correspond to $\{V(m(0), 0; p_j, N_j)\}_{j=1}^{M}$; they do not consider information available from local people and hence variation in hitting probabilities of species within a single site. With the above argument, we argue that the bioprospecting value of species in a given site will be higher than the estimate by Rausser and Small. The crucial parameters in this model are functions m and π: function m represents the degree to which the local people are willing to offer their knowledge to the firms under various amount of payments, and function π represents the degree to which the indigenous knowledge is effective in identifying promising leads out of species in an ecological site.[6] As implied by the ongoing bioprospecting activities by some pharmaceutical firms, m and π considerably affect the bioprospecting values of species. As in the first sub-section of this section it is because of the ethno-botanical information from local

6. Functions π and m may be different across ecosystems or local people due to differences in ecological and economic environment in each region. Hence, different payment schemes may be called for in different regions.

people that these firms collaborating with local people could have been successful in finding promising leads with less cost. Hence, the contribution of indigenous knowledge LC_j given by (2) is likely to be large for the hot spots. The model provided in this subsection can capture such local people's contribution to the bioprospecting benefits.

Implications of Indigenous Contributions to Bioprospecting

Taking off from the arguments above, there is a crucial aspect of bioprospecting that is assumed away in both Simpson *et al.* (1996) and Rausser and Small (2000) and it is of great significance to our concern. It is based on the process through which bioprospecting firms can form their beliefs on the probability of success of each species. Both findings are silent about this process of information gathering. Information on biological resources is available from the local people who are already familiar with the specific use of any biological resources in their communities. In the above model, the payment w to the locals is independent of success in medicinal discovery. However, it may well be the case that the locals prefer a payment scheme where they can share the benefit contingent on 'hit'. The form of π may also depend on the way the firm pays to the locals. Therefore, a bioprospecting firm needs to propose a proper incentive scheme for locals so that they are willing to share their knowledge as well as access to the resource in a given ecological site. In 1991, with the ratification of CBD by 153 countries at Rio, the sharing of benefits has become mandatory in bioprospecting. CBD also entails a bioresources-rich country to obtain a joint patent over discovered drugs. Joint patenting can be an effective way to share the benefits. Alternatively, a contract between the host country and the pharmaceutical firms can also be entered into. In 1991, with the active intermediation of Biochemist Wisner, a leading pharmaceutical firm, Merck Inc. collaborated with the Costa Rican NGO INBio. INBio was given $ 1 million as advance payment besides an undisclosed rate of royalty on the sales of successful drugs, equipment and instrument for sample testing, and other capacity building measures. This agreement opened new vistas in bioprospecting contracts, and it has become a reference point for other countries to follow. In cases where royalty or joint patenting is involved, payment to locals is contingent on success in bioprospecting (rather than fixed independent of the research outcome). It should be noted that whatever happened in the case of Costa Rica can not be duplicated in other countries because of its unique situation in terms of richness of biodiversity (five per cent of the world), competent and robust scientific infrastructure, and stable and conducive political climate. However, this arrangement has aroused the expectation and aspiration levels of the biodiversity rich tropical world. Benefits sharing have been prevalent in one form or the other before CBD; however, it now appears in a more explicit and structured form. This fact itself implies that the contribution by indigenous knowledge is crucial in accounting for the benefits of bioprospecting.

Conclusion

Photochemical from wild plants remain the crucial source of lead for drug discovery. In spite of the ongoing debate regarding the fruitfulness of bioprospecting, a large number of firms such as Merck, Novartis, Glaxo, Sankyo, and SmithKline Beecham are investing considerable amount of resources in the search for drugs and related processes of study and further demonstrating that the bioprospecting potential of biodiversity is substantial. The hypothesis that the value of such marginal species is very small seems to be untenable because its assumption of brute search is unrealistic and far removed from the prevailing practices of the leading pharmaceutical firms of the world. The search process is essentially through a mechanism where prior scientific information from the locals and the ethno-botanical knowledge of the indigenous peoples are incorporated. This information input plays an important role in enhancing the 'strike rate'. Based on the studies by Simpson *et al.* (1996) and Rausser and Small (2000), we proposed a modified framework of bioprospecting evaluation where effective role of ethno-botanical information is acknowledged and assessed. There is still much to be done including the following:

(i) analysing the effect of the market structure and industrial organisation on the efficiency of bioprospecting,

(ii) estimating the gap between private and social bioprospecting value of biodiversity, and

(iii) taking a general equilibrium approach to address the

question of how to allocate industrial effort between non-organic based search and bioprospecting.

So far, the emphasis of the studies has been on how one can estimate the value of biodiversity to a pharmaceutical researcher who faces a competitive market in the product to be discovered. Rausser and Small (2000) argue that (p.175), in the presence of differences in hitting probability among research leads, the market for research opportunities shifts from a purely competitive one to a monopolistically competitive one (points i, and ii above). As Simpson *et al.* (1996) argued in discussing the redundancy of research discoveries, non-organic sources are close substitutes for biological resources as inputs to pharmaceutical production (point iii above).

Finally, if this value of indigenous knowledge in bioprospecting has to be reaped by the international community, an equitable and mutually acceptable mechanism of benefits sharing has to be devised.

10

Marketing of Ayurvedic Medicine[1]

MADHULIKA BANERJEE

In the last few years there appears to have been an upsurge in the use, manufacture and presence of Ayurvedic products in the Indian market. While this might seem to mark the arrival of 'modernised' and user-friendly Ayurveda, the picture looks different when placed in an historical perspective of the 20th century transformation of Ayurveda. Some aspects of this transformation of Ayurvedic medicine have been noticed and widely commented upon: from being dispensed to individual patients to becoming available off the shelf; from being made by a *vaidya* in a small *rasashala* to being mass produced by a manufacturing company; from being identified with a region or a school to becoming 'positioned' as brands; from being a knowledge system accessible to the elite to one available to many; and, above all, from being a medical epistemology to simply a collection of pharmaceutical recipes (Leslie, 1976; Leslie and Young, 1992). This transformation involved on the one hand standardisation of the processes of production, and on the other commercialisation of the processes of distribution. In this chapter, I propose to offer an analytical account of the latter, namely the processes through which Ayurvedic medicines were positioned in the modern market. I do so with the help of a case study of Dabur, the largest manufacturer of Ayurvedic products.

Histories of colonial science and medicine, as also those of the different medical traditions in India, provide a useful frame for this story (Bala, 1991; Sharma, 1992; Arnold, 1993; Muelenbeld & Wujastyk, 2001). Three historical forces combined to shape the context in which Ayurveda entered the modern market in India:

---

1. An earlier version was published as "Power, Culture, Medicine: Ayurvedic Pharmaceuticals in the Modern Market", *Contributions to Indian Sociology*, 36(3), September-December 2002, pp. 435-467.

(1) the trajectory of modernity spread on a global scale, with its own episteme of scientific knowledge, of which modern medicine was a part; (2) that of the globalising market, with its institutions of production and norms of homogenisation and standardisation; (3) the trajectory of the colonial state, a modern institution whose pervasive power over allocating funds and structuring education broke down old forms of patronage and substituted these with new linkages of knowledge and production. Together these three trajectories created an unevenly structured field of power, in which Ayurveda began with a major structural disadvantage, despite early approbation by some elements of the colonial state. Ayurveda was challenged in epistemic, economic and pedagogic arenas, criticism that threatened to relegate it to the margins, if not to erase it altogether.

However, a study of the 20th century history of Ayurveda shows that it was neither erased nor completely relegated to the margins. Ayurveda continued to survive, even to thrive, and has staged something of a resurgence in recent times. Yet the Ayurveda that has survived and thrived is in many ways not the same Ayurveda of a century ago. Hence, the need to understand the story of how Ayurveda encountered and engaged with the modern market. This chapter does not reconstruct the story in any comprehensive sense.[2] Rather, it seeks to bring out the analytical strands in this story by tracing the strategies followed by modern manufacturers of Ayurvedic medicines in the three arenas of profiling, positioning and packaging of their products. In offering this analysis it differs from the prevailing approaches in at least three ways. First, it places the story in the context of an understanding of power and culture. The seemingly mundane and purely economic decisions regarding the profiling, positioning and packaging of the medicines are seen here as expressions of a deep operation of power that are inevitably mediated through culture. Secondly, having recognised the role of power, the analysis seeks to go beyond the simplified mirror images received from the accounts of the history of Ayurveda (Mukhopadhyaya, 1926 and Sharma, 1992;) which, on the one hand present the rise of modern medicine as the inevitable and happy outcome of the onward

2. A fuller account will appear in my forthcoming book, based on my doctoral dissertation, *Power, Culture, Medicine: A Study of Ayurvedic Pharmaceuticals in India*, Department of Political Science, University of Delhi, 1995.

march of scientific rationality and, on the other, those that present Ayurveda, nostalgically, as the sad and helpless victim of modern science. In fact, the story of Ayurveda's encounter with the modern market does not lend itself to either of these simplistic constructions, both of which deny any agency to the victim. Drawing on the recent literature on subaltern agency (Guha, 1997; Rodriguez, 2001), the account offered here, by contrast, focuses on the strategic response of the manufacturers of Ayurvedic medicines to the historical conditions of disempowerment. Thirdly, the account pays special attention to the processes of consumption. For this purpose, it draws upon insights from anthropological studies of consumption (Appadurai, 1986; Miller, 1987; Miller, 1995) to suggest that the transformation in Ayurveda was as much a response to consumer choices as to the choices of technologies of production. In other words, at least a part of a social history of Ayurvedic medicines has to be written as the social history of commodities, reflecting the very complicated shifts in both the organisation of knowledge and the means of production.

The first section introduces the case study by capturing some of the salient points in the history of Dabur, an Ayurvedic pharmaceutical firm that is now more than a 100 years old. The following three sections present the main argument of the chapter by looking, respectively, at product profiling, positioning and packaging-related decisions. The evidence presented in these sections, based largely on interviews with personnel of the marketing division of Dabur and the publicity leaflets put out by the company,[3] show the operation of multiple strategies. These strategies varied, apparently, in response to the changing conditions of what appeared as the market but they can also be viewed as responses to the changing nature of the field of power. Since there was no definite sequence to these

3. There are no archival sources available for the early history of Dabur. The company's own archive was substantially lost and then fully destroyed by its various dislocations, followed by riots and fires. The reconstruction here draws upon the memory of the members of the Burman family and the employees in the company. The description of the marketing strategies draws upon interviews with the personnel in the marketing division and the various leaflets and publicity material put out by the company. A majority of the interviews were carried out in the summer of 1992 at the Delhi and Sahibabad offices of the company. I would like to thank Mr. P.D. Narang, now one of the Directors of the company, for facilitating my access to Mr. A.C. Burman, the then Managing Director of the company, and to a number of serving employees. Much of the information on recent developments is from the company's official website, *www.dabur.com*.

strategies, these are better seen as moments rather than successive phases. These sections bring out the 'moment of confrontation', the 'moment of withdrawal' and the 'moment of diversion' as some of the strategic responses underlying routine decisions regarding product profiling, positioning and packaging. In sum, the complex strategies used by Dabur did succeed in creating and retaining a foothold for Ayurvedic medicines in the modern market. But this success came with a heavy price tag: Ayurvedic medicine had to be cast in the mould of modern medicine and disconnected from its relationship to the knowledge system. The final section summarises the argument of the chapter and brings out some of the ironies and ethical dilemmas inherent in such an encounter.

Dabur: "A 100 Years of Caring"

This chapter focuses on Dabur India Pvt. Ltd., a firm well known for its popular brands of Ayurvedic medicines. Several Ayurvedic medicine manufacturing companies were set up in the 1880s in India, many of which continue manufacture of Ayurvedic products to this day. Dabur is the undoubted leader in the entire industry, both amongst the original manufacturers and those that came after them. The firm was set up in Kolkata, West Bengal, by a physician-entrepreneur, Dr. Burman. The firm formulates, manufactures and markets personal and health care products and is a household name in India. Dabur also manufactures and markets pharmaceutical products (specially oncology products including Paclitaxel), food products, cosmetics and veterinary products, a product portfolio totalling over 450 items. Over time, this portfolio has been variously constituted. First, there were simply Ayurvedic medicines, made in the original forms, as prescribed by the ancient texts. Then, based on Ayurvedic formulations, came a range of traditional cosmetics, like hair oils and tooth powder. With a new focus on diversification in the early nineties, the company announced forays into cosmetics, natural gums, cheese, honey, confectionery, bulk drugs, veterinary medicine products, finance and insurance. The most recent turning point came in May 1997, when Dabur appointed Mckinsey & Co., an international management consultancy firm, to devise its strategic, organisational and operational guidelines. Three years after its report, Dabur divided its business operations into five strategic business units: family products, health care, Ayurvedic specialities, ayurpet, and drugs and pharmaceuticals. Further, it introduced changes in the company's product portfolio, deciding to focus on family products, health care products and foods. The turnover from the first of these was Rs. 325 crore in 1999, while health care products contributed Rs. 275 crore (*www.dabur.com*). While Dabur is now hesitant to launch new brands as such, it is increasing the number of products. For instance, a bigger range of coconut-enriched hair oils and shampoos under the haircare brand Vatika is planned, while new flavours in Dabur Honey, e.g., eucalyptus and plum, are being developed.

Notwithstanding successes in the business of herbal beauty care products, Dabur has found it increasingly difficult to enter the overseas herbal medicine market, which is specially lucrative in both Europe and the United Sates today. The Food and Drug Administration of the United States in particular has employed very stringent criteria, which Dabur finds very difficult to fulfil. This is not for lack of expertise or scientific standards, but on account of the sheer expense of the trials and reports that are required to satisfy the criteria of standardisation required for marketing the products in the USA.[4] However, the laws for another category of products, namely, food supplements or 'nutraceuticals' as they are now known, are easier to comply with. Professing to provide minerals and proteins in their 'pure' forms, these products have become very popular in American and European markets. Spirulina and some seaweed based products are the most well known of these. On the basis of both the knowledge and availability of many plant and mineral raw materials used for Ayurvedic medicines, Dabur can easily create this category of products and establish a presence in the overseas market. Though it has not introduced food supplements/nutraceuticals to the market yet, it has recently presented them as their new product at a conference organised by the Department of Indian Systems of Medicine and Homeopathy.[5] The latest strategy then, is to target this niche.

Over the last 20 years or so, then, Dabur has carefully crafted a series of images seeking to position itself differently. By the early

4. For an account of the engagement of Ayurvedic medicine companies with rules of standardisation, in India and elsewhere, see Banerjee (1995).

5. Conference on 'Good Health in the New Millennium', New Delhi, March 2000. The conference brought together government, nongovernment organisations and the indigenous pharmaceuticals industry, on the same platform.

1990s, it was seen to be moving away from being a 'small-time peddler of Ayurvedic formulations to big-league marketeer of ethnic brands' (Jain, 1990), and by the end of the decade, to a 112 year old fast moving consumer goods (FMCG) company (*www.dabur.com*). In positioning itself in this manner Dabur has not only changed the advertising aimed at the consumer/patient and promotion to the doctor, it has also changed the very construction and orientation of its buildings. Throughout this "100 years of caring", as a publicity leaflet described it, Dabur has emerged as the undisputed market leader of its kind and an extremely innovative firm that is seen to have kept pace with the times. Dabur therefore is a good case study to illustrate the nature of the encounter between Ayurveda and the modern market.

Product Profiling: From Drug to Concept

The principal focus of Ayurveda's entry into the modern market was its product profile. There are broadly six forms in which Ayurvedic medicine was traditionally made: pastes, decoctions, pills, powders, oils and *bhasmas* (ashes). Since biomedicine recognised only tablets/capsules, syrups and injections, decision on the form of the medicinal product has been critical to the encounter of Ayurveda with the modern market. The original range of medicines produced and marketed by Dabur was enormous. These included medicines based on the classical texts, and those created and used by individual families across generations, in the six traditional forms mentioned above. Faced with the requirements of the modern market, Dabur's strategic response was to recast the product appearance to suit the contemporary taste created by biomedicine's tablets, syrups and capsules. In the early phase, in the late 19th century, the recasting needed to be from 'goli' to tablet. Thereafter, there was increasing 'market' pressure to turn even decoctions, pastes and powders into capsules or candy. In Ayurveda the form and content are very closely linked both in terms of how the medication will be administered, and its expected activity. This recasting then, was a transformation in a fairly fundamental sense of the term. The relationship between Ayurvedic medicines and Ayurvedic knowledge was fundamentally altered. This is not the place to go into the story of that transformation. Here we will concentrate on how this transformation affected the market strategies of Ayurvedic pharmaceuticals.

In general terms, four kinds of strategies of product profiling can be identified through this case study. The first strategy was to produce very good quality Ayurvedic medicines in their original forms, but package them better as time went along. The second was to cast old formulations into modern forms like tablets and capsules—a transformation in very real terms. This was accompanied by a focus on cosmetic products like hair oils and dental products. The third strategy was to make new formulations on the basis of old wisdom/ knowledge of the medicinal properties of plants and chemicals, confirmed by extensive research according to the parameters of modern science and medicine. Again, this strategy also included extending the cosmetics line to 'personal care products', the change in nomenclature being evocative of a larger set of decisions. The final strategy was to create a new category of products based on old wisdom about nutrients—the 'nutraceutical' food supplements designed to fulfil daily nutritional requirements.

These strategies were all adopted at different points in time, signifying the particular 'moment' that governed the decision. Since these moments were not sequential or independent of each other, all three strategies might be followed concurrently. In fact many of the original companies that were able to make large profits in the beginning subsequently developed divisions for each and juggled production priorities between them. Thus the first strategy was adopted by most firms that were set up around the late 19th century. The idea then was to make Ayurvedic medicines fulfil two criteria—ready availability and a demonstrated effectiveness—clearly in a spirit of confrontation *vis-à-vis* allopathic medicines. The first could have been achieved by adopting methods of large-scale manufacture and the second by advertising the products—both of which were symbols of modern enterprise. The guiding spirit was one of challenge and confidence in Ayurveda's retaining its position as the hegemonic medical system that it had been for a very long time.

Two factors thwarted the success of this strategy. The available pharmacopoeia was too large and expensive to make and the companies struggled to make profits. Besides, the gathering momentum of allopathic medicines meant that Ayurvedic pharmaceuticals struggled to retain a hold on their target consumers.

Eventually these firms had to make hard choices about the products they were making. Thus they were not able to realise the full potential of the moment of confrontation. This process was further accentuated with the arrival of antibiotics completing, in a sense, the triumph of antiseptics and the antidotes of the 19th century. By the 1940s and 1950s, then, there was a retreat from the earlier response of confrontation. There was an acceptance not simply of the superiority of biomedicine, but also of the parameters of its perspectives. This is what induced academia and pedagogic institutions to validate Ayurveda by the parameters of modern medicine, in order to prove that Ayurveda also was a science, albeit from antiquity.

In the market, this response was associated with the entry of new firms. The Himalaya Drug Company, a company that focused on the second strategy, that is, of the production of new medicines on the basis of old formulations, was set up in the 1940s. It was only later that companies like Dabur sought to demonstrate the scientific validity of the medicines made in the old forms, as also to emulate Himalaya's pathbreaking strategy. This was a moment of withdrawal in the sense of acceptance of the terms of medical discourse being set by biomedicine. This altered the course of modern Ayurveda perhaps irrevocably. It should be noted that this response was already anticipated in what eventually came to be called the 'personal care' products. One of the integral aspects of all traditional medical systems is that they have formulations for skin and hair care, classified as cosmetics by modern industry. These were produced by Ayurvedic pharmaceuticals like Dabur from the very beginning. An interesting angle is the companies' attempt to fit into the categories of the modern market while retaining a flash of defiance, in the form of the label, "This is an Ayurvedic medicine, not a cosmetic product." Himalaya's trajectory is a case in point. Having gathered a fair amount of prestige by the end of the 20th century, Himalaya recognised the enormous profit potential of the 'personal care products' sector and entered it with a new brand name, 'Ayurvedic Concepts'. It was an interesting essentialising of Ayurveda—retaining the pharmacological 'concept', while transforming it for the new market. This is the strategy that has actually seen the burgeoning of the firms and the growth of the sector in the last few years referred to at the beginning of the chapter. Also, this is what lays the basis for the third moment—'the moment of diversion'.

A curious combination of developments make for this third moment. The rise of the critique of Cartesian science in the cognitive realm was complemented by the call for holism and return to nature by the social movements of the 1960s and 1970s. However, these developments were barely able to challenge the hegemonic position of modern science and technology, including modern medicine. What really made a difference to the Ayurvedic sector was the response of the modern market to the rising critique. In a cynical appropriation of the rebellion, the critique was fashioned into a niche and a range of products were developed for the niche 'alternative' consumer, including of alternative medicines. Ayurvedic pharmaceuticals in India have realised the significance of this development over the last decade. Abandoning the difficult project of challenging perspectives, it reworked its profile to target this niche market.

The capturing of this niche required a crucial actor, namely the consumer. The companies would need to confine their sights to a certain section of the market and hope that its volume grew. This was the reverse of the perspective with which they had begun, which was to enlarge the ambit of its market to include more and more consumers. But this is a dimension which can be understood only when the production decisions taken by the companies and the Ayurveda market are supplemented by the consumption decisions being taken. For the demand for commodities is an aspect of the overall political economy of a society, that is, an economic expression of the political logic of consumption (Appadurai, 1986: 29-31). The analysis of demand should thus help us to understand the consumer's relation to the object of consumption (Miller, 1987: 144). The fundamental questions, then, are: Who are the consumers of Ayurvedic medicines? What are their patterns of preference?

Before the colonial period, consumers mostly chose between locally available systems of medicine. The advent of biomedicine radically altered the structure of choices available to them. For the first time, there was a choice between radically different systems of medicine, and the choice put Ayurvedic medicines in an unfavourable light. The new medicines were available in the new form of pills, easy to deal with—to swallow and to carry. This was less cumbersome than traditional formulations, which had numerous requirements of abstinence and accompaniment. The new remedies provided quick, and for most patients symptomatic relief. Expensive to begin with, they slowly became more affordable in comparison with the older medicines. Besides, the latter were also not available readily, off the shelf. Given these constraints, and given the role that the colonial state and its science and industry played against the Ayurvedic manufacturers, it was remarkable that they could establish and retain their identities at all. This was made possible only by the continued consumption of these medicines. Consumption was thus an unrecognised arena of struggle against colonial power.

There were two kinds of consumers of Ayurvedic medicines. First, there was still a large constituency of consumers, particularly the rural poor, who simply could not afford the 'foreign medicine'. But there was also an emerging new urban class of wage-earners, relocated landed owners and traders/industrialists, who attributed cultural value to Ayurvedic medicines and had the crucial 'knowledge about its appropriate consumption'(Appadurai, 1986: 41). They related in this way to a large number of aspects of their traditions—unwilling to let go on the one hand and be seen as pandering to it on the other hand. It was a combination of the two that made it imperative for the tradition to change itself in consonance with the new waves of modernity, if it was to survive. It was this group of consumers that continued to patronise Ayurvedic medicines, while at the same time playing a crucial role in its transformation. This process of transformation involved deploying both evaluative/ideological and technical/empirical criteria to assess these medicines. The evaluative/ideological criteria were to assess how close these medicines were to the prescribed textual norms. The technical/empirical criteria were, increasingly, the extent to which these medicines satisfied criteria of efficacy and uniform standards laid down by biomedicine. These criteria fed into the consumption decisions, which had a direct implication for production and marketing decisions.

In the first 50 years of Dabur, the form of the medicine was not an important issue. The other criteria, that of the content of the medicines, was actually the result of the consumers' engagement with the new biomedical products. The hegemonic discourse of science and rationality on the one hand, and a nagging critique of side-effects and narrowly focussed interventions offered by Ayurveda on the other, had combined to produce a dominant consensus about the character and content of Ayurvedic medicines. This 'common sense' was typically expressed in the form of the following dualisms: (a) while everyday minor problems of coughs and colds and fevers are best dealt with by Ayurveda, the first sign of infection demands no delay in taking allopathic medicines; (b) while Ayurvedic medicines like Chawyanprash are good for building the body, biomedicine can treat the big killer diseases such as tuberculosis and cholera; (c) while Ayurvedic products like *neem*-based products and digestives are good for maintaining the health system, biomedicine is good for emergency interventions; and (d) while long-term health problems like asthma, heart disease and arthritis are best attended to by Ayurveda, only biomedicine can handle surgical intervention. Such is the power of this ideological common sense that no claims to the contrary by practitioners of Ayurveda have succeeded in radically shifting the bases of these assessments. If anything, this commonsense has become more firmly established in the recent times, so that Ayurvedic medicines occupy a low place in the hierarchy of scientific attributes and rational line of treatments. Many studies (e.g., Banerji, 1981; Burghart, 1988) have shown how the rural poor, who actually rely extensively on traditional systems of medicine, feel the need for allopathic treatment and believe in its inherent superiority precisely because the urban rich have access to it.

This common sense passes from one generation to another, one class to another. A senior marketing official reflected Dabur's own estimation of how consumers relate to the products:

> The tastes and preferences of the higher-income segments are steadily percolating down to the middle and lower income groups. As a result, if Dabur does not attract higher-income buyers, even its traditional base could be in jeopardy several years down the line. We have to walk a fine line down our current and future consumer franchises (Business India, 1993: 76).

This was linked with a set of particular problems, such as how to create a brand preference within its product categories, specially those, like hair oils and tooth powders, which fragmented the market shares among many small manufacturers. Focusing on those products which contributed the highest share of returns, Dabur concentrated on advertising these aggressively: 'Scientisation' rather than 'Sanskritisation', or perhaps, Scientisation as Sanskritisation, seems to have become the new formula of upward mobility. This is a point emphasised by Nichter as well, when he argues: "In India, the Sanskritic and the 'scientific' are merging in popular culture apparent in emergent representations of Ayurveda cloaked in the language of science complete with statistical tests and reference to experimental design" (1996: xvi).

With colonialism and the modernised production of Ayurvedic medicines along the lines of allopathy, another category of consumer was created, namely, the *vaidya* or doctor. Earlier, all *vaidyas* by and large made their own medicines—as part of their knowledge and treatment. With medicines being manufactured on a large scale, they moved from being small-scale producers to consumers of large-scale manufactures. In consequence, most *vaidyas*, attempting to be both true to their knowledge of the *shastra* and honest in providing the best medicine to their patients have developed an interesting strategy. Each of them has a personal assessment of the different categories of medicines made by different companies—an informal rating system, on the basis of which they make their prescriptions. Accordingly, they prescribe the oils of one company, the *bhasmas* of another, the *churnas* of a third, and so on. This practice of course involves far more technical/empirical judgement than might be immediately evident, and must be linked to the crucial production questions of technological choice and innovation. What is relevant here, however, is that *vaidyas*, as consumers, are to some extent able to direct product flows in the market.

The allopathic doctors are a different story altogether.[6] They have now grown to be the largest segment among the medical practitioners and therefore the largest consumers of any medicine produced, a crucial consideration for commercial producers of Ayurvedic medicines. Thus this manufacturing sector recognised the need to target allopathic doctors as consumers of Ayurvedic medicines, something they have done since the 1940s. A big stumbling block was the unfamiliarity of doctors trained in modern medicine with the forms of the Ayurvedic medicine, but far more substantial was the fundamental problem of the standardisation and efficacy of these

---

6. In Indian medical parlance, it is invariably the practitioner of allopathy who is called a doctor, while all other medical practitioners are known by their traditional names, like *hakim*, *vaidya*, etc.

medicines. These problems led to a series of debates whose long history is well-known (Arnold, 1993; Bala, 1991; Brass 1972; Leslie, 1976; Leslie and Young, 1992). The same considerations also led to a series of commercial decisions.

In the early years of its manufacture, it was often argued that the primary motivation for manufacturing Ayurvedic medicines was to provide cheaper medicines than the allopathic. This was considered possible because the raw materials used were cheap plant materials, not expensive chemicals, which an unskilled labour force could work on with locally made tools. Progressively, however, the increasingly expensive raw materials, the increasing mechanisation of production and pressures to continuously innovate on the form of the medicines reversed this possibility and resulted in the Ayurvedic medicines manufactured by large companies becoming much more expensive than before. The price of Ayurvedic medicines is now much higher than that of allopathic medicines, beyond the reach of the common person. Yet company representatives do not think that the original intent behind the manufacturing of these medicines has been defeated. Their balance-sheets show that their products are not only selling well, but selling better every year, and Dabur has actually managed to enlarge the market. In a personal interview the Marketing Manager of Dabur claimed that they were the overall leaders in the market and that even though they lag behind in a couple of products, they are not really worried because of their sound overall position. When asked why they are proud of their high prices, he immediately responded that it is because they maintain high standards, which do not come cheap.[7] Thus the benefits of economies of scale—a major argument in favour of mechanised, large-scale, 'modern' production—do not reach the poor consumer/patient.

Nichter (1996) argues that the development of new health products is really a response to the population's felt need and desire for health products. This ties in with Miller's (1995) argument about consumption complementing production in influencing the creation of new products. The production of what Nichter calls 'ayurpathic' medicines (1996), actualises the desire for a modernised tradition acceptable in the changed contexts of the daily lives of urban and

7. This links with the next issue in the commercialisation process, i.e., image-building or positioning.

semi-urban Indians. This development, with its prime focus on food supplements, would directly contribute to producing what Nichter calls "cosmopolitical medicine"—an index of 'subtle dimensions of capitalist ideology associated with the exchange of labour capital for health through medical fixes in a secular cosmopolitan world. ... Knowledge about body processes is increasingly replaced by knowledge about medicine products, leading to new patterns of health problem solving..."(1996: 298). Thus, in the context of Dabur, the response to nutraceuticals in the domestic market remains to be seen, but judging by the success of the cooking pastes introduced some time ago, the nutraceuticals should be able to build up a market as well. The urban consumer is very conscious of the low levels of nourishment and high levels of adulteration and pesticide present in everyday food products and vegetables, and will find it easier to include food supplements as a part of regular expenditure rather than undertake a larger mobilisation for fundamental changes on these issues.

In the modern market then, Ayurveda finds itself moving from medicines to FMCG, from drugs to candy and now, from drugs to concepts.[8] Clearly, both the company and the consumers are working towards creating these new products in a complex interplay of 'demand and supply' forces. But only a particular segment of the consumers—mainly urban, upper class professionals—can afford to be a part of this process of transformation.

Positioning and the Politics of Images

If the 'hard core' economic decisions regarding product profiling conceal a play of culture and power, the process is most clearly visible in the decisions regarding product positioning. It should be noted right at the outset that 'positioning' is much more than simply advertising a given product. The process of finding or creating an appropriate market slot for a medicine often involves creating a new product altogether. This aspect of positioning is crucial to the Dabur story. Besides, positioning is not confined to these products alone. It involves creating an image for the brand name through advertising and other strategies. Creating an image is of course deeply political,

8. Dabur advertisement no. d89/DIL/161.

for any attempt to create a favourable image must endorse or challenge dominant standards and values. This section attempts to uncover the politics of images by looking at the way Dabur constructed the now popular image for itself, that of a modern company that sells tradition.

The basic decision to enter the modern market of mass produced medicines dictated the ingredients of the strategy followed by Dabur and the rest of the industry: advertising strategies had to be used to convince a remote and abstract consumer of the availability and efficacy of the medicine, as well as of the reliability of the manufacturer. This was a radical departure from the earlier practice where the image of the medicines was inseparable from the skills of the *vaidya* prescribing and making these. In this sense the developments in India were parallel to the transition in the West itself. Image production was already a major issue with medical formulations and preparations in Britain and in the United States by the time the Ayurvedic companies were established in India (Abraham, 1995). Claims and counter-claims of the virtues of these medicines were rife in the newly emerging public spaces in Europe—newspapers, magazines, walls, banners and exhibitions. In many ways the response of the Ayurvedic pharmaceuticals in India drew upon this precedent.

Let us begin the story of the production of images from a recent example. There is a fascinating advertisement being aired on television in the last three years to promote 'Ayurvedic Concept', a range of personal care products from the Himalaya Drug Company. A very savvy, but clearly old, lady is being used to 'hard-sell' shampoos to young girls, foot creams to her daughter-in-law and a health tonic to a natty young executive sitting next to her on a flight. She tells them about hair stimulators and what to find in them, body toxins and how to do away with them and, for good measure, how the executive could do with a faster microprocessor for his laptop! But then, this is no ordinary old lady. She looks and dresses in a traditional way, but is clearly comfortable with the modern, both in form and substance. So she is seen 'chatting' online, and speaking with great authority on medical matters in a language replete with scientific concepts and explanations that easily roll off her tongue. She is kindly, with a touch of amusement at the incredulity on the faces of her quarry, yet undoubtedly confident of her ideas and their ability to win in the end. Always, however, the final cut is an expression of kindly triumph—of being able to stump the younger generation with her solutions to their problems. Though this sleek advertisement is not from Dabur, it brings out very well the image strategy followed by Ayurvedic pharmaceutical companies, including Dabur, for the last several decades: their products are presented as a living tradition that is at once modern and scientific. If foregrounding the image of tradition appears as a gesture of defiance, the attempt to seek its legitimacy in 'modern' images and scientific vocabulary points to a deeper submission that defines this strategy.

This however was not always the case. In the early years, Dr. Burman, the founder of Dabur, used mail-order sales for the allopathic formulations with which he began his venture. Such a practice, which was also common in the case of other Ayurvedic medicines companies at the time, might well have been used by Dabur. The most well-known and oft-cited early Dabur advertising strategy is that of a Bonanza two-seater aircraft which showered the pilgrims of the Kumbh and Pushkar *melas* with leaflets extolling the virtues of its products. The target was well-chosen not only for its size—these being the largest-known congregation of people at one predictable point in time—but also for its composition. The predominantly Hindu pilgrims to these fairs could safely be assumed to be tradition-minded Ayurveda users, and Dabur could attract this niche through the sheer novelty value and power equation conveyed by this communication. The other two well-remembered methods of advertising, used to target the rural consumer in particular, were wall paintings, and two elephants carrying banners of Dabur products. The wall-paintings depicted the product, in the particular bottle or jar in which it was packaged. Advertising personnel at Dabur suggested that this was for the convenience of the illiterate consumer, who could easily identify a product displayed this way. Initially the hair oil bottle carried the face of a woman, with long, wavy hair, the index of beauty of those who used hair oil. Such advertisements used modern media and some of the spaces in the emerging modern public sphere, but the message did not invoke a modern outlook or ideology, a strategy suggestibe of indifference to its modern competitor. This could not be the dominant strategy for too long, for ultimately the Ayurvedic medicinal products could not but compete with the modern medicines, but it is worth noting that some of these strategies survived still in targeting the rural consumers. Of late, the face on the oil bottle has been replaced by the photograph of a well-known film-star, whose lustrous, long hair, does not look oily, but is endorsed by her to be a result of regular use of oil! The switch to endorsement was timed to coincide with the outreach of television to millions of homes in India. On balance, this confident response is now limited only to personal care products that do not directly compete with modern medicinal products.

The most interesting strategic moves are to be witnessed in the case of core medicinal products that cannot avoid competing with modern medicine. Dabur's repositioning of their products, specifically, Chyawanprash and Hajmola, is a case in point. The early advertising for Chyawanprash is a good example of the moment of confrontation: a regular advertisement to appear during the first decade of the 20th century, in the *Anand Bazar Patrika* said "Chyawanprash is better than cod liver oil." Over the years this confrontation has given way to a retreat. Chyawanprash is now positioned as a 3000-year old health tonic. Its positioning as a tonic makes it a respectable and harmless supplement to modern medicine rather than a potential rival. The advertisement seeks to draw legitimacy from modern and scientific images: it claims that Dabur Chyawanprash recreates the secret recipe of the *rishis* "... in a highly automated plant, with more than 40 natural ingredients like *amla, dashmool* and *ashwang*." More importantly, the advertisement goes on to offer a defence in modern scientific terms: *Amla* juice has 20 times more vitamin C than orange juice', and further, that:

> Modern science confirms this about the richest known source of Vitamin C. Dr. Linus Pauling, twice winner of the Nobel Prize, made an amazing discovery. That Vitamin C revitalises body tissues, slows down ageing process and builds up your natural resistance to coughs and other common ailments.[9]

Thus, clear linkages between modernity and tradition are being drawn, wherein tradition is translatable and legitimised in the dominant 'modern' language. By announcing modern science's knowledge about *amla*, there is a clear response to its epistemic

9. Dabur advertisement no. d89/DIL/161.

trajectory. *Amla* juice is at the heart of Chyawanprash, which is really a tonic for maintaining good health, claiming to do precisely what Linus Pauling had suggested Vitamin C does.

The story of Hajmola, a digestive tablet, is in some ways even more interesting. Dabur produced a *churan* 'Kshudhavardhak Bati'—literally, appetiser—and marketed it under its textual name for many years. In 1984, a consensus emerged in the company that the name was a tongue-twister, and so it was rebranded as Hajmola—a linguistic innovation that drew upon the popular Hindustani expression, *hajam,* for digestion. The rebranding was accompanied by an endearing visual which repositioned it to a completely different audience—children. The advertisers used the well-known fact that children love to eat all kinds of *churan* regardless of their value as digestives. The visual, showing errant kids in a hostel dormitory winning over a stern master with Hajmola, was an instant hit, and Hajmola a runaway success. Following this campaign, Hajmola's sales went up from Rs. 1 crore in 1984 to Rs. 9 crores in 1990. This visual has remained unchanged and has created a history of sorts in Indian advertising by posting a close parallel to the 'Lifebuoy' soap jingle, the longest-running jingle for any product.

The Hajmola story brings out a highly complex strategic response. The repositioning from an esoteric medicinal product to a popular digestive candy is clearly a modern marketing strategy. At the same time, Dabur did not use an anglicised name like 'Digene', (The name of an allopathic digestive tablet.) Nor did the justification for Hajmola use any modern medicinal parameters. This was because its most serious competitor in the market was actually Pachnol, a Unani preparation from Hamdard. Digene's flavours were mostly unfamiliar to the Indian palate, while Pachnol's were not. Besides, both 'Hajm' and 'pach', the root words of these two brand names, mean digestion in Hindustani. Here is a case of an encounter with the modern market transforming the character of Ayurvedic medicine without necessarily involving a competition with modern medicine.

Selling 'tradition' can have its problems too, as Dabur discovered to its consternation in their promotion campaign for Shilajit capsules. Shilajit is a Himalayan exudate of rocks, rich in minerals, hormones, enzymes and vitamins and well known as an aphrodisiac. Using the photograph of a suggestive posture from the sculptures at the

Khajuraho temple, Dabur's advertisement invited the consumer to "discover the power of nature for a fuller life. Kindle the fire in you".[10] The strategy was successful in that sales went up from Rs. 50 lakhs to Rs. 124 lakhs within a couple of years, but in 1989-90, after a complaint was lodged against Dabur 'on moral grounds', the campaign had to be withdrawn and a much more staid advertisement substituted. There were thus clear limits to the modern outlook that Dabur would have taken for granted as part of the consciousness of its consumers. Successful advertisements for traditional 'rejuvenating' medicines have had to be couched in hints, transparent to the target audience, without disturbing their sensibilities.

Besides strategies of confrontation and retreat, the arena of product positioning also shows the operation of diversion as a strategy. Although this response has gained currency in the last few years, with the opening up of the global herbal market, the basic strategy could be seen much earlier. Dabur started advertising its products in specialty magazines, aimed at the hotel industry, in the mid-80s itself. This shift was occasioned by the introduction of some new products. A cooling summer drink called Sharbat-e-Azam (clearly a counterpoint to Rooh Afza, a very popular cooling drink produced by the leading Unani pharmaceutical company, Hamdard), Capsico (red pepper) Sauce and a cardamom extract called Instent, were among these new products. The advertisement for Capsico reads: "While a common Western recipe, it is also an asset in the Bar—a dash or two makes Bloody Mary, gin and lime or vodka punchier and sensational."[11] On the one hand, this could well be understood as simple capacity utilisation—each of the raw materials used in these are also used for making medicines. On the other, this could be interpreted as a repositioning of the company—as one that makes a wider range of consumer goods, specially for the modern, urban middle class consumer. Hereafter, Dabur undertook a complete reorientation of the company profile from an exclusive focus on Ayurvedic medicines to include 'natural products' as well.

This was well reflected in advertisements for two of Dabur's products, 'Clean-n-Clear' and 'Hajmola Candy'. Hajmola Candy was actually developed to counter the digestive candy called 'Swad'. 'Swad'

10. From a copy of the advertisement made available from Dabur's files.
11. From a copy of the advertisement made available from Dabur's files.

introduced two new ideas in the market: (i) that digestives could be made available in candy form; and (ii) that they could be packaged in handy wrappers, which made them easier to carry— while retaining the flavours familiar to the consumer. This way, it threatened to capture a segment and the imagination of the urban digestives market. On both counts, Hajmola lagged behind because it continued in its old tablet form and was packaged in a large glass bottle with a tablets hundred in each. Dabur responded by developing a candy with well-loved flavours and used the brand name of Hajmola to legitimise the product in terms of its Ayurvedic origins, eventually driving Swad out of the market. In a conversation with one of the scientists at Dabur, it was revealed that Dabur had considered producing a Chyawanprash eclair, if the candy market proved to be competitive.

Clean-n-Clear gel capsules were based on extracts from *neem*, the well-known medicinal plant of India, used by all the medical systems. It promised a 'cure, rather a cover', for skin problems, whereas 'pimple creams provide the illusion of good looks'. The advertisement is worth quoting in detail:

> You need much more than a cosmetic to cleanse your blood and clear away those unsightly blemishes. Purifying syrups may provide the answer. But Yuck! difficult to down. Only Clean-n-Clear capsules of *neem* lock the bitter and bring out the best of you. Modern medicine accolades Nimbidin and Nimbidol, the bitter principles of *neem* as anti-bacterial and highly effective in various skin conditions like Furunculosis, Arsenical dermatitis...[12]

It must be noted that the reference to purifying syrups directly refers to another widely advertised Unani product, Safi. Its dismissal is swift and complete, while a laboured explanation of the virtues of the capsule in the terminology of 'modern medicine' is offered thereafter. Advertising for mass consumers is only one of the sites of product positioning, especially for medicinal products. In the market for modern medicines, advertising the products with the doctors is considered a far more effective way of positioning the products that the consumer knows little about. In this category the 'modern' *vaidyas* and the allopathic doctors define the market for Ayurvedic products, forcing Ayurvedic pharmaceuticals to adopt a defensive strategy. They had little option. The overall trend in Ayurvedic teaching, research and practice since the 1950s had been to measure and demonstrate the efficacy of Ayurveda by the parameters and standards of

12. From the booklet accompanying the launch.

biomedicine. In that sense, Ayurveda had already given in to the hegemonic knowledge claims of modern medicine.

This acceptance was translated into market strategies in the late 1980s, when Dabur's marketing focus moved to modern doctors as much as modern patients. By the mid-1990s, therefore, Dabur's strategy took the form of 'Ethical Promotion'[13]—an exercise to promote their drugs in exactly the same way as mainstream pharmaceutical companies promote drugs amongst allopathic doctors. This requires engaging a team of medical representatives and providing them with a booklet listing their products and their qualities. Both the exercise itself, and the booklet designed for the purpose, use a careful combination of formulations, presented in the languages of Ayurveda and allopathy. For instance, Chandraprabha Bati, a formulation for urinary tract infection in women, is illustrated over two pages. The first shows the smiling faces of two women, with a drawing of the urinary tract, as represented in modern anatomical figures. The text claims that the product is "a potent diuretic, keeps the urinary tract and urine sterile and [is] a safe bactericidal agent," establishing that it is "a drug of choice for UTI, [and also for] Dysuria, and Spermatorrhoea." This language is easily understood by modern *vaidyas*, B.A.M.S. graduates, who have learnt both Ayurveda and modern medicine in the concurrent teaching system of most Ayurvedic colleges. On the second page of the booklet is the photograph of a woman clad in a white overall, standing inside a laboratory, complete with various instruments, a computer terminal and gleaming work-surfaces. An inset illustration carries a certificate, 'Chandraprabha Bati is a clinically tried therapy in acute UTI', signed by two doctors from the prestigious KEM Hospital in Bombay. The use of a certificate by practitioners of biomedicine to establish the credibility of Ayurvedic medicines illustrates the defensive positioning of Ayurvedic medicines in the modern market.

In doing so Dabur was conditioned both by the changing nature of medical practice and its practitioners, as well as by the competition it faced from its rival manufacturers of the Ayurvedic pharmaceuticals.

13. A strategy adopted by modern pharmaceutical firms to distance themselves from the hyperbolic claims made in the popular media by the old apothecaries. The firms now claimed scientific validation of the efficacy of their medicines, and only on this basis sought to promote them amongst doctors and practitioners of medicines. Both their methods and target audience were different from each other.

The changing nature of the Ayurvedic medical practitioner was indicated in a remark by the head of advertising in Dabur:

> The modern *vaidya* is very different—they have slick offices, with B.P. instruments and stethoscopes... No *dhoti*-clad old men in dingy rooms.... They have become very conscious of brand names. So we have to adopt strategies of ethical promotion accordingly.[14]

Allopathic doctors had already been successfully cultivated for nearly two decades as a new user category for Ayurvedic medicines, principally by the Himalaya Drug Company to promote its Ayurvedic formulations presented in modern drug forms like tablets, syrups, etc. Dabur's products were different from Himalaya's, in that they made Ayurvedic medicines both in their original and in modern forms, but they took ethical promotion a step ahead of Himalaya. They sought to sell both forms of Ayurvedic medicine—old and new—to this new group. A physician who is an important advisor to the Dabur Research Foundation, admitted that "Himalaya has shown how effective ethical promotion can be—we cannot afford to lag behind."[15] However, Dabur's new ethical promotion exercise was prompted not only by the success of the Himalaya Drug Company, but also by the initiative taken in this regard by their traditional rivals, Zandu and Baidyanath. These two, which have the same target audience, took to promoting the generic Ayurvedic medicines on a regional basis. Dabur decided to do it on a national scale, to take care of the competition all at once. Yet another site of the positioning of the medicines is the manufacturing space itself or the architecture and environs of the factory, features which Dabur has used strategically to position itself as different from the rest of the crowd. This comprises a large number of small concerns that are involved in manufacturing Ayurvedic medicines. Their advantages are that their costs of production are low, particularly on the labour-intensive processes and so they are able to price their medicines low. But there is one crucial drawback that many of them suffer from—the premises are dingy, lacking even the basic norms of hygiene and raw material standards. This is of course against the traditional norms for making the medicines, and indicates a degeneration in those norms over time. This was one of the points on which they invariably compared unfavourably with the biomedical pharmaceutical companies. The 'moment of withdrawal' in the

14. Interview with Dr. C.K. Katiyar, Medical Advisor to Dabur, June 1992.
15. Interview with Dr. C.K.Katiyar, Medical Advisor to Dabur, June 1992.

encounter of Ayurveda with modern market meant that the bigger companies became very conscious of the need to comply with some manufacturing standards in order to establish a credibility and legitimacy in the market. Therefore, some of them took the initiative to actively establish new norms, in a clear effort to alter the image of Ayurvedic medicine manufacture.[16]

In the early nineties, when they shifted their headquarters from Kolkata to Delhi, the precinct of the Dabur complex was built at Sahibabad, Uttar Pradesh, very close to the border of Delhi. In the last few years, they have shifted their manufacturing to Baddi in Himachal Pradesh, and the Sahibabad unit is now used for other purposes. The complex, designed by Dabur, houses the offices of the head of the manufacturing unit, the company secretary and other financial divisions, the main manufacturing unit and the Dabur Research Foundation. Over the four years that the company was visited for interviews, etc., the premises became increasingly like that of the biggest companies of the Indian market—gleaming floors, indoor plants, muted lighting, central air-conditioning, men and women dressed in vogue, hushed voices and noiseless lifts. Computer terminals were to be found in most offices, as were most other modern facilities. The main manufacturing space comprised a number of buildings which housed different kinds of machinery and separate units for the production of different items. Large sleek trucks brought in consignments of raw materials. The personnel of the factory, particularly those who worked at the machines at the shop-floor, wore rubber boots, blue overalls and white caps covering their hair. There were charts next to most machines which recorded time or temperatures, as required, making supervision easy even when the actual factory-hands were not present. There was an air of brisk efficiency, and white work-surfaces gave an impression of antiseptic cleanliness.

Similar to this is the Dabur Research Foundation (DRF). Corridors of glass-partitioned work-spaces, revealed all manner of modern equipment for experimentation, along with row upon row of bottled

16. In order to standardise some norms of production, however, and to maintain the overall image and legitimacy of the industry, the government has recently introduced what it calls Good Manufacturing Practices. These will have to be implemented by the entire industry by the year 2003 (GoI 2001, *The Drugs and Cosmetics Act*, 1940 (Schedule T : Good Manufacturing Practices).

herbs and plants. Here, too, all those inside these spaces wore white overalls, spoke the language of modern chemistry and pharmacy and responded to queries from a political scientist with an air of bemused and impatient incredulity. The DRF had a library too, housing a research collection on different aspects of Ayurveda, where efforts were on to accession the available material on a computerised on-line facility.

Ayurvedic medicine manufacturing units do not invariably look like this, even in the case of relatively big companies like the Ayurveda Rasashala of Pune. The Rasashala looks like a larger version of what the old *rasashalas* or pharmacies making Ayurvedic medicines must have looked like, possibly even Dabur in its early years. A large number of tasks are done by hand, and many by women who, at most wear an apron over their *saris*. But they sit on the floor as they sift and sort, that being the posture they are most comfortable with. There are some machines, designed to exactly duplicate what the human hand would have done, and some designed to approximate natural conditions (e.g., those used to control temperature conditions). The extensive use of firewood and dung-fuel had turned the walls in some of the rooms black from the smoke, as were those parts of the floor where the burning had been done. But the attitude of those at the Rasashala was that all visitors would have to just accept and get used to the Rasashala's form of cleanliness, rather than the Rasashala transforming itself to theirs.[17] On the other hand, the self-image that Dabur wishes to project, is of a modern, 'scientific' and efficient establishment. This is directly linked to the predilections of the particular category of consumers that Dabur has in mind whenever such decisions are taken. For them, the first and lasting impression should be that it is 'like any modern medicine manufacturing unit'.

As we said at the beginning of this section, creating an image is deeply political and reading off the semiotics of Dabur's trajectory of advertising would, at one level, provide the analytical basis for understanding this politics. Tracing the history of its advertising strategies at least traces "the development from processes of specific

17. This was actually experienced first hand when visiting the Rasashala at the same time as a delegation of American pharmacy students. They were heard extolling their visit to Dabur at Delhi, principally in terms of how 'modern' it looked, despite making 'traditional', medicines. I overheard a wry response from one of the workers about different cultural parameters.

attention and information to an institutionalised system of commercial information and persuasion" (Williams, 1980); as also "...trace the changes in society and in the economy, and to trace changes in the method in the context of changing organisations and intentions' (Williams, 1980). This analysis is hinged on the argument that there is a typical way in which Ayurvedic business interests constructed their consumer and then projected their estimations on them by the kind of products they released in the market. In this way, they set the parameters for the way in which Ayurvedic products shape up in the modern market. While it has its insights, its assumptions about consumption patterns and consumer images has come in for criticism wherein, the creation of images is not only a question of production, but also that of consumption. Miller argues "Those with knowledge of business have invented an abstract aggregate consumer"(1995: 52) and that "At present the concept of the consumer is becoming fetishised as mere purchaser. But this is led by a commercial desire to construct persons reduced to their buying behaviour" (1995: 54). In order to counter this and other 'economistic' trends of analysing consumer behaviour and consumption patterns, he suggests a radically new approach, best understood as the politics of consumption. Analysing the history of capitalism in the hundred years after Karl Marx, he points out that the "contradictions of dialectical development are increasingly manifest within the individuals whether of the first or third worlds, in their dual existence as labour and consumer. The emphasis upon consumption today does not therefore resolve the contradictions analysed by Marx, but rather extends them" (1995: 49-50). Intended as complementary to the politics of production, rather than counter to it, a preliminary application of this approach will be attempted henceforth in this article. The next aspect of Ayurveda in the modern market that will be considered is that of packaging.

Packaging the Social Character of a Commodity

Fine (1995) argues that consumption is dependent on the shifting relationship between the physical and social properties of commodities. That is, commodities are constituted by two kinds of criteria: of form and packaging on the one hand, and content on the other. Here we consider especially the way in which consumption responds, *via* packaging, to the physical and social properties of Ayurvedic medicines, arguing that the trajectories of consumption were as vital to deciding the direction of 'shifts' as the trajectories of production.

Packaging is meant to serve two basic purposes. First, it must make the product easy to handle and attractive to the eye. At the same time, for medicines, certain strict norms need to be followed, for instance, that medicines should not be packed in containers of materials that might react to their particular chemical composition. Most metals are therefore unacceptable for packaging Ayurvedic medicines. Originally, all such products were packed in earthenware vessels, while glass was used for *asavas, arishtas* and *awalehas,* and paper for *bhasmas* and *churnas*. This packaging was meant for small quantities for specific patients. In the early stages of mass production, the shift was made to glass packing for all products, along with tin. The industries that produced these materials had been set up quite early in India, being used in packaging mass produced allopathic medicines around the same time. Packing of the other range of products, cosmetics, which Dabur now call personal care products, follows slightly different criteria, for the reason that continuity in the 'look' of a product is crucial. For instance, until recently Dabur's hair oils continued to be packed in glass bottles, with more or less the same kind of labels as before.

In the beginning, Dabur had bottles of differing shapes for different medicines, the idea being that identification of specific products with certain packaging proves a strong association for the consumer. In the 1950s, Dabur had 90 different kinds of bottles, all made by hand, but ultimately a decision had to be made between the principle of customer-association and the long-run profits of the company. Those who believed a change was necessary 'had to virtually steamroll' the decision (Bahal, 1994) because of strong opposition from the marketing division, which believed that some products sold well precisely because of the fancy shapes and designs of the bottles. According to reports, the Managing Director of the time, "cut down the number of bottles to 19....The results: increased automation of bottles, an increase in sales, more shapely bottles, less breakages and slick packaging" (Bahal, 1994).

In the 1970s, came the shift to plastic which soon began to occupy pride of place among packaging material in the Indian market. It was introduced mainly because the urban consumer was choosier about packaging, in terms of both looks and convenience. Since plastic was still expensive, the company had to decide which products would be 'privileged' with this packaging. Significantly, they chose to put their main revenue earner, Chyawanprash in a plastic container and also worked painstakingly on the label of the container, which features a *rishi*, the rising sun and line drawings of *amla*, in four different colours. On the other hand, Hajmola, even when repositioned, was not repackaged. However, as soon it started to face competition from the candy market, it was transformed into a candy and packaged, like its rivals, in the form of single units.

The most important aspect of Dabur's achievement in the packaging of Ayurvedic medicines is that it has successfully standardised the look of the plastic containers which contain *bhasmas* and *churnas*, so much so that almost all companies now use exactly the same kind of jar for packaging Ayurvedic medicine formulations. Conceived originally as a remaking of the image, the new packaging, must also have acquired significance in terms of economies of scale. A modern air-conditioned packing line has been commissioned at Sahibabad for Dabur's homemade brands of ethnic pastes and lime juices, as also for PET jars.

While most medicines were packaged in plastic jars, hair oils for a long time continued to be in glass bottles on the understanding that the market for this product was in rural areas, where glass would be acceptable and familiar. In the last few years however, the urban elite has become exposed to the 'international' look, while, a host of international cosmetics companies have entered the Indian market supplying both regular and 'herbal' cosmetics. Since the elite consumer is not unwilling to continue the use of hair oil, provided it is 'non-stick' (to keep the 'look' right), Dabur developed a 'non-stick' hair tonic, which is packaged in a very slick bottle, with an expensive trendy label. The product did so well in the market that it is proposed that all hair oils will now be packaged in plastic bottles. In any case, plastic and its convenience is now known (through Pan Masala pouches and bread packaging) in the rural areas, satellite to modern metros, which comprise a sizeable part of Dabur's market.

The very latest of Dabur's strategies is the packaging and marketing of honey. While retaining the packaging in glass bottles, though with a new label for about two years, it has now been repositioned as an energy provider for children, sold with an offer of a plastic mug free. What is most telling is the picture printed on the mug—it is that of the fictional character of A.F.Milne's well-loved children's tales, Winnie-the-Pooh, the bear that loves honey. That this company is also targeting the children of the class being referred to throughout this chapter, is clear from this choice, since it is only this elite class that would know of Winnie-the-Pooh's existence. The irony is greater because Dabur has been a prominent sponsor of the major mythological serials on Doordarshan in the eighties. Almost every child in the country is familiar with some of the better-known figures of these mythologies and would have no difficulty identifying strength and energy with a large number of them. Alternatively, there is a great variety of secular symbols to choose from, and the fact that they were not chosen clearly indicates Dabur's targeted consumer and not a desire to uphold traditions of any particular kind.

Conclusion: Power, Culture, Medicine

Let me draw together the various strands of argument implicit in the preceding sections. The encounter of Ayurveda and modern market gave rise to a new industry, with the same framework of pharmaceutical manufacturing companies as had become the norm in Europe and the United States by the end of the 19th century.[18] The commercial decision makers of this new industry had to negotiate between two givens: the norms of its own medical pharmacopoeia/ pharmacology, and the demands of the modern market. It was not an easy negotiation, for Ayurveda was made to play on a field of power tilted against it. Yet entrepreneurs like the founders of Dabur came up

18. The pharmaceutical, as commodified medicine available in an open market, accessible to anyone, doctor or patient, who makes an assessment of its properties and wants to make use of it, is a 19th century idea. It develops in the context of the values and gains of large scale manufacture applicable to any commodity: economies of scale, homogenisation of products and convenient packaging for the consumer. Over time, it acquires the other characteristics: standardised quality, attractive packaging and, eventually, creating new consumers. The medicines that developed in 19th century Europe and the United States evolved through these stages, pharmacopoeia/ pharmacology and medical practice being in tandem with the market (Abraham, 1995).

with a series of strategies to face this challenge. The founding moment and the fountainhead of all the changing strategies was the basic decision to enter the modern market of mass-produced medicines. It meant that the Ayurvedic medicinal product had to be disconnected from the *vaidya* and sold off-the-shelf in the market, that modern advertising strategies, rather than the skills of the *vaidya,* had to be used to sell the availability and efficacy of the medicine, and that the product had to be packaged in 'respectable' and attractive ways, as was the case with modern medicinal products.

The unfolding of this encounter resulted in various specific strategic moments. In the early stages of this encounter, one can discern a moment of confrontation, where Ayurvedic medicine seeks to take on the commercial might of 'English' medicine. Ayurvedic medicines are profiled and positioned so as to rival some of the well-known modern medicines. The advertisements make a direct claim to being more efficacious than modern medicine and the glass packaging seeks to be contemporary without giving up the requirements of the Ayurvedic pharmacopoeia. With these strategies Ayurveda tried to retain and win back both the traditional and the newly modernising consumers. Implicit in this moment is the ambition to make Ayurvedic medicines available to all the sections of society for the first time in history. If this ambition was not realised, it was not a failure of these strategies. It is just that these were not compatible with the changes in the field of power within which Ayurvedic pharmaceuticals operated. The policy decisions of the colonial and then the post-colonial Indian state did not leave any room for the infrastructure of knowledge and skills that this strategy required. The emergence of the giant establishment of modern medicine and the arrival of antibiotics meant that this strategy had to be abandoned.

The second strategic moment is more difficult to label. In many ways it does represent a retreat from the aggressive strategy of the moment of confrontation, though it is obviously not presented as such. The Ayurvedic pharmaceuticals began to work out their strategy by accepting the dominance of the biomedicine. No longer did the Ayurvedic pharmaceuticals aim at defeating modern medicine at its own game; the goal was now to work out a breathing space for Ayurveda in a market dominated by the products, standards and consumers of modern medicine. Thus the profile of Ayurvedic medicines was maintained in the range and diversity always available, but there was an acceptance that no one could challenge the wonders of antibiotics. Accordingly, the strategy shifted to emphasising those products that did not conflict with the mainstream allopathic medicines and could be used to supplement them. There was one small assertion though. Ayurveda tried to use the one chink in the armour of allopathic medicines to its advantage—those of 'side-effects'. But the declaration that Ayurveda has no side-effects was a negative assertion, and so the trade-off between effect and side-effect was invariably in favour of the former. Linking this with 'holism' as a positive medical perspective was possible only much later, in the larger context of epistemic challenges to the perspectives of modern science.

In terms of positioning, the prestige of modern science was invoked to validate the claims of Ayurveda. For years, both academia and industry assiduously undertook the 'validation' of Ayurvedic knowledge by parameters defined by the pharmaceutical and knowledge industry of modern medicine in Europe and the United States hence the kind of advertising and decisions of 'ethical promotion' discussed above. The acceptance of plastic packaging that went against the canonical wisdom of the Ayurvedic pharmacopoeia symbolised this strategy of retreat. In that sense it can be characterised as the 'moment of withdrawal'. This moment did not result in any commercial decline. In fact, Ayurvedic pharmaceuticals in general, and Dabur in particular, gained in market share and made commercial gains by this strategic retreat. It should also be noticed that this moment is present in some ways throughout the history of mass production of Ayurvedic medicines. In more ways than one, this moment continues to define the response of this industry even today.

The 'moment of diversion' is clearly a recent development, though its elements were present in the earlier decades as well. The very success of modern medicine has created its own discontent in the advanced capitalist world of the West. As a result there has appeared a space in the market and the imagination for alternative or herbal medicine. The global orientation of Indian Ayurvedic pharmaceuticals in recent years is a strategic response to this opportunity. It is neither a step forward nor a retreat; it can be seen more as a step sideways or a diversion. This is what has resulted in the creation of a new category of products, namely food supplements. The attempt to package and export raw material rather than finished products also represents another face of this strategy. The positioning and packaging changes according to the tastes of a new consumer group. This strategy is not necessarily oriented towards the external market. A similar approach can be adopted for the niche consumer of the domestic market as well. In narrow terms of the turnover and profit, the moment of diversion is a golden moment. But if viewed as a cultural and political response to a certain field of power, it is a cynical appropriation of the ideology of holism and naturalism that have been recently reiterated by the 'traditional' systems as part of a larger critique of modern science and technology.

This leads to a consideration of the irony and the dilemmas mentioned earlier. Is this a success story or not? What yardsticks do we use for a judgement like this? Indeed, how can we judge whether the successful Ayurvedic pharmaceuticals of today are in any serious sense the successors to the Ayurveda that faced a crisis more than a century ago? Or does this phenomenon deserve a name other than Ayurveda? These are difficult questions to answer, not only because the evidence is insufficient and disputed, but also because the very terms of the debate are essentially contested. The key categories of standardisation and validation (not discussed in detail here) are inextricably enmeshed in the political disputes of knowledge that they seek to resolve.

Instead of engaging in the impossible and pointless exercise of answering this question, it may be more useful to conclude by explicating the gains and losses of Ayurveda's encounter with modern market as evident from the material examined here. The most obvious success is that entering modern market prevented Ayurveda from complete erasure. It is possible that given the way the field of power was structured, any other response would have led to a sharper disappearance of Ayurveda than has been the case in the 20th century. For an ordinary consumer there is a much wider range of products available today than was the case a few decades ago. Arguably, too Ayurvedic formulations have been available to all sections of society, not just caste Hindus. From the point of view of the industry as well the success is quite evident. The Ayurvedic medicinal sector has had a growing market and yielded attractive profits. Dabur is indeed a success story in this regard. But it is not clear if this positive picture holds for Ayurveda as a whole, since much of the increase in the market of mass-produced, off-the-shelf Ayurvedic medicines has taken place at the expense of the Ayurvedic drugs being prepared and dispensed by the *vaidya*.

There are more serious entries on the negative side. The evidence presented above shows that, as the price of its success Ayurveda had to cast itself in the mould of modern medicine. The attempt to commercialise mass-produced Ayurvedic medicines affected the internal order of the Ayurvedic knowledge system. The original purpose of mass production was to take advantage of its democratising potential, but the logic of that system now works against itself. It is now clear that only a small section of consumers, that is, those with purchasing power and thus the power to make choices between different products, are being catered to. The encounter with modern market is successful only to the extent that Ayurvedic pharmaceuticals accept the ground rule, the industry responds and caters only to those who could afford its products.

A further set of issues stems from the requirements of 'standardisation' of the medicines. They are about the validation of the claims of efficacy of existing forms of medicines; the clinical trials necessary to make the second and third forms (of casting old formulations into modern forms like tablets and making new formulations on the basis of old wisdom/knowledge of the medicinal properties of plants and chemicals) legitimate for the market; and those for the fourth category nutraceuticals, are slowly evolving in the market and international institutions. All of these criteria have been simply transferred from those in use for biomedicine and the dominant pharmaceutical industry. They pose significant epistemic problems and ignore the available norms of Ayurveda, notwithstanding scientists' opinion to the contrary (Roy Chaudhury, 1992). Apart from the epistemic question, the expense of the required trials makes it impossible even for most of the bigger companies to undertake them. Furthermore, making major investments of this sort is economically feasible only in those products of which the manufacturers are sure of a ready market. Thus the situation comes full circle. Only certain parts of Ayurveda—the tonics, 'vitality' medicines and recipes for beauty care—a motley collection of handy hints or grandmothers' recipes 'a bag from which products had to be taken out' (Nandy and Visvanathan, 1990: 170) can be modernised. Concomitantly, a large number of products of Ayurveda—those that cannot be disconnected from the accompanying regimen, restrictions and treatment and made to fit standardisable categories, are left out. Ultimately, these could simply fade away from usage/availability, and eventually from the medical imagination.

The very real conflict and differences between Ayurveda and biomedicine on these issues, mostly dismissed as unscientific aspects of Ayurveda, lurk as grey areas, reinforcing the consumers' categorisation of illness and medicines I referred to earlier. So the part of the story of Ayurveda that is a success is that of its marketable aspects. The defeat that it encounters is in the loss of its larger perspectives, which can be established by not simply the medicines but also regimen for the body and the line of treatment. So even if it were to be argued that 'holistic' and 'natural' perspectives are returning to the consciousness of both consumers and doctors, a catch must be recognised. Dominant epistemic and economic trajectories require anything good and worthwhile to be available in a bottle, preferably an attractive one. Is well packaged tradition capable of transforming the fundamental directions of our lives, as a focus on holism or the natural would be expected to do? This is certainly one of the important questions of our times.

11

Pollution Control by Natural Dyes[1]

G. BADRI NARAYANAN[2]

Introduction

Historically, natural dyes were used to colour clothing or other textiles, and by the mid-1800s chemists began producing synthetic substitutes for them. By the early part of this century only a small percentage of textile dyes were extracted from plants. Lately there has been increasing interest in natural dyes, as the public becomes aware of ecological and environmental problems related to the use of synthetic dyes. Use of natural dyes cuts down significantly on the amount of toxic effluent resulting from the synthetic dye process.

Natural dyes generally require a mordant, which are metallic salts of aluminum, iron, chromium, copper and others, for ensuring the reasonable fastness of the colour to sunlight and washing. Customers who have become accustomed to the dazzling colours and wash and light fastness of synthetic dyes are hard to convince, as only a few of the natural dyes have good all round fastness. Most of the natural dyes produce comparatively dull shades. But there are chemicals and methods available now, which can enhance the colour and fastness of the natural dyes. This raises the question of whether the natural dyes really reduce emissions or not, since some additional inorganic chemicals are required for them.

---

1. Originally prepared as a term paper on "An Analysis of Long-run Environmental Impacts and Multi-criteria-based Prioritisation of the Natural Dyes in the Indian Textile Industry", submitted as a partial requirement for the completion of a course on Environmental Economics at the Indira Gandhi Institute Of Development Research, November, 2003.

2. I would like to thank Dr. Sudhakar Yedla for providing an opportunity of submitting this term paper, and also for his valuable suggestions and comments, which have resulted in enhancing the quality of the paper. My sincere gratitude is also due to Dr. Nirmal Sengupta, who motivated me to work on this area and provided some valuable literature. I should also thank my friends who helped me in literature collection and who encouraged me during this work.

In this chapter, the following sectors and dyes have been chosen for analysis of emissions.

Sectors: Natural Fibres: Cotton, Wool and Silk

Synthetic Fibres: Polyester and Nylon

Dyes: Natural dyes: Fenugreek Yellow, Golden Dock Brown, Gallnut Black, *Dolu*, Gum Arabic, Indigo, Shellac, Kamala, Madder, and Pomegranate

Synthetic dyes: Acid dyes, Reactive dyes, Sulphur dyes, Azo dyes, Disperse dyes, and Direct dyes.

The following is a short note on each of the natural dyes listed above:

Fenugreek Yellow: It is a yellow dye produced from fenugreek seeds (*Trigonella foenum-graecum*). Fenugreek is used in food preparation in India and has therapeutical value. This vegetable dye has affinity for cotton fibres.

Golden Dock Brown: This is derived from Golden Dock (*Rumex maritimus*) seeds extracted in alkaline water, giving a brown colour, with an affinity for cotton.

Gallnut Black: This is a natural dye for yellow, grey and black with good light, wash and rub fastness. The dye is obtained from Gallnuts of *Quercus infectoria*, which is dried secretion of an insect living on the tree. It has strong astringent properties. The galls are crushed to designed particle size and extracted in aqueous media. The extract is filtered and spry to produce the dye.

Dolu: *Dolu* (*Rheum emodi*) root and bark yields a yellow colouring matter suitable for silk, wool, nylon and polyester dyeing. The alkaline extract (brown coloured powder) gives yellow, brown and grey shades of good fastness on mordanted substrate. The Indian rhubarb is also used as a purgative and astringent tonic, teeth cleaner and in treatment of ulcers.

Gum Arabic: The bark of *Acacia nilotica* (Indian Gum Arabic) tree yields the colouring matter of good fastness properties. Dye is extracted in alkaline medium from dry powdered bark. It gives brownish black extract and has affinity for cotton treated with metallic salts. Shades obtained from this dye range from brown to grey with Aluminium sulphate, Ferrous sulphate and Copper sulphate. *Babool* bark yields tannin, which finds use in leather tanneries. Decoction of bark is also used as a gargle.

Indigo: This is a blue natural dye obtained from the leaves of *Indigofera tinctoria* plant. The leaves are fermented in fermentation pits. The dye is precipitated by oxidation or by passing the air. The precipitated dye settles down at the bottom. The cake is dried in the air and sun. The dye converted into leuco form with caustic soda and sodium liquor hydrosulphite in soft water. The dyeing is carried out in the reduced and exposed to air. By oxidation the dye slowly changes into blur on the fabric.

Shellac: Lac mud is the by-product of shellac Industry. The dye is extracted in alkaline medium from the mud cakes. The purplish black dye powder gives tones of purple on cotton, wool and silk with the help of metallic salts.

Kamala: It is a natural bright golden yellow colour with moderate light and good wash fastness. The dye is obtained from ripe fruit of (*Mallotus philippensis*) by beating and shaking or also by stirring the fruits vigorously in water, settled dye sediment is collected for the production of dyes. Kamala is used in Ayurvedic preparations as wormicide and antiseptic. The dye is dissolved in alkaline water and applied on treated and salts untreated fabrics and yarns.

Madder: The roots of Indian Madder (*Rubia cordifolia*) have traditionally been used for dyeing cotton fabrics, blankets and carpets. Red coloured dye powder is extracted from roots in alkaline medium. With alum it gives pink to orange shades. Roots are known to have tonic astringent, antiseptic, antidysentric and deobstruent properties and are a part of various Ayurvedic preparations.

Pomegranate: This is a natural dye with reasonably good light, wash and rub fastness. The dye is obtained from pomegranate (*Punica granatum*) fruit rind. Rind is used as an astringent, and cure for diarrhoea and dysentry. The dye is dissolved in soft water and applied on treated fabric, fibres, or yarns with the metal salts like Aluminium sulphate to get yellow or post treatment Ferrous sulphate for grey shades.

The objectives of this study are as follows:

1. To analyse the environmental emissions that could be reduced by the introduction of natural dyes in the Indian textile industry by the year 2020 under various scenarios.

2. To prioritise the dyes for different fibres based on their emission levels, costs and fastness.
3. To propose some policy implications for emission reduction using the natural dyes in the Indian textile dyeing sector.

Literature Review

A wide range of literature is available in the context of various technological research and developments taking place in the field of the natural dyes. But very few published papers are available in the area of emission analysis of the dyes as a whole. There is almost no significant work done in the comparison of emission levels due to natural dyes and those due to synthetic dyes.

G.R. Pophalia *et al.* (2003) analyse the emission levels of synthetic dyes in India to compare them with those resulting from the application of CETP technology in the dyeing houses. This data was useful in checking whether the theoretically calculated emission levels of different dyes lie within the practical range.

An Internet site, namely, *www.alpsind.com,* of the Alps Industries Limited, Ghaziabad, was the source of data for the dyeing procedures for different natural dyes. Many other websites[3] have been useful for the data regarding the dyeing procedures of synthetic dyes, production figures, and the standards of emission levels.

T. Bechtold *et al.* (2003) discusses the various merits and demerits of natural dyes in the current Maddertrial situations in a technical manner. Dheeraj *et al.* (2003) have tested the eco-friendliness of natural dyes using the values of effluent concentrations obtained from informal sector-dyers in Rajasthan. Agarwal (2003) analyses the compatibility of natural dyes to the modern dyeing houses. Holme (2003) lists the recent developments in the textile dyes, of which some facts and figures about natural dyes sound significant. Rubeena (2002) has analysed the biochemical features of the natural dye effluents such as toxicity and their bio-degradability. Patra *et al.* (2002) have studied the performance of some natural dyes on the cotton fabrics in terms of fastness and depth. Teli *et al.* (2000) have given an overall account of natural dyes—their classification, technology, and future prospects. Roshan *et al.*

---

3. *www.alpsind.com; www.emich.edu/textiles/PDFs/wfacid/hot.pdf; www.metricchemical.com/tmetagenas.pdf; www.chinadyestuff.com; www.aurorasilk.com/info/naturaldyes_faq.shtml* and *www.swicofil.com/setilawidnaucationic.html.*

(1996) have a description of extraction and application of various natural dyes on different fibres.

Nousianen (1997) has a detailed explanation of the natural dyes. According to this author, environmental awareness is setting tough demands for textile dyeing technology, at the same time as keen competition in the world of fashion textiles requires quick responses, quality and low production costs. Demand is increasing for eco-textiles, certified with various official labels defining colour fastness and the maximum concentration of toxic or harmful impurities. The standard methodologies that have been developed for certification are also ensuring the use of best available technology (BAT) in production processes. Although natural dyes can serve as models, there is no way that the annual consumption of 0.5 metric tonne of textile dyes can be met by natural dyes.

According to Parham (1994), new technology in application of natural dyes allows a wide range of shades with good fastness properties, no salt use, elimination of heavy metals in processing, safe effluent, and rational methods for sourcing raw materials with positive effects to the environment. Glover (1995) argues that synthetic dyes are more user- and environmentally friendly than natural dyes. The arguments put forward are those related to the excessive use of supporting chemicals, possible over-intensification of agriculture and low quality of natural dyes.

Sewekow (1988) gives a detailed description on the use of natural dyes instead of synthetic ones, for environmental protection. The origin, availability, dyeing methods and fastness, as well as ecology and toxicity of natural dyes are discussed. Natural dyes are not suitable as an alternative in textile dyeing due to technological and ecological problems, inferior fastness, and elevated cost.

Kharbhade and Agarwal (1988) have described the identification of natural dyes in historic textiles from the mid-19th century. Seventy samples taken from museum textiles were compared with reference materials prepared in the laboratory as well as with CP major dye components of natural dyes. One yellow, two brown, one blue, and two red natural dyes were identified in different primary and secondary coloured samples. It is also seen from the results that mixtures of two dyes have been used to obtain desired shades. Bahl and Gupta (1988) have developed a method for mordant dyeing of silk with cutch natural dyes in the presence of different mordants (alum, chrome, $CuSO_4$, and $FeSO_4$) for a wide variety of colours. The dyed fabrics exhibited fair-to-good wash fastness and light fastness. Moses and Ravi (2003) have applied the waste grape skin for the application on protein textiles such as silk and wool in combination with other similar natural resources like pomegranate rind, orange rind and annatto seed and has observed that the results such as colours obtained, fastness towards rubbing, light, heat and washing are very much convincing.

In Auslander *et al.* (1977), naturally occurring dyes were discussed in form of a monograph with screening studies on their stability. Duff *et al.* (1977a) have assessed wash fastness of natural dyes on wool by the tests conducted under standard conditions. A number of the dyes underwent marked changes in hue on washing that was due to the effect of small amounts of alkali in washing mixtures. In Duff (1977b), the colour changes accompanying light fading were followed visually and instrumentally and characterised in terms of light-fastness grades, grey-scale differences, colour differences in CIELAB colour space, and in Munsell colour coordinates. The light-fastness grades were similar to those previously reported for daylight exposures. The various methods of expressing colour change gave detailed and quantitative measures of the effects of light on the colour of natural dyes; this type of information could be of value in predicting the original colour of ancient textiles.

Kirtikar (1947) and Gulati (1949) have analysed the Indian indigenous natural dyes in terms of their eye appeal, colour value and fastness and found them to be less valuable than the synthetic dyes. An interesting study by Furry (1945) has shown that the cotton fabrics dyed with natural dyes such as osage orange and quercitron showed excellent mildew-resistance, that persisted even after six weeks' weathering.

Based on the above sources of literature, the following inferences could be made:

1. The natural dyes are, in general, inferior to synthetic dyes in colour value or eye appeal and colourfastness.
2. However, there has been a significant progress in the research of enhancing the dyeing characteristics of the natural dyes for the past five decades and as of now, there are many natural

dyes with colour value and fastness comparable to those of the synthetic dyes.

3. There is a debate among various technologists, researchers and scientists regarding the utility of natural dyes. While some of them claim that natural dyes can be widely used as 'better substitutes' for the synthetic dyes in terms of emissions and cost, others claim that the colour value is not as good in the case of natural dyes as in the synthetic dyes. A betterment of colour value of natural dyes would involve use of some chemicals, which in turn, would cause pollution again.
4. Some researchers have even expressed their doubt over the validity of the widely spoken idea that natural dyes essentially reduce the pollution levels.
5. A small proportion of the scientists predict that substitution of the synthetic dyes with the natural dye would cause serious problems of environmental concern in terms of over-intensification of agricultural land, deforestation, etc.
6. Hence, to end up with a meaningful decision, a balanced multi-scenario approach that considers all relevant aspects of natural dyes and synthetic dyes in a macro-level, for the entire sector in the country, with proper projections about the future with different assumptions on the adaptation rates of natural dyes, is necessary.

Methodology

Steps Involved for the Multi-Scenario Analysis

Step 1: The Indian production figures of the dyed yarn and cloth made of cotton, silk, wool, polyester, and nylon are projected for the years 2005, 2010, 2015, and 2020, based on the average annual growth rate calculated from the data available for the years 1985-1999.

Step 2: The inorganic chemical composition or total dissolved solids (TDS) of the effluents generated by dyeing different fibres for different colours using natural and synthetic dyes is calculated using the procedure explained in the Appendix A-11.1. Inorganic chemicals are, in most cases, considered to be the source of water pollution since they are not bio-degradable and some of them have toxic effects on the health of human beings and other living organisms. Hence, TDS would be a good measure of pollution.

Step 3: The emission levels (in terms of grams of inorganic chemicals per gram of the material produced and grams of TDS per litre of the effluent) calculated as above are compared with the standards fixed by the Government of India.

Step 4: **Construction of scenarios**: A scenario is a well-defined set of assumptions regarding a system in terms of its probable growth, development and changes that would take place in the future. In this study, the purpose of construction of the scenarios is to determine the pollution levels in the future under different assumptions on the rates at which the industry would adapt to the natural dyes. The adaptation rate would be the proportions of natural dyes and synthetic dyes in the total amount of dyes used for dyeing in different years. The following scenarios are constructed in this study:

- **BAU (Business As Usual)**: 100 per cent of the dyes used for all the categories of materials are synthetic throughout the period of analysis, except for silk, in which 70 per cent are natural dyes. For the proposition that natural dyes reduce emissions to be true, BAU should cause maximum emissions.
- **OPTI,** Scenario1 (optimistic): The shares of natural dyes and synthetic dyes for different years are in Table 11.1, except for silk for which 70 per cent natural dyes is assumed for all periods. This is optimistic because of the fact that in this scenario, synthetic fibres have been assumed to adapt to natural dyes as fast as the natural fibres do, which is not very realistic as natural dyes are not very much applicable to synthetic fibres. This scenario would be expected to cause least emissions if natural dyes were 'pollution-reducers'.

Table 11.1

Features of Scenario 1 (OPTI)

Year	*Natural Dyes (Per Cent)*	*Synthetic Dyes (Per Cent)*
2005	20	80
2010	30	70
2015	40	60
2020	50	50

- **REAL,** Scenario 2 (realistic): For cotton, wool and silk, the same percentage of dyes are maintained as in Scenario1, while for synthetic fibres, the rates in Table 11.2 are assumed. Hence, this scenario is realistic given the lower applicability of natural dyes on natural fibres. To claim that natural dyes reduce pollution, REAL scenario should give second least level of emissions, since it has the second fastest adaptation rates for the synthetic fibres and fastest rates for the natural fibres.

Table 11.2

Features of Scenario 2 (REAL)

Year	*Natural Dyes (Per Cent)*	*Synthetic Dyes (Per Cent)*
2005	0	100
2010	10	90
2015	20	80
2020	25	75

- **PESSI,** Scenario 3 (pessimistic): In this scenario, the assumption is that the natural dyes are not adapted to synthetic fibres throughout the period of analysis and that they are adapted to natural fibres at a pace at which they were assumed to be adapted to synthetic fibres in the Scenario 2. Silk is assumed to use natural dyes at 70 per cent throughout the period.

  Though this scenario is termed as pessimistic one, it should be noted that even this is not as pessimistic as the BAU, in which the natural dyes were assumed to be totally absent in all sectors throughout the period of study. Hence, this scenario should give the second largest level of emissions. However, this is more pessimistic than the other scenarios, since the growth rate of natural dyes is zero per cent for synthetic fibres and lower for the natural fibres, than those in all other scenarios, including the next scenario, which also assumes the deprivation of synthetic fibres from natural dyes.

Table 11.3
Features of Scenario 3 (PESSI): Only for Natural Fibres (Cotton and Wool)

Year	*Natural Dyes (Per Cent)*	*Synthetic Dyes (Per Cent)*
2005	0	100
2010	10	90
2015	20	80
2020	25	75

- **NOSYN,** Scenario 4: (No synthetic fibres with natural dyes.) Natural dyes are adapted by the natural fibres at a pace defined in Scenario 1, while synthetic fibres do not at all adapt them. As the natural fibres adapt to natural dyes at higher pace in this scenario than in PESSI, this scenario should cause less emissions than PESSI, i.e., third largest level of emissions.

Step 5: Based on the emission levels obtained under each scenario, the following queries should be addressed:

1. Is there any reduction in emissions by adapting natural dyes?
2. What is the magnitude of reduction in emissions under different assumptions on the pace of adaptation in different sectors?
3. What is the maximum possible reduction in emissions for the different years considered for the analysis? (Difference between the emission levels under BAU and Scenario1-OPTI).
4. What would be the reduction in emissions if, in addition to promoting the natural dyes for the natural fibres, the application of natural dyes on synthetic fibres is also promoted equally? (Difference between emissions under Scenario 1 and 4).
5. What would be the reduction if they were adapted to synthetic fibres to some extent and to natural fibres to a much greater extent? (Difference between emissions under Scenarios 1 and 2).
6. What would be the reduction if they were not at all adapted to synthetic fibres and to natural fibres to some extent? (Difference between emissions under Scenarios 1 and 3).

7. What are the priorities of dyes for each material, taking into consideration only the emission levels?

Assumptions Involved in the Multi-scenario Analysis

1. The production of the materials grows at an average annual rate calculated from data for the years 1985 to 1999.
2. For the synthetic dyes, 40 per cent of the chemicals added in the recipe are retained in the effluent.
3. For both the synthetic and natural dyes, 10 per cent of the chemicals remain in the effluent after proper treatment in ETP.
4. For the natural dyes, 70 per cent of the chemicals added in the recipe are retained in the effluent. This is reasonable because of the fact that natural dyes are not included in the TDS, whereas the synthetic dyes are included. Hence, one can expect a higher proportion of chemicals added to be retained in the case of natural dyes than in that of synthetic dyes since most of the dye is adsorbed into the materials, reducing the percentage retained in the latter case. This is because most of the additive chemicals are washed away in the dyeing process, while most of the dye is retained in the material. In short, inclusion of dye as a component of TDS has decreased the percentage retained in the case of synthetic dyes.
5. Light, medium and dark shades are obtained for equal proportions of the total materials dyed.
6. Silk is dyed with 50 per cent natural dyes now and it may not go beyond 70 per cent in the future.
7. The measure of emissions is GPL of TDS (total dissolved solids–only inorganic) and hence it does not include any organic material in the effluent. Hence, natural dyes are assumed to be non-polluting in nature as they are organic.
8. The rates of adaptation have been designed based on the fact that many synthetic dyes are being banned (e.g. azo dyes) in the international market and many more are anticipated to be banned in the future. The extent to which the sectors are expected to adapt the natural dyes is based on the expectation of the other dyes to be banned and there is no concrete set

of data available in this regard. Hence, we assume some reasonable adaptation rates and the inclusion of different scenarios would serve the purpose of including all possible ranges of adaptation.

Steps Involved in the AHP-based Ranking of the Dyes

Step 1: The emission levels of different dyes for different shades in the case of different sectors are calculated in terms of GPL (grams of TDS per litre of effluent).

Step 2: For each shade, dye and sector, the values of GPL, cost and fastness index (average of light fastness, wash fastness and rubbing fastness) are listed.

Step 3: The reciprocals of GPL, cost, and the fastness index value are used for the AHP analysis. A matrix is formed for each dye-shade-sector combination, whose rows are the different dyes and columns are 1/GPL, 1/cost, and fastness index.

Step 4: Assuming equal weights for the criteria, a vector of three equal normalised elements (0.333), each of which indicates the weights imputed on each of the criteria, is constructed. A better analysis could be done by obtaining these weights by Eigen value-method based on different weights assigned by different sets of people, for e.g., environmental experts, industrialists, researchers. The matrix obtained in Step 3 above is multiplied by this vector.

Step 5: The vector resulting from the Step 4 above is normalised and based on the values of this normalised vector, the dyes are ranked. The higher the value, the higher is the rank. Appendix A-11.2 contains an example calculation for AHP-ranking.

Assumptions Involved in the AHP-based Ranking of the Dyes

1. Cost, GPL of emissions and fastness values are of exactly equal importance for ranking the dyes for a particular shade in a particular fibre.
2. All criteria are quantitative, i.e, possibilities of taking durability (rather than fastness) or pollution/health hazards (rather than emission level in GPL) as a qualitative criteria are ruled out.

3. The three criteria considered here are assumed to be the only ones for the ranking of dyes used for a same type of shade.
4. International prices are taken as the cost criteria.

Results

Emission Levels of Different Dyes

The tables in the Appendix A-11.3 show the GPL of TDS caused by different dyes in different sectors. The following are summary tables prepared from those.

Table 11.4

Ranking of Dyes for Different Sectors based on Emission

Sector	*Rank*	*Light Shade*	*Medium Shade*	*Dark Shade*
Cotton	1	Fenugreek*	Sulphur	Gallnut*
	2	Sulphur	Golden Dock*	Sulphur
	3	Direct	Acid	Reactive
Wool	1	*Dolu**	Golden Dock*	Gum Arabic*
	2	Acid	Acid	Acid
Silk	1	Pomegranate*	Madder*	Shellac*
	2	Azo	Azo	Azo
	3	Reactive	Reactive	Reactive
Polyester	1	Disperse	Disperse	Disperse
	2	Kamala*	Indigo*	Shellac*
Nylon	1	*Dolu**	Golden Dock*	Gum Arabic*
	2	Disperse	Disperse	Disperse

Note: Dyes marked with '*' are natural dyes.

Table 11.4 shows that natural dyes are the most preferable for cotton, at least in the context of the environmental emissions for the light and dark shades. This is not so in the case for the medium shade since Golden Dock is a natural dye requiring many supporting chemicals and sulphur dye causes less TDS in all cases. Table 11.4 indicates that natural dyes cause less emission than the synthetic dyes in the case of wool. For silk, as seen in the Table 11.4, natural dyes are least polluting and the difference in GPLs of TDS for natural and other dyes is significant. Table 11.4 however, shows the fact that for polyester, natural dyes are more polluting than the synthetic disperse dyes. This is to be taken as evidence in favour of the proposition that dyeing of natural dyes, on synthetic fibres, is so complicated and cumbersome a process that it would necessitate the addition of quite a few supporting chemicals, due to which the pollution caused by natural dyes turns out to be higher than that caused by the corresponding synthetic dyes.

In the case of nylon, unlike polyester, the natural dyes are again less-polluting than synthetic dyes because of the fact that nylon requires so high a concentration of the synthetic dyes and its supporting chemicals for its dyeing, that even the natural dyes, despite causing a higher level of pollution than in other sectors, cause a lower level of pollution than the synthetic dyes.

LEAP Results of the Scenario-analysis

LEAP (Long-range Energy Alternatives Planning) is a software package used to calculate the pollution levels and energy consumption levels of any system based on its various branches and for different years in the future for different scenarios. The system may consist of different sectors, each of which may, in turn, be comprised of subsectors. Each subsector would have different end-uses and each of which would make use of different pollution-causing elements. In this study, the sectors are the different fibres, the subsectors are the different shades and the end-use is the 'type of dye'. The last level in this hierarchy tree, called the 'LEAP demand tree', is the name of the particular dye, for which the emission level is fed as input in GPL. This exercise is repeated for each of the scenarios mentioned earlier with proper feeding of the data regarding the adaptation rates for the different years. The data of production in each sector, with its share in each level, is also fed into LEAP. The Figure 11.1 shows the LEAP Demand Tree.

It is possible to run LEAP without considering changes in demand patterns. But this would give a static picture without including the fact that the demands change with time. Here a simple demand forecast model is used. The average annual growth rates were calculated using MS-Excel, based on the data available for the years 1985 to 1999. Table 11.5 shows the forecast of future demands using present demands and the estimated average annual growth rates.

Figure 11.1

The LEAP Demand Tree

Sector	*Shade*	*Type of Dye*	*Name of Dye*
+---Cotton-----	Light Shade----------	Natural---------------	Fenugreek Yellow
		+-Synthetic----------	Direct Dye
			+-Sulphur Dye
	+-Dark Shade-------	Natural---------------	Gallnut Black
		+-Synthetic----------	Reactive Dye
			+-Sulphur Dye
	+-Medium Shade-----	Natural---------------	Golden Dock Brown
		+-Synthetic----------	Acid Dye
			+-Sulphur Dye
+-Wool----------	Light Shade----------	Natural---------------	*Dolu*
		+-Synthetic----------	Acid Dye
	+-Dark Shade-------	Natural---------------	Gum Arabic BR.B
		+-Syntheic----------	Acid Dye
	+-Medium Shade----	Natural---------------	Golden Dock Brown
		+-Synthetic----------	Acid Dye
+-Silk-----------	Light Shade----------	Natural---------------	Pomegranate Yellow
		+-Synthetic----------	Azo
			+-Reactive
	+-Dark Shade-------	Natural---------------	Shellac
		+-Synthetic----------	Azo
			+-Reactive
	+-Medium Shade------	Natural---------------	Madder Orange
		+-Synthetic----------	Azo
			+-Reactive
+-Polyester---	Light Shade----------	Natural---------------	Pomegranate Yellow
		+-Synthetic----------	Disperse
	+-Medium Shade-----	Natural---------------	Indigo
		+-Synthetic----------	Disperse
	+-Dark Shade-------	Natural---------------	Shellac
		+-Synthetic----------	Disperse
+-Nylon--------	Light Shade--------	Natural----------------	*Dolu*
		+-Synthetic----------	Disperse
	+-Medium Shade------	Natural--------------	Golden Dock Brown
		-Synthetic------------	Disperse
	+-Dark Shade-------	Natural---------------	Gum Arabic
		+-Synthetic----------	Disperse

Table 11.5

Production of Dyed Fabrics & Yarns in the Sectors in Billion Kg

Sector	*1990*	*Growth Rate (%)*	*2005*	*2010*	*2015*	*2020*
Cotton	1.306	5.51	2.92	3.818	4.592	6.528
Wool	0.024	4.11	0.047	0.058	0.073	0.091
Silk	0.02	11.33	0.1	0.171	0.293	0.5
Polyester	0.21	22.06	4.117	11.316	30.659	83.065
Nylon	0.021	0.33	0.022	0.022	0.023	0.023

A glance at the rates and figures would confirm that polyester would dominate the textile industry, comprising more than 90 per cent of the total production in 2020. This, in turn, would imply that polyester sector, in addition to being one with high pollution intensity, is going to be the major contributor to the pollution because of its side effect. This observation, when linked with another note made in the previous section 4.1, that the technology of application of natural dyes on polyester is not very advanced, would imply that a concrete policy to encourage the technical research in this area is essential for a significant emission reduction.

Based on Table 11.6, many inferences can be made. For example, the reduction of emissions that would be caused by adapting to natural dyes uniformly in all sectors is the difference between the emission levels under BAU and OPTI. Similarly, the reductions that could be caused by different scenarios can be observed, as inferred below in Table 11.6.

The following inferences can be made from the above results of LEAP:

1. Maximum possible reductions in the emission of TDS by the penetration of natural dyes (at the most optimistic pace) = E(BAU)-E(OPTI) = 4.96167 billion kg. E(X) is the emission levels in scenario X, as seen in Table 11.6.
2. Emission reductions by promotion of natural dyes for both synthetics and natural fibres at equal pace (rather than depriving synthetic fibres of natural dyes) = E(NOSYN)-E(OPTI)= 3.56296 billion kg (equivalent to a reduction in GPL of 1.98).

Table 11.6

Overall Results (LEAP) of Emissions of TDS under Different Scenarios

		2005	*2010*	*2015*	*2020*
BAU	Total billion kg)	0.64	1.56	4.05	10.86
	GPG	0.088081	0.101397	0.112375	0.12039
	GPL	4.64074	5.069873	5.618757	6.019489
OPTI	Total (Billion Kg)	0.51945	1.12147	2.54437	5.89833
	GPG	0.071491	0.072894	0.070599	0.065387
	GPL	3.574525	3.644686	3.529925	3.269331
PESSI	Total (Billion kg)	0.64	1.55	4.02	10.81
	GPG	0.088081	0.100747	0.111543	0.119835
	GPL	4.64074	5.037374	5.577137	5.991774
REAL	Total (Billion kg)	0.59164	1.31611	3.07075	7.67981
	GPG	0.081426	0.085545	0.085204	0.085135
	GPL	4.071291	4.117251	4.110197	4.116771
NOSYN	Total (Billion kg)	0.59164	1.41343	3.59714	9.46129
	GPG	0.081426	0.091871	0.09981	0.104884
	GPL	4.071291	4.113533	4.590483	5.244211

3. Emission reduction if natural dyes are adapted to synthetic fibres to some extent and to natural fibres to a much greater extent=E(BAU)-E(REAL)=3.1802 billion kg
4. Emission reduction if natural dyes are not at all adapted to synthetic fibres and to natural fibres to some extent, as compared to the BAU=E(BAU)-E(NOSYN)=1.3987 billion kg
5. With relatively realistic assumptions, emission reductions as compared to BAU are 3.1802 billion kg. Hence, the natural dyes cause a clear drastic reduction in emissions of TDS.
6. Emission reductions in the case of equally fast promotion measures of natural dyes for both natural and synthetic dyes, compared to:
   a) BAU: 4.96167 billion kg (45.69 per cent reduction)
   b) PESSI: 4.9117 billion kg (45.44 per cent reduction)
   c) REAL: 1.782 billion kg (23.2 per cent reduction)
   d) NOSYN: 3.56296 billion kg (37.66 per cent reduction).

7. Even in terms of grams of TDS emitted per gram of dyed material (GPG) and GPL of TDS in the effluent, the reductions are significant. As compared to the different scenarios, the final reduction in GPL by the year 2020 if the OPTI scenario is implemented are as follows:
   a) BAU: 2.75 gpl (45.69 per cent reduction)
   b) PESSI: 2.72 gpl (45.44 per cent reduction)
   c) REAL: 0.987 gpl (23.2 per cent reduction)
   d) NOSYN: 1.98 gpl (37.66 per cent reduction)

The basic purpose of the above inferences is to quantify the benefits of adapting to natural dyes in terms of TDS and percentage. More importantly, this exercise aims at precisely disaggregating the consequences of adaptation in different sectors at different rates, which is solved by the definition of scenarios. For example, the reductions by not adapting to natural dyes only in synthetic fibre-sectors compared to those by uniformly adapting to all sectors would be as shown in inference 2. Thus, to be concise, this analysis is an attempt to pinpoint separately the reductions caused due to various levels of adaptation to natural dyes in various sectors.

As seen in the Table 11.7, the cotton sector has least emissions in three scenarios—OPTI, REAL and NOSYN. This is because of the fact that the adaptation rates for this sector have not changed in these scenarios. The emission reductions are about 30 per cent by the adaptation of natural dyes, i.e., from 302.53 million kg or 2.317 GPL in BAU to 212.26 million kg or 1.626 GPL in these scenarios. Even in the PESSI scenario, the reductions are almost 20 per cent, i.e., from 302.53 million kg or 2.317 GPL in BAU to 257.4 million kgs or 1.972 GPL in PESSI. This implies that, by 2020, the cotton sector would reduce its emissions by 20 per cent under pessimistic rates of adaptation of natural dyes and 30 per cent under normal rates of adaptation.

As seen in the Table 11.8, the wool sector has least emissions in three scenarios—OPTI, REAL and NOSYN. This is because of the fact that the adaptation rates for this sector have not changed in these scenarios. Just similar to the cotton sector, by 2020, the wool sector would also reduce its emissions by 20 per cent under pessimistic rates of adaptation of natural dyes and 30 per cent under normal rates of adaptation.

Table 11.7

Emission of TDS in Cotton Dyeing Sector

Scenario		*2005*	*2010*	*2015*	*2020*
BAU	Total emissions in million kg	135.32	176.94	231.37	302.53
	GPG	0.046342	0.046344	0.046348	0.046343
	GPL	2.317123	2.317182	2.317408	2.317172
OPTI	Total emissions in million kg	119.17	145.27	176.14	212.26
	GPG	0.040812	0.038049	0.035284	0.032515
	GPL	2.040582	1.902436	1.764223	1.625766
PESSI	Total emissions in million kg	135.32	166.38	203.75	257.4
	GPG	0.046342	0.043578	0.040815	0.03943
	GPL	2.317123	2.178889	2.040765	1.971507
REAL	Total emissions in million kg	119.17	145.27	176.14	212.26
	GPG	0.040812	0.038049	0.035284	0.032515
	GPL	2.040582	1.902436	1.764223	1.625766
NOSYN	Total emissions in million kg	119.17	145.27	176.14	212.26
	GPG	0.040812	0.038049	0.035284	0.032515
	GPL	2.040582	1.902436	1.764223	1.625766

Table 11.8

Emission of TDS in Wool Dyeing Sector

Scenario		*2005*	*2010*	*2015*	*2020*
BAU	Total emissions in 1000 kg	2045.73	2556.68	3195.24	3993.3
	GPG	0.043526	0.044081	0.04377	0.043882
	GPL	2.176309	2.204034	2.188521	2.194121
OPTI	Total emissions in 1000 kg	1793.52	2084.31	2409.66	2767.11
	GPG	0.03816	0.035943	0.033009	0.030408
	GPL	1.908	1.797164	1.650452	1.52039
PESSI	Total emissions in 1000 kg	2045.73	2400.69	2805.34	3384.11
	GPG	0.043526	0.041391	0.08429	0.037189
	GPL	2.176309	2.06956	1.921466	1.85944
REAL	Total emissions in 1000 kg	1793.52	2084.31	2409.66	2767.11
	GPG	0.03816	0.035943	0.033009	0.030408
	GPL	1.908	1.797164	1.650452	1.52039
NOSYN	Total emissions in 1000 kg	1793.52	2084.31	2409.66	2767.11
	GPG	0.03816	0.035943	0.033009	0.030408
	GPL	1.908	1.797164	1.650452	1.52039

Table 11.9

Emission of TDS in Silk Dyeing Sector

Scenario		*2005*	*2010*	*2015*	*2020*
BAU	Total emissions in million kg	0.42	5.86	10.01	17.13
	GPG	0.0342	0.034269	0.034164	0.03426
	GPL	0.4275	0.428363	0.427048	0.42825
OPTI	Total emissions in million kg	3.42	5.86	10.01	17.13
	GPG	0.0342	0.034269	0.034164	0.03426
	GPL	0.4275	0.428363	0.427048	0.42825
PESSI	Total emissions in million kg	3.42	5.86	10.01	17.13
	GPG	0.0342	0.034269	0.034164	0.03426
	GPL	0.4275	0.428363	0.427048	0.42825
REAL	Total emissions in million kg	3.42	5.86	10.01	17.13
	GPG	0.0342	0.034269	0.034164	0.03426
	GPL	0.4275	0.428363	0.427048	0.42825
NOSYN	Total emissions in million kg	3.42	5.86	10.01	17.13
	GPG	0.0342	0.034269	0.034164	0.03426
	GPL	0.4275	0.428363	0.427048	0.42825

Table 11.10

Emission of TDS in Polyester Dyeing Sector

Scenario		*2005*	*2010*	*2015*	*2020*
BAU	Total emissions in billion kg	0.5	1.37	3.8	10.53
	GPG	0.119703	0.121068	0.123944	0.126768
	GPL	5.985157	6.053376	6.197201	6.33841
OPTI	Total emissions in billion kg	0.39224	0.96568	2.35347	5.66411
	GPG	0.093905	0.085338	0.076763	0.068189
	GPL	4.295236	4.116879	3.838139	3.409444
PESSI	Total emissions in billion kg	0.5	1.37	3.8	10.53
	GPG	0.119703	0.121068	0.123944	0.126768
	GPL	5.985157	6.053376	6.197201	6.33841
REAL	Total emissions in billion kg	0.46387	1.15975	2.87927	7.44484
	GPG	0.06896	0.07743	0.08021	0.0896
	GPL	4.1023	4.1067	4.1065	4.118
NOSYN	Total emissions in billion kg	0.5	1.37	3.8	10.53
	GPG	0.119703	0.121068	0.123944	0.126768
	GPL	5.985157	6.053376	6.197201	6.33841

In the case of the silk dyeing sector, as seen in Table 11.9 above, there is no change in emission level because of the fact that the assumptions on the adaptation rates of natural dyes for the silk sector are the same for all scenarios.

As seen in the Table 11.10, the polyester sector has least emissions in OPTI scenario. The emission reductions are about 45 per cent by the adaptation of natural dyes, i.e., from 10.53 billion kg or 6.338 GPL in BAU to 5.66 billion kg or 3.41 GPL in OPTI scenarios. Even in the REAL scenario, the reductions are almost 30 per cent, i.e., from 10.53 billion kg or 6.338 GPL in BAU to 7.44 billion kg or 4.118 GPL in REAL scenario. This implies that, by 2020, the polyester sector would reduce its emissions by 30 per cent under modest (as in REAL) rates of adaptation of natural dyes and 45 per cent under OPTI rates of adaptation. This indicates the significance of development of technology of applying the natural dyes on the polyester sector, arising out of the huge potential of emission reductions in this sector.

Table 11.11 shows that a maximum of 42 per cent reduction of TDS is possible by 2020 in the case of nylon, since the difference

Table 11.11

Emission of TDS in Nylon Dyeing Sector

Scenario		*2005*	*2010*	*2015*	*2020*
BAU	Total emissions in 1000 kg	3390.51	3446.82	3504.07	3562.27
	GPG	0.154114091	0.156674	0.152351	0.154881
	GPL	7.705704545	7.833682	7.617543	7.744065
OPTI	Total emissions in 1000 kg	2824.7	2583.12	2333.34	2074.11
	GPG	0.128368636	0.117415	0.10145	0.090198
	GPL	6.418431818	5.870727	5.072478	4.69891
PESSI	Total emissions in 1000 kg	3390.51	3446.82	3504.07	3562.27
	GPG	0.154114091	0.156674	0.152351	0.154881
	GPL	7.705704545	7.833682	7.617543	7.744065
REAL	Total emissions in 1000 kg	3390.51	3158.92	2918.7	2818.41
	GPG	0.154114091	0.143587	0.1269	0.12254
	GPL	7.705704545	7.179364	6.345	6.126978
NOSYN	Total emissions in 1000 kg	3390.51	3446.82	3504.07	3562.27
	GPG	0.154114091	0.156674	0.152351	0.154881
	GPL	7.705704545	7.833682	7.617543	7.744065

between the emissions of BAU and OPTI scenarios is 1488.16 (3562.27-2074.11) million kg or 3.044 (7.744-4.7) GPL. Considering the REAL scenario, the possible reduction is 21 per cent. Thus the potential to reduce the emissions in the nylon sector by adapting the natural dyes is high (21-42 per cent).

A striking observation from the tables of standards of TDS concentration and emission levels in different sectors (Table 11.12) is that in most of the scenarios of almost all sectors, the emission levels are too high to be within the standards. Only in the case of silk, in which the natural dyes are most predominant, the standards are satisfied. In the cotton and wool sectors, the emission levels are relatively lower than others because of their better adaptability to natural dyes. Polyester and nylon cause the highest GPL emissions of TDS, because of their non-compatibility with natural dyes, being synthetic fibres.

Table 11.12

Indian Standards of TDS Concentration in Effluents

Standards	*Inland Surface Water*		*Public Sewers*		*Land for Irrigation*		*Marine Coastal Areas*	
M:L	1:20	1:80	1:20	1:80	1:20	1:80	1:20	1:80
GPG	0.0113	0.0452	0.0279	0.1116	0.0137	0.0548	0.0133	0.0532
GPL	0.5652		1.3952		0.6854		0.6654	

Most significantly, cotton and wool sectors can be, on an average, developed as the sectors with emission levels conforming to the standards under the optimistic scenario (OPTI). All these observations, in addition to the previous inferences from the overall and sector-wise results, lead us to conclude that natural dyes not only reduce the emissions significantly, but also to an extent that at least the natural fibre-sectors can conform to the Indian standards for the effluents. As for the synthetic fibres, it would depend on the technological developments that could improve the compatibility of natural dyes with them.

4.3 Ranking of the Dyes based on AHP

For the different sectors, the dyes have been ranked based on three criteria for each shade—cost, colourfastness and emission level. The international prices and fastness indices of various dyes have been tabulated in Table 11.13.

Table 11.13

Cost and Fastness Indices of Different Dyes

S. No.	*Dye*	*Cost (US$/Lb)*	*Fastness Index*
1.	Acid Dye	25	5
2.	Azo Dye	20	5
3.	Direct Dye	20	5
4.	Disperse Dye	26	5
5.	Reactive Dye	30	5
6.	Sulphur Dye	19	5
7.	Gallnut	43	4
8.	Kamala	8.25	3
9.	Gum Arabic	18	4
10.	Fenugreek	43	4
11.	Dolu	27.5	4
12.	Madder	25	4
13.	Indigo	28	4
14.	Pomegranate	19	4
15.	Shellac	14	4
16.	Golden Dock	14	3

Source: www.alpsind.com and other websites cited in footnote 3.

The following table shows the results of ranking based on the AHP analysis.

A comparison of Table 11.4 with Table 11.14 would highlight the fact that the inclusion of cost and fastness as the criteria for ranking the dyes, in addition to the emission levels, has changed the order of ranking. The natural dye has moved to second and third place respectively for dark and medium shades. This may be due to the fact that the cost of Golden Dock and Gallnut is not low enough to compensate their low fastness value.

Table 11.4, when compared to Table 11.14, shows that only Golden Dock natural dye has been rejected for the first place due to its low fastness, relatively high cost and not low enough emissions. The other natural dyes have retained their first place despite the inclusion of the new criteria.

Table 11.14

Ranking of the Dyes for Different Sectors based on AHP

Sector	*Rank*	*Light Shade*	*Medium Shade*	*Dark Shade*
Cotton	1	Fenugreek*	Sulphur	Sulphur
	2	Sulphur	Acid	Gallnut*
	3	Direct	Golden Dock*	Reactive
Wool	1	Dolu*	Acid	Gum Arabic*
	2	Acid	Golden Dock*	Acid
Silk	1	Pomegranate*	Azo	Shellac*
	2	Azo	Reactive	Azo
	3	Reactive	Madder*	Reactive
Polyester	1	Disperse	Disperse	Shellac*
	2	Kamala*	Indigo*	Disperse
Nylon	1	Dolu*	Disperse	Gum Arabic*
	2	Disperse	Golden Dock*	Disperse

Note: Dyes with * are natural dyes.

A comparative glance of the Tables 11.14 and 11.4 would again support the proposition that natural dyes are better than synthetic dyes even when cost and fastness are included as criteria, but for the fact that Madder natural dye has become least preferred after the inclusion of these criteria. An important note to be made here is that, though azo dye causes low emission of TDS, the content of this effluent is highly toxic and hence azo dye has been banned widely. In this case, a measure of toxicity such as LC_{50} should have been included in the analysis. However, this would matter much only in the case of azo dyes and since the objective is more towards checking for the feasibility of natural dyes, it can be safely concluded that, for the medium shade, Madder natural dye is clearly not the preferable one, and is inferior at least to the reactive dye.

In the case of polyester, the natural dye shellac has become a better dye than disperse dye with the inclusion of additional criteria, because of its sufficiently low cost and/or sufficiently high fastness and/or sufficiently low emission. For light and medium shades, natural dyes retain their last rank. This reiterates the importance of encouragement of innovations in the area of application of natural dyes to synthetic fibres especially polyester.

As in the most other cases, the natural dye Golden Dock has been found to be less preferred to synthetic dyes with the inclusion of other criteria for nylon. For light and medium shades, natural dyes still dominate the first place.

Conclusions

The following are the brief conclusions that could be made from this analysis:

1. The adaptation to natural dyes would cause a significant reduction 20 per cent to 50 per cent in the emission of TDS by the year 2020 depending on the rate of adaptation.
2. A reasonably fast (OPTI scenario) adaptation would bring the emission levels for the natural fibres (cotton, wool, and silk) well within the Indian standards.
3. For reducing the emissions within the standard limits in the case of synthetic fibres (polyester and silk), a combination of fast adaptation and encouragement of research in the application of natural dyes on the synthetic fibres are required.
4. Polyester, being the single major polluting sector, requires maximum attention in this context, in terms of research as well as adaptation policy.
5. An individual analysis of the dyes for each sector-shade pair shows that natural dyes cause significantly lower emissions in all cases except a very few, for example, polyester, which is due to not-so-developed technology.
6. The fact that the ranking of the dyes, after the inclusion of the criteria of cost and fastness, has changed in some cases and unchanged in quite a few, reiterates the overall feasibility of natural dyes. Other than the natural dye Golden Dock, most other natural dyes have been able to retain their ranks even after including these criteria.
7. The policy implication of this analysis would be that a well-designed policy should be framed for the promotion of natural dyes in particular and reduction of emissions in the textile dyeing sector in general. The features of such a policy, based on this analysis, would be as follows:

- This should include features that would encourage the research in the application of natural dyes on the synthetic fibres and improvement of the colouring properties of the natural dyes.
- A meticulous action plan comprising of rates of adaptation to the natural dyes should be framed.
- A set of rules and regulations should be designed for the dyeing factories throughout the country for the adaptation of natural dyes.
- The natural dyes, which are found to be outstanding based on different criteria, as analysed in this study, should be chosen and promoted commercially.
- If, as found in this study, the natural dyes are not feasible for certain applications, then synthetic dyes that are less-polluting or are better than others as per the ranking, should be promoted in such cases.
- Techno-economic feasibility analysis of natural dyes would prove useful in tracking the practical issues involved in the adaptation of natural dyes and hence should be encouraged.
- The standards of emissions in the effluents should be fixed in a scientifically reasonable manner and implemented strictly. One way of promoting natural dyes could be a systematic setting of the emission standards in such a way that the adaptation of natural dyes would be mandatory to achieve such standards.

Possible Extensions

1. An AHP analysis could be done by including other criteria such as quality of the colour, durability and health hazards, and collecting the opinion of experts from different areas.
2. A cost-benefit analysis of natural dyes could be done by including various factors such as savings in effluent treatment plant (ETP) costs, cost-differences of dyes and environmental costs.
3. Environmental costs of natural dyes, due to over-intensification of the land for their cultivation, could be analysed.

4. Organic dyes, which are currently under development and are claimed to be eco-friendly and better in quality and fastness than natural dyes, could be compared with natural dyes in terms of costs, emissions, etc.
5. Inclusion of a measure of toxicity of the effluent, such as LC_{50}, could be done so that the toxicity of some natural dyes would also be internalised in the analysis.
6. The extension of this analysis to some more sectors, dyes and scenarios based on different assumptions on the production could be done.

Appendix A-11.1

Calculation of TDS for the Dyes

The following data has been collected from the dyeing procedures of various dyes on various fibres to obtain different shades:

1. Percentage of different chemicals used in solid form on the weight of the material (OWM). For e.g., 3 per cent OWM of a chemical 'x' means that 0.03 g of that chemical is needed to dye 1 g of the material.

2. GPL and concentration of the chemicals added in solution form. GPL is the grams per litre of the solution in the dye liquor, while concentration is the grams per litre of the chemical in the solution that is added to the dye liquor. In some cases GPL is directly given, while in some other cases concentration of the chemical solution and its amount in the dye liquor (in ml per litre) are given. In the latter case, the effective GPL is: GPL = (conc/1000)*(ml/litre).

3. M:L ratio: This is the ratio of the weight of the material to be dyed to the volume of the dye bath required. Hence, this is in g per ml. For e.g, if M:L = 1:20, it means that 1 g of material requires 20 ml of dye bath, which in turn, means that the equivalent GPL of the material is (1/20)*1000 = 50.

Calculation of grams of chemical per gram of the material dyed (gpg) if OWM is known: gpg = OWM/100.

Calculation of gpg if GPL and M:L are known: gpg = GPL/[(M:L)*1000].

The sum of gpg values of all chemicals would give the total gpg of TDS in the dyebath. For synthetic dyes, the dye is included in the calculation, while it is not done for natural dyes, based on the fact that natural dyes being organic, do not come under TDS. This value is then multiplied by 0.04 and 0.07 for synthetic and natural dyes, respectively to obtain the TDS in the final effluent. The gpg can be converted into GPL by multiplying the value by [(M:L)*1000].

A similar set of calculations can be done for the determination of standard levels of TDS in terms of GPL and in terms of gpg for different M:L ratios.

Appendix A-11.2

Calculation for Ranking of the Dyes: AHP

(Ranking of Dyes for Cotton—Light Shade)

Dye	*1/gpl*	*1/Cost*	*Fastness*	*Vector to Multiply*	*Priority Vector*	*Normalised Priority Vector*	*Rank*
Direct	0.83612	0.05	5	0.33	1.94242	0.292901	3
Sulphur	1.5625	0.052632	5	0.33	2.182993	0.329178	2
Fenugreek	3.571429	0.023256	4	0.33	2.506246	0.377921	1

The columns 2, 3 and 4 form a matrix and this matrix is multiplied with the vector of column 4, which represents the weights assigned to each of the criteria. The resultant priority vector is then normalised and ranks are obtained based on this vector.

Appendix A-11.3

Emission Levels for Different Sectors

Appendix A-11.3.1a

Cotton-Emission Levels of TDS with Different Dyes for Different Shades

Dye	*Shade*	*GPL*
Direct Dye	Light	1.196
Acid Dye	Medium	5.02
Reactive Dye	Dark	5.26
Sulphur Dye	Light	0.64
Sulphur Dye	Medium	0.72
Sulphur Dye	Dark	0.8
Natural Dye–Fenugreek	Light	0.28
Natural Dye–Golden Dock	Medium	1.14
Natural Dye–Gallnut	Dark	0.455

Appendix A-11.3.1b

Wool-Emission Levels of TDS with Different Dyes for Different Shades

Dye	*Shade*	*Gpl*
Acid	Light	2.12
Acid	Medium	2.18
Acid	Dark	2.24
Natural Dye–Dolu	Light	0.28
Natural Dye–Golden Dock	Medium	1.14
Natural Dye–Gum Arabic	Dark	0.21

Appendix A-11.3.1c

Silk-Emission Levels of TDS with Different Dyes for Different Shades

Dye	*Shade*	*Gpl*
Azo	Light	1.14
Azo	Medium	1.14
Azo	Dark	1.14
Reactive	Light	1.205
Reactive	Medium	1.211
Reactive	Dark	1.222
Natural Dye–Pomegranate	Light	0.28
Natural Dye–Madder	Medium	0.56
Natural Dye-Shellac	Dark	0.46

Appendix A-11.3.1d

Polyester-Emission Levels of TDS with Different Dyes for Different Shades

Dye	*Shade*	*Gpl*
Disperse	Light	0.59
Disperse	Medium	1.39
Disperse	Dark	2.19
Natural Dye–Kamala	Light	2.065
Natural Dye-Indigo	Medium	3.57
Natural Dye-Shellac	Dark	0.2625

Appendix A-11.3.1e

Nylon-Emission Levels of TDS
with Different Dyes for Different Shades

Dye	*Shade*	*Gpl*
Disperse	Light	7.615
Disperse	Medium	7.648
Disperse	Dark	7.714
Natural Dye–Dolu	Light	0.385
Natural Dye-Golden Dock	Medium	3.08
Natural Dye-Gum Arabic	Dark	0.315

12

From Carcass Disposal to Social Empowerment

T. RAMASAMI

Leather has many features that make it unique and unmatched by synthetic materials. It is used worldwide in a variety of consumer products ranging from footwear to fancy fashion product/goods. Since the conversion of leather into products is labour intensive, Asia has emerged the most dominant continent in the manufacture of leather products.

One of the main problems facing the farmers is what to do with animal carcasses. In the socioeconomic context of India, cattle live long and a significant percentage (about 8.5 per cent) of the population die of natural causes. Disposal of fallen animals is a challenge. Some extremely poor people in India gain access to the fallen carcasses. They have no facilities for transporting carcasses or disposing of animal remains after the skin and hide have been removed. As a result, skins and hides often get damaged in transport, while other animal byproducts are left to rot, fouling thereby the environment. A survey made in 1987 estimated that the poor recovery of fallen carcasses in India caused annual losses of US$ 350 million.

The Central Leather Research Institute (CLRI), in Chennai, under the Council of Scientific and Industrial Research, came up with a basket of innovative technologies that were particularly suited to the varied Indian context. Technologies span the entire range of activities pertaining to establishment of microenterprises starting from improved handling of carcasses to the complete utilisation of fallen carcasses. Activities focused on the establishment of microenterprises. For example: technologies for carcass utilisation centres which deal with 4-6 animals per day, were innovated and implemented in 15 different geo-social contexts, under the leather Technology Mission (LTM). Technology packages have included both hardware for low investment potentials and small economic sizes and software for manufacturing quality products for all byproducts. A technology campaign for vegetable-tanning of leather has been reached to 177 families in Athni, near Kolhapur in Karnataka.

This chapter will highlight two innovations: (1) the recovery and total utilisation of the fallen carcasses, leading to social empowerment of a particularly vulnerable section of society; and (2) the vegetable-tanning process which has revived a dying, traditional craft of making Kolhapuri footwear into a flourishing trade.

Background of the Project

Cattle wealth of India amounts to a population of 220 million. Animal farms are small sized. They are mostly in villages numbering about 600,000. When they die or are slaughtered, skins and hides are obtained as byproduct. In the case of natural death, disposal of the carcass is a problem for the farmer. Some poor people who do not have access to other means of employment collect carcasses and have no means of transporting the dead animal from place of collection to any shed for flaying. Therefore they drag the dead animal along the ground manually. Due to limitations of resources, they then flay the skin or hide and discard the rest of the animal carcass to rot. The situation cried out for an S&T innovation that would gain recoverable value for the farmer and the flayer and avoid negative environmental consequences.

Along with the farmer and the flayer, there is the tanner. Village tanners gain access to such hides and skins which are rejected on account of poor quality by organised tanning industry. Village tanners tan these into leather for making a kind of open footwear called *chappal*. Traditionally, the village tanner used a process of tanning with vegetable barks. The traditional tanning practice has been passed down through the generations of tanning families over centuries. This process is slow (it takes 35 days) and afford low yields (23 per cent). Village tanners were often unable to pay creditors and meet their other needs of livelihood. It is estimated that about 200,000 families live in the fringes of village leather sector in India. CLRI identified a priority need for a shorter, tanning process with a better yield which would not strain the environment. Technology that eminently suits the small, rural tanner was developed by CLRI, but its diffusion was not easy.

In January 1995, India took stock of her strengths in the leather sector. These included the ready availability of carcasses and the existence of high-quality technical manpower. There were 1.7 million people earning their livelihood from the leather sector, yet a large number had no access to usable technical knowledge. To address this shortfall, LTM was launched with a range of appropriate technologies supported by world-class research and development (R&D) facilities and infrastructure. CLRI was given the responsibility of relating the best of the modern technology to the needs of the leather sector, while LTM provided the thrust to outreach the grassroots. A technology partnership of CLRI with the grassroot leather workers facilitated by non-governmental organisations (NGOs) was soon established.

Carcass Recovery and Utilisation

It was estimated that if the loss caused by the poor recovery of fallen carcasses could be recovered, the carcass collectors would see a rise of US$ 700 in per capita income. CLRI identified areas where such losses were especially high. Arranging for the dead animals to be carried to centralised locations appeared to be infeasible and unwise given the socioeconomic context of India and the decentralised population base of livestock as well as flayers. It was considered desirable to take the technology to the people rather than forcing people to move to places where the technology could be practiced.

In 1992, CLRI itself had already started to concentrate on downsizing of technologies to suit recovery and total utilisation of fallen carcasses in decentralised production centres. The funding for the project was sourced from the Department of Biotechnology of the Government of India. A critical requirement was the downsizing of technology, which is suitable for application in a decentralised mode in villages and is economically viable at low sizes of production. A capacity to process three or four animals a day was considered appropriate. By the time the LTM was up and running in 1995, a complete technology package was already in place—from transporting animals, cooking the meat and separating the bones, to wastewater treatment and utilisation of wastes. The technology was ready. LTM had been commissioned. Plausible locations for technology intervention had been identified. Yet the flayers were not yet ready for embracing the changes needed.

To overcome users' lack of interest, a strategy of referencing technologies to the social context of India was adopted, for this, field demonstration centres were necessary. The first centre was built in Bakshi-ka-Talab, near Lucknow, the capital of Uttar Pradesh. Although it attracted some attention from the general public, flayers continued to ignore it and came only with reluctance. However, as word spread that the centre could be worthwhile and may even help them improve their lot, the flayers' reluctance changed to interest. The centre taught them how to flay without cuts. Flaying was made easy using simple ergonomics. The benefits of flaying a hoisted carcass became evident to experienced flayers. The quality of the hide improved. And all of these developments translated into money savings and improved earnings, which brought user confidence. Scientists also benefited. They adapted the equipment and technology as new insights into users' needs and problems were gained. Now a simple device for peeling off the hide from a carcass has emerged. Mr. Sam Setter, a UNIDO expert designed Static Flaying Frame device. It has been developed at a cost of Rs. 7500 for application in India with the consent and participation of the innovator. Similarly improvements were made by CLRI to the design of the wet rendering cooker, used to cook the meat, float the tallow and separate the bones, by using it to cook under slight positive steam pressure. A facility to admit variation in fuel inputs was introduced. An energy-efficient drier was designed and developed to dry the meat quickly and well, while equipment for processing bones was developed in collaboration with the Centre for Technology Development, a NGO, and the Central Mechanical Engineering Research Institute, a sister laboratory under CSIR.

Real-time data have been collected for working with 4/6 animals per day in as many as 16 different locations. Plants operating at 4 animals per day are eminently bankable, while the payback period for those with capacity for 6 animals per day, is only 3.5 years.

A total of 31 centres were built within two years so that the technology could be tested in a wide variety of social conditions. Referencing the technology to the social context of the flayers had its own challenges and lessons. The right to collect carcasses has been with a specific social group in most villages and they resisted change. The techno-social innovation was challenging and demanding, yet it had its benefits. This intervention made a significant change in the social empowerment of about 600 people in villages in India. This was a proof of concept. Now the Government of India is developing suitable schemes for wide scale propagation of the successful models of fallen carcass recovery units.

The Kolhapuri Footwear

The traditional art of making footwear had survived, untouched by any modern influences, in a small community of about 1200 families in a cluster of villages in and around the town of Athani in Western Karnataka, about 200 kilometres from Kolhapur. The families made a living from it. They had skill and a certain innovative capability, yet they knew nothing about the modern technology that could improve their leather and products and still less about marketing and selling.

An entrepreneur from Kolhapur started to market the footwear made in these villages, taking it to towns and cities to sell and marketing a profit for himself; the village artisans also benefited. However, market acceptance soon dwindled as the product quality varied from piece to piece and batch to batch. The quality of the leather also left much to be desired. LTM launched a technology campaign, accelerating CLRI's effort to take the benefit of modern indigenous leather technologies to the leather workers.

The Athani tanners used vegetable-tanning, which makes use of local resources. They employed a traditional and slow process needing about 35 days of processing time. CLRI targeted 177 tanning families and taught them about an improved process which would save 60 per cent of the process time and increase the yield by 30 per cent. The CLRI efforts were met with distrust and scepticism in the beginning. The tanners were comfortable with what they already knew and were doing and did not welcome outside intrusion into their life and work. Although this initial response came as a dampner to the scientists, they were tenacious. They sought to borrow some support facilities from a tanner so that they could demonstrate the benefits of the new processes. However, the tanner demanded rent for the facilities and refused to provide raw materials for the trials. The scientists went to another, senior tanner and succeeded in assuring him that the demonstration would be made at the cost of the laboratory if he could provide the facilities at no cost. He agreed to lend the equipment but not to supply raw hide for the trials. The first trial did not attract much attention, but the senior tanner noticed the difference in the quality of the leather coming out of the demonstration experiment. The process time had been reduced from 35 to 15 days and the yield was 30 per cent higher. The tanner was convinced and, for scientists, this was a breakthrough in gaining the community's confidence. The tanner sought another demonstration, but still would not risk any of his own raw materials. However, 12 people had become sufficiently curious to come to watch this second demonstration. The senior tanner wanted yet another demonstration and this time he agreed to supply the raw material.

The success of the third trial in a row convinced the tanners, who came in large numbers to see what was going on. All 177 of them, in batches of 20 people at a time, were given a demonstration and training in the new technology. At this stage, four fully trained young men trained in Gandhi Ashram of the dignity of labour were selected. The selection was on the basis of their attitude and enthusiasm towards change, to help and sustain implementation of the technology in small rural environment.

The new process was easy and adaptable. It accelerated the diffusion and led to better use of tannins. The challenge lay not so much in devising the technology as in gaining the acceptance and confidence of the tanning community. The process had to be adapted to the existing infrastructure. The demonstrations and the scientists' determination won that confidence. Its cost advantage immediately impressed the tanners who could now reduce interest burden and give the footwear artisans a better material which the market accepted with readiness. Both tanners and footwear makers now demand (and get) more money for their improved products. Kolhapuri footwear now commands a better market and a higher price as there is greater consistency in the quality of the leather and greater standardisation of the product.

CLRI benefited from the user interaction which helped them to identify areas and needs for product improvement. Two artisans were invited to CLRI for two weeks and asked to make the footwear using their own traditional methods. A CLRI scientist, who knew both the tradition as well as the power of scientific methods, explained the traditional methods to a team of footwear experts who in turn helped to design the right kind of last and bottom template using the most modern methods. The two artisans were given the modern last and template and, after trying them out, suggested how they could be made easier to use. CLRI experts acted on these suggestions to adapt the new tools. This direct involvement increased the artisans' confidence.

All the artisans were given a set of lasts and templates under a National Leather Development Programme (NLDP). The computer-aided design of the standard-size lasts eliminated the problem of size variation of the earlier handmade products, and a set of lasts for men's and women's footwear meets all the requirements of size standardisation. During training, each family of artisans made 13 pairs of footwear in three weeks. Productivity increased by 20 per cent. The market for the product needs to be consolidated and an NGO is working with the artisans to build market links.

Costs and Benefits

Implementation period of Athani experiment was one year (1997), and the cost Rs.10 lakhs. Leather Technology Mission (setting up of Carcass Utilisation Centres) lasted from January 1995 to January 2000 (including a consolidation phase of one year). A budget of Rs. 9.0 lakh was made for each fallen carcass recovery centre.

Innovative procedures have led to a 120 per cent reduction in process time, a 30 per cent increase in product yield and a 15 per cent gain in product value owing to the improved quality of leather. In the traditional artisanal sector, the quality of handmade, open-type footwear has been standardised without changes having to be made to the equipment infrastructure used by household tanning units. Special lasts and construction methods have been developed to ensure quality improvements and consistency. About 1,200 families have already benefited from these developments.

The experience of taking science and technology (S&T) innovations right to the doorsteps of artisans has led to a synergy between formal and informal applications of technology in India's leather sector. The experience is eminently replicable in different regions in India and other developing countries.

Patenting and Commercialisation

Social empowerment through technology tools has been the focal theme of LTM. It aimed at the poorest sectors in India for intervention on fallen carcass recovery and village tanning. Commercialisation of technologies with return on investment was not the focal theme.

There has been a direct, commercial impact, however, on the 600 flayers, 177 tanners and 1,200 footwear artisans already involved in the experience. They are now the agents of change and it is hoped that, in a period of two to three years, 30,000 flayers and 20,000 tanners across India can be reached and encouraged to adapt to changed technologies and practices.

The experiment has been a harbinger of a social change which would sustain itself possibly with some minor support from outside. A network of people engaged in different microenterprise activities has emerged and all participants share the benefits. The leather workers interact with CLRI scientists in a mutually rewarding relationship where scientists learn from leather workers about their methods and needs and then go back to them with improved technology and designs.

Several lessons were learnt as a part of an innovative S&T experience in the microenterprise sector of leather. First, traditional artisans are apprehensive of change and reluctant to adopt new technologies; they are initially unwelcoming when outsiders approach them with supposedly better ways of doing thing and asking them to change their ways. Overcoming of this initial mistrust and winning confidence and acceptance are major challenges during the introduction of changes to a traditional community. However, once confidence is won, the enthusiasm of target groups is reward enough for the agents seeding technology changes.

Second, modern practices have much to gain from the traditional ways of doing things in terms of insight into what is wrong and what needs to be done. Although CLRI had all the processes and ideas, it benefited greatly from the two artisans who were invited to stay on its premises and demonstrate the traditional methodology. This experience enabled CLRI in selecting appropriate tools, which helped the leather workers.

Third, a national commitment, such as National Leather Mission was a great help in giving focus and urgency to the task of taking modern technology to tradition-bound communities. Without such a focus, the diffusion of technology to the target groups would have been delayed.

Fourth, management may often not be aware of the problems that arise from a really close interaction with target groups. In carcass utilisation, a significant insight gained was that the right to collect carcasses has traditionally been given to special social groups in most villages and these groups resisted any move towards a more scientific collection of carcasses as it affected them directly. The situation needed direct intervention from district officials and required great tact and understanding. It was of the utmost importance to gain understanding and cooperation before any progress could be made. Social changes through technology tools are harder to achieve because resistance to social change in weak economic structure is much higher than those prevalent in other social segments.

Fifth, training and demonstration are the basic instruments for carrying innovation forward. It helps if NGOs that are well-respected in the area can be convinced of the benefits and enlisted for propagation of the innovation, which they can be trained to do. The people's goodwill towards these NGOs is a helpful factor.

Summary

CLRI has been a reliable source of modern technologies to the organised leather industry. The experience of CLRI in relating technologies to the grassroots through Leather Technology Mission has made CLRI richer and more purposeful. Saving and adding values to skin through application of size matching technologies in rural India have been a rewarding S&T experience to CLRI.

13

Crafts in a Globalising World[1]

APARNA BHAGIRATHY AND
NIRMAL SENGUPTA

I

The World Bank estimates that two-thirds of the world's population cannot survive without foods provided through indigenous knowledge of plants, animals, insects, microbes and farming systems. The World Health Organization informs that up to 80 per cent of the world's population depends on traditional medicine for its primary health needs. No international organisation has brought out, as yet, the importance of crafts in the livelihoods of poor people.

We know that in India the crafts sector comes second in employment generation, outranked only by agriculture. Led by such facts, crafts are usually viewed as relics of the past, still existing only to cater to the livelihoods of the poorer sections. The promotional activities in this sector have been directed towards decorative production or for tourist attraction. People like Kamaladevi Chattopadhyay put crafts on the map and gave the sector its prestige. Only in one area of policy—employment, income generation and poverty alleviation programmes—are crafts taken seriously. While agreeing that this emphasis is just, we must also pay attention to the other potentials of crafts.

The commercial potential of crafts in modern markets is immense. Crafts and craft based industries are India's highest export earners. This is not surprising since the competitive edge in today's globalised world is obtained primarily by capitalising on specific skills rather than mere labour intensive production. Along with the skill content,

---

1. Originally published as "Surviving in a Globalizing World", *Seminar*, Issue No 523, March 2003.

the crafts sector also embodies valuable traditional knowledge that is rarely appreciated. No doubt, macro industries and hi-tech mechanised production are favoured over small-scale village industries and indigenous technologies. But with the development of new technologies and global markets, elements of traditional knowledge are also being appreciated as resources of actual or potential value.

A related question that arises in the context of value addition and technological development of crafts is regarding the role and recognition of rights of the craft persons. Global efforts for protection of intellectual property rights over such valuable knowledge are also on the rise. This is better known for indigenous genetic and medicinal knowledge, but on a lesser scale, is also present in craft. Like in the case of biodiversity and folk medicine, consolidation of commercial potential of crafts in a globalising world has two dimensions: (a) creation of value through technology improvement and (b) sharing of the benefits by means of intellectual property protection. This chapter discusses these two issues, indicating some of the support measures that are necessary for reaping the commercial potential of crafts in an increasingly globalised world.

Some of these may appear as largely export oriented measures which, one may feel, need not be the primary purpose for the production of crafts. But this is no longer true, for globalisation has brought with it more competition. Even if export is not the purpose of production, crafts still have to be export worthy to survive. In the WTO regime the distinction between domestic and export markets is becoming increasingly vague. In the domestic market itself, many crafts will have to compete with freely imported foreign goods, just as much as they have to in any foreign market. So, even if the primary purpose of craft development is poverty alleviation, the programmes have to take into account this globalised feature of markets.

II

Every area, every community has a different tradition, a different need and a different capacity. In the past, the craft community was linked to a consumer community that was close by, and locally accessible materials were used to cater to the local demand for products. Globalisation has changed the need for localised activities.

The value of crafts must be perceived in the light of new potential uses in these changing contexts. But before we enter into a discussion about value creation, from a commercial perspective we must take note of the significance of crafts in culture and religion.

Many craft items have both use value and cultural value. Market, or globalisation in any form, may come into conflict with the cultural standards. Neglect of the intrinsic and inherent value to owners/artisans resulted in severe discontent which, of course, found expression only in those countries where rights of crafts-people are recognised. The nature of debates over the use of some Australian aboriginal designs that were considered as sacred, outside the traditional context, without gaining prior consent from the concerned community may be appraised from the following cases.

III

As early as in 1974, reproduction of a painting by Bulun Bulun on T-shirts was challenged as a copyright violation under the breach of the Trade Practices Act of Australia. The court granted injunctions and the dispute was settled for the sum of A$ 150,000. The landmark judgment extended the copyright law for the protection of community rights of the indigenous Australians in artistic creations. Bulun Bulun admitted that he owed a fiduciary duty to the traditional owners to preserve the knowledge by guarding against infringements of copyright in the painting. If he did not, the custodians had rights to compel him to preserve the integrity of the community's culture and ritual knowledge.

In 1991, the Dolina Fashion Group was accused of copying an aboriginal painting onto fashion dresses. This case was settled out of court and the remaining stock destroyed. Yumbulul alleged that no permission had been granted to reproduce the totem pole, 'Morning Star', onto the $ 10 bank notes. Action against the Reserve Bank was settled by agreement.[2] There are numerous such designs/motifs specific to communities, such as in the northeast region of India that are not open to use by non-members or outsiders of the community. Their valuation must not be made in market prices.

2. See *http://www.mq.edu.au/hoa/briefhistory.htm* (for Australia) and *http://www.state.gov/p/wha/rt/oas/20827.htm* (for US situation).

IV

Commercial value of knowledge and skill is related to its application and market potential. Value may be enhanced either through an improvement in technology and/or by linking the production to the market requirements through efforts to market the product. There is no single model applicable for all crafts. The processing and manufacturing of craft products like leather goods evolved over centuries, responding to local needs, using locally available materials and creating local variations. The markets were typically small and sharing of knowledge and techniques limited in the absence of strong links with larger, modern markets. The traditional communities preserving and practising the techniques were unfamiliar with the methods of commercialisation of ethnic products in relation to the tastes and preferences of the modern market. Trade was not global, designs were static and restricted to the local market.

Modern markets are just the reverse. These are very dynamic and the demand for ethnic leather products temporal. In complete contrast is the textiles sector that has been extremely dynamic and globally linked over centuries. In world textile trade, India was once a world leader. Techniques that originated in India are now widely found in other parts of the world. In domestic demand and exchange of technological knowledge, the textile sector has remained vibrant. Technology upgradation and development need to be based on an understanding of the current position and requirements of the sector.

V

The leather technology upgradation mission of the Central Leather Research Institute synergised the traditional wisdom of the leather artisans with relevant modern science and technology and industry requirements. The problem was in linking the production of leather products to the requirements of the modern market. The development and marketing of the Kolhapuri footwear, an ethnic product, is an interesting example. The main problem with the Kolhapuri footwear is the lack of standardisation in quality. This is due to a mismatch in the material and the variations in size. On analysis of the conventional practices, it was found that it was the practice of having to first wet the leather and consequently wait for it to dry that resulted in lower productivity.

As a first step it was demonstrated that this process was actually not required and doing away with it by procuring better quality leather would automatically result in higher productivity. Pertaining to the problem of size variations, standard size lasts were designed with computer-aided methods and templates for the bottom patterns cut out from metal sheets and distributed to the artisans. With support from NGOs, the required market links were also established.

A question that is frequently asked[3] is, "Why do craftspeople with centuries of skilled tradition need outside intervention at all?" Tradition must be a springboard, not a cage; and if craft is to be utility based and economically viable, it cannot be static. Crafts are constantly evolving, but they must also respond to changes in markets, consumer lifestyles, fashion and usage. In responding to these changes in markets, lifestyles and usage, it is the role of designers and other agencies that serve as mediators that assumes significance in sensitively interpreting these changes to the craftspeople.

Craftspeople cannot afford to keep samples and have rarely seen what their forefathers made. The value of crafts may be enhanced by incorporating modern techniques where suitable, after a careful analysis of the processes involved and the requirements of the markets. In some cases even modern techniques are not required—forgotten old techniques may need to be revived. But again, this is an area where outside intervention is necessary.

VI

Following a ban by the European Union on imports of products using azo dyes, the potential for using natural dyes in a number of export earning sectors is immense. One of these is the large Indian carpet exporting sector. Use of natural dyes is an old technique but almost forgotten. An NGO, the Society for Employment Welfare and Agricultural Knowledge (SEWAK), engaged in a project for reviving traditional carpet weaving among the Bhotia community in the Kumaon region of Uttar Pradesh is trying to revive use of natural dyes. It finds that the price of these natural carpets are 300 per cent

3. L. Tyabji, *http://www.coop4coop.org/highlight/dastkar/product.htm*.

higher than the synthetic ones today. The project that started in 1996 with two families now involves more than 50 families.

In the globally linked textiles sector, the technology upgradation programme of the government is one of mindless imitation of technology prevalent elsewhere, without paying attention to the requirements of the processes in the sector. As a contrast, we will cite here some private initiatives directed to use traditional knowledge of craftsmen. There is an old proverb among the artisans claiming that the quality of the fibres in the cotton bud is far superior to those in any other stage of subsequent processing. The group investigated and came to believe that there is some truth in the saying. The spinning mills in the five largest cotton producing states are able to absorb only half of what is produced. Cotton is transported in bales to the mills for the production of yarn. A careful study of the process revealed that cotton was transported in bales in the past only for the purpose of ease of transport, for it had to be shipped all the way to England.

The AU-PPST group decided to use the folk knowledge of the cotton craftsmen as the prior art for technology development.[4] By now the group has developed a machine building on this basic fact. The processing is initiated at the seed level itself, thereby minimising the damage and cost due to baling and transportation. Further, since the quality of the cotton at the start is also higher, a much simpler process is sufficient. If the machine is deployed in the five largest cotton producing states and the yarn produced at the place where the cotton is grown, instead of having to export it to other states, it is estimated that the returns are likely to be much higher. This example highlights the importance of a careful study of the current technology and identifying the requirements of the sector before adopting or applying new technology. The needs of this sector were of localising the technology, in sharp contrast to the needs of the leather sector.

VII

Will the benefits from such technological developments and additional value generated reach the craft persons and artisans? Is

4. As described by L. Kannan of AU-PPST at the Workshop on *Traditional Knowledge—Appreciation for Policy Making*, 25-26 March 2002, IIC, New Delhi.

there a mechanism to ensure that the benefits are transferred to them? In the seminar on traditional knowledge,[5] Deborah Thyagarajan exposed our indifference by describing an incident. Art prospectors popularise Indian designs with the support of craft organisations. In one such programme at the Delhi Craft Museum, an artist from Madhubani demonstrated the techniques of Madhubani paintings. A French designer purchased the demonstration piece at a small price, which she subsequently used in one of her designs in her country. As acknowledgement of the original contribution by the Madhubani artist, she sent a cheque of above Rs. 100,000 back to the artist. On further usage of the design, she sent an additional amount of Rs. 250,000.

This is something of a precedent in our country, where it is usually assumed that designs are common domain for everyone and imitation is rampant. Not many may feel the necessity or the obligation to pay for using someone else's design for commercial exploitation. In the process the design is made cheap, and everybody loses.

VIII

Consequent upon the long history of protection of intellectual property rights, in Australia a substantial share of fund goes to the custodians. The total value of the aboriginal art market in Australia is around A$ 200 million per year. Half of the sales are related to the tourism market and of the total aboriginal art trade, A$ 50 million is estimated to reach the aboriginal producers directly.

In the US, a 1935 Act adopted criminal penalties for selling goods with misrepresentations i.e. when they misled people into believing that they were (American) Indian produced. Although this law was in effect for many years, it provided no meaningful deterrent to those who misrepresented imitation arts and crafts as being (American) Indian produced. In addition, it required 'willful' intent to prove a violation, and there was very little enforcement. In response to growing sales of products misrepresented or erroneously represented, in the billion dollar US indigenous arts and crafts market, the Congress passed an Act, essentially a truth-in-advertising law designed

5. Roundtable on *Indigenous (Traditional) Knowledge* held on 28 August 2001, at the Madras Institute of Development Studies, Chennai.

to prevent marketing products as 'Indian made' when the products are in fact, not made by (American) Indians as defined by the Act.

IX

India has introduced and modified its IPR laws to take care of traditional knowledge—largely biodiversity and medicinal knowledge. Crafts have not been given much consideration. We will discuss what protective provisions exist or are needed for crafts. In extending IPR protection to the crafts sector, several legal and operational issues arise. Identification of the craft sectors for protection, documentation for creating a record of rights, improvement so as to conform to the requirements of IPR laws, comparing the existing customary laws, protocol regarding access and use and transfer of folklore are some of the issues under discussion.[6]

Even the terminology is open to many explanations: Crafts are taken to include handlooms, handicrafts and other rural based cottage industries. What items can be given intellectual protection? The 'indigenous' or 'local' parts alone qualify for IPR protection. Indigenous knowledge (IK) not only refers to the knowledge of indigenous peoples, but also to that of any other defined community. The connotations vary across regions. Often, crafts are subsumed under the larger category of folklore. For the purposes of the World Intellectual Property Organization (WIPO) activities, expressions of folklore include handicrafts and other tangible cultural expressions. WIPO defines 'tangible expressions' to include "drawings, paintings, carvings, sculptures, pottery, terracotta, mosaic, woodwork, metal ware, jewellery, basket weaving, needlework, textiles, carpets, costumes, musical instruments, architectural forms."

X

Existing international provisions include several international agreements that have been formed for the protection of folklore and rights of the holders of expressions of folklore. An Intergovernmental Committee on Intellectual Property and Genetic Resources, Traditional

6. UNCTAD-background note on Systems and National Experiences for Protecting Traditional Knowledge, Innovations and Practices.

Knowledge and Folklore was established under WIPO to specifically consider the emerging issues of intellectual property protection pertaining to the three themes. The Tunis Model Law on Copyright for Developing Countries (1976) is an earlier effort towards protection of works of folklore. The Model Provisions for National Laws on the Protection of Expressions of Folklore Against Illicit Exploitation and Other Prejudicial Actions were adopted in 1982 under the auspices of WIPO and the UNESCO.

Several countries have used the model provisions as a basis for national legal regimes for the protection of folklore. However, it is recognised that the scope and impact of the model provisions is limited and it has been suggested that they be updated. There exist other similar initiatives to extend legal protection of folklore. However, these are often limited in scope and impact. There is no internationally binding legal agreement for the protection of crafts and the rights of the artisans. Where the existing mechanisms can be interpreted in a manner such that legal protection is extended to crafts, there is absence of an enforcement mechanism.

XI

With the standardisation of IPR regimes across countries through the Agreement on Trade Related Intellectual Property Rights (TRIPS), there has been discussion on possibilities for extending the existing IPR provisions for the protection of crafts. Some that may be applicable are industrial designs, geographic appellations of origin, copyrights and trademarks. Some of the state governments are already involved in extending protection to some traditional craft products. The Geographical Indications Act was passed in 1999; however, in the absence of Rules for the Act, there is still uncertainty regarding the procedure through which such protection may be claimed and used.

Geographical Indications is a commercial right that can be used to enhance the ethnic value of a craft product or design. It does not protect the knowledge or the underlying technology but it does prevent the use of the name in a way that misleads people about the true geographic origin of the product. The Tamil Nadu State Government Department for Handlooms and Textiles has identified some traditional craft products and studied their characteristics and techniques of production in detail so as to determine if they can qualify for GI protection. One such product is the Kancheepuram *sari*.

One of the basic requirements for claiming protection for traditional designs under industrial designs is the documentation of the tradition-based designs in conformity with the requirements of industrial designs, along with a classification of the designs. It is also important that the industrial property offices in different countries recognise such documents as a searchable database in the process of examination of applications for industrial design titles. The Government of India has undertaken such an exercise for medicinal plants in India—The Traditional Knowledge Digital Library is expected to be completed soon. A similar exercise for designs or natural dyes may also be considered. These are already well documented independently across institutes and organisations in the country.

XII

There also exist alternatives outside the conventional IPR laws for the protection of collective rights for works of art are often the product of collective efforts. Conventional IPR mechanisms have mostly been used for protection of individual or private rights. Collective rights organisations such as artist unions or performing rights societies provide for the recognition of the contribution of collective efforts. Neighbouring rights is a specific legal provision that recognises the efforts of the several different contributors to a work of art or performance and guarantees certain rights to them. In France, these rights were introduced in 1985 to recognise the moral and remunerative rights of performing artists and the rights of record producers to authorise or forbid reproduction of the records.

The need for intellectual property protection of crafts arises in the context of: (a) prevention of misappropriation or unauthorised use of traditional crafts and designs, (b) ensuring sharing of benefits on commercialisation of the crafts, and (c) for recognition of collective rights of the holders of expressions of folklore or crafts persons. As yet, no thought has gone into the two later issues: benefit distribution and customary rights. In a country where we are just becoming aware of acknowledging intellectual knowledge and rights over designs, little advance is expected on these matters. Here, however, we may cite the

Australian experience as an example. The Australian courts have approached such claims with sensitivity to customary laws, traditions and practices of the indigenous communities in Australia. The court acknowledged cultural sensitivity and awarded exemplary damages for culturally based harm. To enable aboriginal clans to take account of collective ownership of the designs, damages awarded were lump sum. Additional damages were awarded for humiliation or insulting behaviour to a particular cultural group.

XIII

In approaching the questions of creating additional value in crafts through technology improvement and sharing of benefits through IPR protection, there is utmost need for sensitivity to the position and requirements of each of the crafts sectors and the rights of craft persons. For technology intervention and laws for benefit sharing to be truly beneficial to the artisans and crafts persons, these have to be introduced by thinking for them and understanding their traditional and cultural contexts. Recognition of their contribution and their rights and a mechanism for actual distribution of benefits will go a long way in not only reaping the commercial potential of crafts but also in helping the craft persons to sustain their occupations and enjoy a position of prestige in today's globalised markets.

References

Abraham, J. (1995). *Science, Politics and the Pharmaceutical Industry: Controversy and Bias in Drug Regulation*, UCL Press, London, p.42.

Acheson, J.M (1972). "The Territories of Lobstermen", *Natural History*, 81, pp.60-69.

———. (1979). "Variations in Traditional Fishing Rights", in Raoul Anderson (ed.), *North Atlantic Maritime*, Cultures, The Hague, Mouton.

———. (1981). "Anthropology of Fishing", *Annual Review of Anthropology*, Vol. 10, pp.257-316.

Agarwal, K.K. (2003). "Problems and Prospects of Using Natural Dyes in an Maddertrial Enterprise", *Colourage*, Vol. 50(6), pp.37-40, Alps Maddertries Limited, Ghaziabad, India.

Anderson, Raoul (1972). "Hunt and Deceive: Information Management in New Foundland Deep Sea Trawler Fishing", in R. Anderson, and C. Wadel (eds.), *North Atlantic Fishermen: Anthropological Essays in Modern Fishing*, New Found land, St.John's Mem. University.

Anuradha, R.V. (1998). *Sharing With Kanis: A Case Study from Kerala, India*, Kalpvriksha, *Mimeo*, New Delhi.

Appadurai, A. (ed.), (1986). *The Social Life of Things: Commodities in Cultural Perspective*, Cambridge University Press, Cambridge.

Arnold, D. (1993). *Colonising the Body: State Medicine and Epidemic Disease in Nineteenth Century India*, Oxford University Press, Delhi.

Arrow, K.J. (1962). "Economic Welfare and the Allocation of Resources for Invention", in *The Rate and Direction of Inventive Activity*, National Bureau of Economic Research Volume, Princeton University Press, Princeton, pp.609-625.

Auslander, D.E., M.Goldberg, J.A. Hill and A.L.Weiss (1977). "Naturally Occurring Colorants: A Stability Evaluation", *Drug & Cosmetic Industry*, Vol. 121(5), pp.36, 38, 40, 105, 114, Squibb Inst. Med. Res., New Brunswick, NJ, USA.

Bahal, A. (1994). "Gunning for an Ayurvedic Empire", *Financial Express*, September 18, p.3.

Bahl, Deepti and K.C.Gupta (1988). "Development of Dyeing Process of Silk With Natural Dye-Cutch", *Colourage*, Vol. 35(22), pp.22-4, Department Clothing Textiles, G. B. Pant Univ. Agriculture Technology, Pantnagar, India.

Baker, H.G. (1965). "Characteristics and Modes of Origin of Weeds", in H.G. Baker and G.L. Stabbins (eds.), *The Genetics of Colonizing Species*, Academic Press, New York, pp.147-172.

Bala, P. (1991). *Imperialism and Medicine in Bengal: A Socio-historical Perspective*, Sage Publications, New Delhi.

Balick, M.J., E. Elisabetsky and S. A., Laird (eds.) (1996). *Medicinal Resources of the Tropical Forest: Biodiversity and its Importance for Human Health*, Columbia University Press, New York.

Banerjee, M. (1995). "Power, Culture, Medicine: A Study of Ayurvedic Pharmaceuticals in India", *Ph.D. Dissertation*, University of Delhi.

Banerji, D. (1981). "The Place of Indigenous and Western Systems of Medicine in the Health Services of India", *Social Science and Medicine*, Vol. 15A, pp.109-114.

Banuri, T., and F. Apffel-Marglin (eds.) (1993). *Who Will Save the Forests? Knowledge, Power and Environmental Destruction*, Zed Books, London.

Barrow, Chris (1987). *Water Resources and Agricultural Development in the Tropics*, Longman Scientific and Technical, Essex.

Bavinck, Maarten (2001). *Marine Resource Management-Conflict and Regulation in the Fisheries of Coromandel Coast*, Sage Publications, New Delhi.

Bechtold, T., A. Turcanu, E. Ganglberger and S. Geissler (2003). "Natural Dyes in Modern Textile Dyehouses—How to Combine Experiences of Two Centuries to Meet the Demands of the Future?" *Journal of Cleaner Production*, Vol. 11, pp.499–509.

Berry, Suman and R.K. Shukla (2003). "NCAER's Market Information of Households: Statistical Properties and Applications for Policy Analysis", *Economic and Political Weekly*, Vol. XXXIII(4).

Boojh, R. and P.S. Ramakrishnan (1983). "Sacred Groves and Their Role in Environmental Conservation", in *Strategies for Environmental Management*—Souvenir Vol., Department of Science and Environment, Government of Uttar Pradesh, Lucknow, pp.6-8.

Borthakur, D.N., A. Singh, R.P. Awasthi and R. M. Rai (1978). "Shifting Cultivation in the North-Eastern Region", in *Resources Development and Environment in the Himalayan Region*, Department of Science and Technology, Government of India, pp.330-342.

Brass, P. (1972). "The Politics of Ayurvedic Education: A Case Study of Revivalism and Modernisation in India", S.H Rudolph and L.I. Rudolph (eds.), *Politics and Education in India*, Harvard University Press, Cambridge, pp.342-371.

British Medical Journal (1996). Vol. 313, p.7048.

Brokensha, D., D. Warren and O. Werner (eds.) (1980). *Indigenous Knowledge Systems and Development*, University Press of America, Lanham.

Burghart, R. (1988). "Penicillin: An Ancient Ayurvedic Medicine", van der Geest, S. and Whyte, S. R. (eds.), *The Context of Medicines in Developing Countries: Studies in Pharmaceutical Anthropology*, Kluwer Academic Press, Dordrecht, pp.289-298.

Chacko, P.I., G.K. Kurien and A.T. Sherief (1960). "Fishing Calendar for Madras Presidency", in S. Aruldas (ed.), *A Handbook on Deep Sea Fishing in Madras*, Government Press, Madras.

Chang, H. (1995). "Patent Scope, Antitrust Policy, and Cumulative Innovation", *RAND Journal of Economics*, Vol. 21, pp.34-57.

Chattopadhyaya, Debiprasad (Sr.), (1964). *Indian Philosophy: A Popular Introduction*, People's Publishing House, New Delhi.

Commission of Intellectual Property Rights (2002). Report on "Integrating Intellectual Property Rights and Development Policy", DFID.

Cordell, J.C. (1974). "The Lunar-tide Fishing Cycle in North Eastern Brazil", *Ethnology*, Vol. 17, pp.1-24.

Cox, P.A. and M.J. Balick (1994). "The Ethnobotanical Approach to Drug Discovery", *Scientific American*, June 84.

Current Science (1996). Vol. 70, pp.976-986

David, Paul A. (1993). "Intellectual Property Institutions and the Panda's Thumb: Patents, Copyrights, and Trade Secrets in Economic Theory and History", in Mitchell B. Wallerstein, Mary Ellen Magee, and Roberta A. Schoen (eds.), *Global Dimensions of Intellectual Property Rights in Science and Technology*, National Academy Press, Washington DC.

Denicolo, V. (1996). "Patent Races and Optimal Patent Breadth and Length", *The Journal of Industrial Economics*, Vol. 44, pp.249–265.

Department of Fisheries (1958). "Statistical Survey of Kanyakumari District, 1956-57", in *Administrative Report of the Dept. of Fisheries*, Government Press, Madras.

Development Department (1929). *Report of the Committee on Fisheries in Madras, 1929*, Government Press, Madras.

Dharampal (2000). *Indian Science and Technology in the Eighteenth Century*, Other India Press, Goa.

Directorate of Fisheries (1982). *A Census Report on Marine Fisheries*, Government Press, Madras.

———. (1986a). *A Census Report on Tamil Nadu Marine Fishermen*, Government Press, Madras.

Duff, David, G. Sinclair, S. Roy and David, Stirling (1977a). "The Fastness to Washing of Some Natural Dyestuffs on Wool", *Studies in Conservation*, Vol. 22(4), pp.170-6, Department Chemistry, Paisley College Technology, Paisley/Renfrewshire, UK.

———. (1977b). "Light-induced Color Changes of Natural Dyes", *Studies in Conservation*, Vol. 22(4), pp. 161-9, Department Chemistry, Paisley College of Technology, Paisley/Renfrewshire, UK.

Environment Protection Authority (1998). *Environmental Guidelines for the Textile Dyeing and Finishing Industry*, Environment Protection Authority, Australia.

Fagerlin, Helen (1999). *Report from Roundtable Meeting on Intellectual Property and Traditional Knowledge*, WIPO, Geneva, November.

FAO, (1987). "Soil and Water Conservation in Semi-Arid Areas", *FAO Soils Bulletin*, Vol. 57, Rome.

Farnsworth, N.R. and D.D. Soejarto (1985). "Potential Consequences of Plant Extinction in the Unites States on the Current and Future Availability of Prospecting Drugs", *Economic Botany*, Vol. 39(3).

Farnsworth, Norman (1988). "Screening Plants for New Medicines", in E.O.Wilson (ed.), *Biodiversity*, National Academy Press, Washington DC, pp.83-97.

Fine, M. (1995). "From Political Economy to Consumption", in D. Miller (ed.), *Acknowledging Consumption: A Review of New Studies*, Routledge, London and New York, pp.127-163.

Forman, S. (1967). "Cognition and Catch: The Location of Fishing Spots in a Brazilian Coastal Village", *Ethnology*, Vol. 6(4), pp.417-426.

Furry, Margaret S. (1945). "Some Natural Dyes Give Long Life to Cotton Fabric", *Rayon Textile Monthly*, Vol. 26, pp.603-5, Bureau of Human Nutrition & Home Economics, Agriculture Research Administration, U.S. Department of Agriculture.

Gadgil, Madhav (1987). "Restraints on Exploiting Nature", *Development*, Vol. 1, pp.26-30.

Gilbert, Richard J. and Carl Shapiro (1990). "Optimal Patent Protection and Breadth", *Rand Journal of Economics*, Vol. 21, pp.106-112.

Glover, Brian (1995). "Are Natural Colorants Good For Your Health? Are Synthetic Ones Better?" *Textile Chemist and Colorist*, Vol. 27(4), Dundee Textiles Limited, Dundee, UK, pp.17-20.

Gopalan, C., B.V. Ramasastri and S. S. Bala Subramanium (1989). *Nutritive Value of Indian Food*, revised and updated by B.S. Narasingha Rao, Y.G. Deothala and K.C. Pant, National Institute of Nutrition, Indian Council of Medical Research, Hyderabad, India.

Government of India (1908). *Nimar District Gazetteer*, Government Printing Press, Allahabad.

———. (1924). *Agricultural Statistics of India*, series later renamed *Indian Agricultural Statistics*.

———. (1962). "Records and Agricultural Statistics" (*Mimeo*), Directorate of Economics and Statistics, Ministry of Agriculture.

———. (1966). *Irrigation Team All-India Preview of Minor Irrigation Works Based on State-wise Field Studies*, Planning Commission, Committee on Plan Projects, Irrigation Team, New Delhi.

Govindan, V. (1916). "Fishery Statistics and Information, West and East Coast", *Bulletin* No. 9, Madras Fisheries Bureau, Government Press, Madras.

Green, Jerry R. and Suzanne Scotchmer (1995). "On the Division of Profit in Sequential Innovation", *Rand Journal of Economics*, Vol. 26, pp.20-33.

Grifo, F.T. and D.R. Downes (1996). "Agreement to Collect Biodiversity for Pharmaceutical Resource: Major Issues and Proposed Principles", in S. Brush and D. Stibansky (eds.), *Valuing Local Knowledge*, Island Press, Washington DC.

Guha, R. (1997). *Dominance Without Hegemony: History and Power in Colonial India*, Mass Harvard University Press, Cambridge, *http://indianmedicine.nic.in*.

Gulati, A.N. (1949). "Natural Indian Dyes and the Art of Their Application", *Indian Textile Journal*, Vol. 60, pp.223-9.

Gupta, A. (2000). "Rewarding Traditional Knowledge and Contemporary Grassroots Creativity: The Role of Intellectual Property" (Draft).

Haksar, P.N. *et al.* (1981). *A Statement on Scientific Temper*, July 19, Nehru Centre, Bombay, reprinted in *Mainstream*, July 25, pp.6-10.

Holme, I. (2003). "Recent Developments in Colorants for Textile Applications", *Colourage Annual*, pp.81-106, Adel, Leeds, UK.

Hornell, James (1927). "The Fishing Methods of the Madras Presidency, Part-1, Coromandel Coast", *Bulletin* No.18, Government Press, Madras.

Howes, M. and R. Chambers (1980). "Indigenous Technical Knowledge: Analysis, Implications And Issues", in D. Brokensha *et al.* (eds.), *Indigenous Knowledge Systems and Development*, University Press of America, Lanham, pp.329-340.

Indian Water Resources Society (1990). *Souvenir* published on Water Resources Day. IWRS Publication.

Jain, P. (1990). "Dabur Brews a Winning Potion", *The Economic Times*, October 31.

Kawasaki T. (1985). "Fisheries", in R., Kates, J. Ausebel, and M. Berberian (eds.), *Climate Impact Assessment*, John Wiley and Sons, New York.

Kharbade, B.V. and O. P. Agrawal (1988). "Analysis of Natural Dyes in Indian Historic Textiles", *Studies in Conservation*, Vol. 33(1), pp.1-8, Natural Research Conservatory Cultural Property, Lucknow, India.

King, S.R. (1996). "Conservation and Tropical Medicinal Plant Research" in M. B. Balick, E. Elisabetsky and S. A., Laird (eds.), *Medicinal Resources of the Tropical Forest: Biodiversity and its Importance for Human Health, Balick*, Columbia University Press, New York.

Kirtikar, D.B. (1947). "Indigenous Indian Dyes", *Indian Textile Journal*, Vol. 58(137), pp.159-60.

Klemperer, Paul (1990). "How Broad Should the Scope of Patent Protection Be?" *Rand Journal of Economics*, 21: 113-130.

Kosambi, D.D. (1965). *The Culture and Civilization of Ancient India in Historical Outline*, Routledge and Kegan Paul, London, p.243.

Kumar, Devendra (1989). *Rural Housing Crisis: Wardha*, SPA, New Delhi.

Kumar, P. (2001). "Valuation of Medicinal Plants for Pharmaceutical Uses: Review of Literature and Issues", *Working Paper* 33, Institute of Economic Growth, Delhi.

Kumar, Pushpam and Nori Tauri (2003). "Does Indigenous Knowledge Contribute Towards the Benefits from Bioprospecting?" *Working Paper* E/234/2003, Institute of Economic Growth, New Delhi.

Kurien, John (1985). "Technical Assistance Projects and Socioeconomic Change: Norwegian Intervention in Kerala's Fisheries Development", *Economic and Political Weekly*, Vol. XX (25&26), pp.A70-A88.

Kurien, John and Mathew Sebastian (1982). "Technological Change in Fishing: Its Impact on Fishermen", *Status Paper* for ICSSR, Centre for Development Studies, Trivandrum.

Leslie, C. (ed.), (1976). *Asian Medical Systems: A Comparative Study*, University of California Press, Berkeley.

Leslie, C. and A.Young (eds.), (1992). *Paths to Asian Medical Knowledge*, University of California Press, Berkeley.

Llobet, G. (2002). "Patent Litigation When Innovation is Cumulative, CEMFI, Madrid, Spain", International *Journal of Industrial Organisation* (forthcoming).

Lofgren. O. (1972). "Resource management and Family Firms: Swedish West-coast Fishermen", in R. Anderson and C. Wadel (ed.), *North Atlantic Fishermen: Anthropological Essays in Modern Fishing*, St. Johns Mem. University, Newfoundland.

Macilwain C. (1998). "When Rhetoric Hits Reality in Debate on Bioprospecting", *Nature*, Vol. 392, pp.535-40.

Marx, Karl (1984). *Capital*, Volume 1, Progress Publishers, Moscow.

Marx, Karl and Frederic Engels (1964). *The German Ideology*, Progress Publishers, Moscow.

Mathur, Ajeet (2003). "Who Owns Traditional Knowledge?" *Working Paper* No. 96, Indian Council for research on International Economic Relations (ICRIER).

Mathur, P.R.G. (1978). *The Mappilla Fisherfolk of Kerala: A Study in Inter-Relationship between Habitat, Technology, Economy, Society and Culture*, Kerala Historical Society, Trivandrum.

Maurer, S.M. (1999). *Raw Knowledge: Protecting Technical Databases for Science and Technology*, National Research Council (National Academy of Sciences), Committee on Promoting Access to Scientific and Technical Knowledge.

Mc Cay, B. J. (1979). "Systems Ecology, People Ecology and the Anthropology of Fishing Communities", *Human Ecology*, Vol. 6(4), pp.397-422.

Mendelsohn, R. and M. J. Balick (1995). "The Value of Undiscovered Pharmaceutical in Tropical Forests", *Economic Botany*, Vol. 49(2).

Menell, Peter S. (2000). "Intellectual Property: General Theories", in Boudewijn Bouckaert and Gerrit De Geest (eds.), *Encyclopedia of Law and Economics*, Cheltenham, Edward Elgar.

Menon, T.R. (1980). "Inventory of Catamarams and Their Fishing Gear in Andhra Pradesh and Tamil Nadu", *Working Paper* 2, Bay of Bengal Programme, Madras.

Merges, R.P. and R.R. Nelson (1990). "On the Complex Economics of Patent Scope", *Columbia Law Review*, Vol. 90(4), pp.839–916.

Miller, D. (1987). *Material Culture and Mass Consumption*, Basil Blackwell, Oxford.

———. (1995). *Acknowledging Consumption: A Review of New Studies*, Routledge, London and New York.

Ministry of Urban Development (MoUD), (1990). *National Housing Policy*, New Delhi.

———. (1994). *National Housing Policy*, New Delhi.

Misra, B. (1976). "A Positive Approach to the Problem of Shifting Cultivation in Eastern India and a Few Suggestions to the Policy Makers", in B. Pakem, J.B. Bhattacharji, B.B. Dutta, and B. Dutta Ray (eds.), *Shifting Cultivation in North-East India*, North-East India Council Social Science Research, Shillong, pp.80-91.

Mishra, B.K. and P.S. Ramakrishnan (1981). "The Economic Yield and Energy Efficiency of Hill Agro-Ecosystems at Higher Elevations of Meghalaya in North-Eastern India", *Acta Oecologia-Oecologia Applicata*, pp.369-389.

———. (1982). "Energy Flow through a Village Ecosystem with Slash and Burn Agriculture in North-Eastern India", *Agricultural Systems*, Vol. 9, pp.57-92.

———. (1983a). "Slash and Burn Agriculture at Higher Elevations in North-Eastern India: Sediment, Water and Nutrient Losses", *Agriculture, Ecosystems and Environment*, Vol. 9, pp.69-82.

———. (1983b). "Slash and Burn Agriculture at Higher Elevations in North-Eastern India: Soil Fertility Changes", *Agriculture, Ecosystems and Environment*, Vol. 9, pp.83-96.

———.(1984). "Nitrogen Budget Under Rotational Bush Fallow Agriculture (Jhum) at Higher Elevations of Meghalaya in North-Eastern India", *Plant and Soil*, Vol. 81, pp.37-46.

Mitchell, R. (1979). *The Analysis of Indian Agro-Ecosystems*, Interprint, New Delhi, p. 180.

Moore, R. (1975). *Man in the Environment*, McGraw-Hill, New York, p.155.

Moses, J. Jeyakodi and Nirmala Ravi (2003). "Application of Grape Skin Powder Extract on Protein Textile Fabrics", *Man-Made Textiles in India*, Vol. 46(8), pp.295-300, PSG College of Technology, Peelamedu, Coimbatore, India.

Muelenbeld, G. Jan and D. Wujastyk (eds.), (2001). *Studies on Indian Medical History*, Motilal Banarsidass Publishers, Delhi.

Mukhopadhyaya, G.N. (1926). *History of Indian Medicine*, Volumes 1-3, Calcutta University Press, Calcutta.

Myers, N. (1980). *Conversion of Tropical Moist Forests*, National Academy of Sciences, Washington DC. p.205.

———. (1988). "Threatened Biotas: Hot Spots in Tropical Forests", *Environmentalist*, Vol. 8(3).

———. (1997). "Biodiversity's Genetic Library", in G. C. Daily (ed.), *Nature's Services*, Island Press, Washington DC., pp.255-74.

Nandy, A. and S. Visvanathan (1990). "Modern Medicine and Its Non-modern Critics", in S. A. Marglin and F.A. Marglin (eds.), *Dominating Knowledge: Development, Culture and Resistance*, Clarendon Press, Oxford, pp.145-184.

National Buildings Organisation (NBO), (1996). *Handbook of Housing Statistics*, New Delhi.

National Remote Sensing Agency (1983). "Mapping of Forest Cover in India from Satellite Imagery, 1972-75 & 1880-82", *Summary Report-North-eastern States/Union Territories*. Deparment of Space, Government of India, Hyderabad, p.8.

National Sample Survey (NSS), (1989). *44th Round*, New Delhi.

Newman, Katherine S. (1983). *Law and Economic Organisation*, Cambridge University Press, London.

Nichter, M. and Nichter, M. (1996). *Anthropology and International Health: Asian Case Studies*, Gordon and Breach Publishers, Netherlands.

Nordhaus, William D. (1969). *Invention, Growth and Welfare: A Theoretical Treat*, MIT Press, Cambridge, MA.

North, Douglass C. and Thomas, Robert P. (1973). *Rise of the Western World: A New Economic History*, Cambridge University Press, Cambridge.

North, Douglass C. (1981). *Structure and Change in Economic History*, W.W.Norton & Company Inc., New York.

Nousiainen, P. (1997). *Modern Textile Dyeing Takes Note of the Environment*, Kemia – Kemi, Finland, Vol. 24(5), pp.376-380.

O'Donoghue, Ted (1998). "A Patentability Requirement for Sequential Innovation", *RAND Journal of Economics*, Vol. 29(4), Winter, pp.654-679.

O'Donoghue, Ted, Suzanne Scotchmer and Jacques-Francois Thisse (1998). "Patent Breadth, Patent Life, and the Pace of Technological Progress", *Journal of Economics and Management Strategy*, Vol. 7(1), Spring, pp.1-32.

Parham, Rita J. (1994). *Elimination of Production and Environmental Problems in Cellulose Dyeing: Neutral Dyeing Reactives, Bifunctional Reactives, and Natural Dyes*, Rite Maddertries, Inc., High Point, NC, USA. Book of Papers-International Conference & Exhibition, AATCC, pp.398-403.

Patra, A.K., Aditi Sareen and Deepti Vohra (2002). "Performance Studies of Some Natural Dyes on Cotton", *Man-Made Textiles in India*, Vol. 45(8), pp.319-323, The Technological Institute of Textile & Sciences, Bhiwani, India.

Pearce, D.W. and D., Moran (1994). *The Economic Value of Biodiversity*, Earthscan Publications Ltd., London.

Plant, Arnold (1934). "The Economic Aspects of Copyright in Books", *Economica*, Vol. 1, pp.167-195.

Planning Commission (1996). *Draft Mid-Term Appraisal of the VIII Five-Year Plan*, New Delhi.

Platteau, J.P. (1989). "The Dynamics of Fisheries Development in Developing Countries: A General Overview", *Development and Change*, Vol. 20(4).

Pophalia, G.R., S.N. Kaula and S. Mathurb (2003). "Influence of Hydraulic Shock Loads and TDS on the Performance of Large-Scale Cetps Treating Textile Effluents in India", *Water Research*, Vol. 37, pp.353–361.

Principe, Peter (1989). "The Economic Significance of Plants and Their Constituents as Drugs", in H. Wagner, H. Hikino and N. R. Fransworth (eds.), *Economic and Medicinal Plants Research*, Vol. 3, Academic Press, London and San Diego.

———. (1996). "Monetizing the Pharmaceutical Benefits of Plant" in M.J., Balick, E. Llisabetsky and S.A. Laird (eds.), *Medicinal Resources of Tropical Forests*, Columbia University Press, New York.

Pushpakumara, D.K.N.G., H.B. Kotagama, B. Marambe, G. Gamage, K.A.I.D. Silva, L.H.P. Gunarathna, S. S. D. K. Karaluvinne (2002). "Prospects of Pharmaceutical Prospecting to Finance Biodiversity Conservation in Sri Lanka", *Sri Lankan Journal of Agricultural Economics*, Vol. 4(1).

Ramakrishnan, P.S. (1984a). "Let the Tribals Decide What They Want", *Science Age*, Vol. 2, pp.8-11.

———. (1984b). "The Science Behind Rotational Bush Fallow Agriculture System (Jhum) (Golden Jubilee Number)", *Proceeding of Indian Academy of Science (Plant Science)*, Vol. 93, pp.379-340.

Ramakrishnan, P.S., O.P. Toky, B.K. Mishra and K.G. Saxena (1981). "Slash and Burn Agriculture in North-Eastern India", in H.A. Mooney, T.M. Bonnicksen, N.L. Christensen, J.C. Lotan and W.A. Reiners (eds.), *Fire Regimes and Ecosystem Properties, USDA Forest Service General Technical Report*, WO-26, Honolulu, HI, pp.570-586.

Ramakrishnan, P.S., R.P. Shukla and R. Boojh (1982). "Growth Strategies of Trees and Their Application to Forest Management", *Current Science*, Vol. 51, pp.448-455.

Ramakrishnan, P.S. and O.P. Toky (1981). "Soil Nutrient Status of Hill Agro-Ecosystems and Recovery Pattern After Slash and Burn Agriculture (Jhum) to North-Eastern India", *Plant and Soil*, 60: 41-64.

Rausser, G.C. and A.A. Small (2000). "Valuing Research Leads: Biodiversity Prospecting and the Conservation of Genetic Resources", *Journal of Political Economy*, Vol. 108(1), pp.173-206.

Revi, Aromar (1987). "The Role of Appropriate Technology and Local Enterprise for Shelter in Rural India", *Proceedings of Habitat Forum*, Berlin, in *TRIALOG* Number 25 Darmstadt.

———. (1990). *Shelter in India*, Vikas Publication, New Delhi.

Roche, A. Patrick (1984). *Fishermen of the Coromandel: A Social Study of the Paravas of the Coromandel*, Ramesh Jain Publishers, New Delhi.

Rodriguez, I. (ed.), (2001). *The Latin American Subaltern Studies Reader*, Duke University Press, Durham and London.

Roshan, Paul, Jayesh Malanker and Sandeep R. Naik (1996). "Natural Dyes: Classification, Extraction and Fastness Properties", *Textile Dyer & Printer*, Vol. 29(22), pp.16-24, Department of Chemical Technology, University of Bombay, Mumbai.

Roy Chaudhury. R. (1992). *Herbal Medicine for Human Health,* World Health Organization, New Delhi.

Rubeena S., R.C. Sharma, G.P. Pandey (2002). "Biochemical Analysis of Natural Dyes: An Empirical Study", *Research Journal of Chemistry and Environment*, Vol. 6(4), pp.67-72.

Sahu, S.D. (1978). "Energy Requirement for Some Selected Cultural Practices in a Hilly Region of Meghalaya", *M. Tech. Thesis*, Department of Agricultural Energy, Indian Institute of Technology, Kharagpur.

Saxena, K.G. and Ramakrishnan, P.S. (1984). "Herbaceous Vegetation Development and Weed Potential in Slash and Burn Agriculture (Jhum) in North-Eastern India", *Weed Research*, Vol. 24, pp.135-143.

Scotchmer, Susan (1991). "Standing on the Shoulder of Giants: Cumulative Research and the Patent Law", *Journal of Economic Perspectives*, Vol. 5(1), pp.1929-1941.

———. (1998). "Incentives to Innovate", in *The New Palgrave Dictionary of Economics and the Law*, Macmillan Press, London.

———. (1999). "Cumulative Innovation in Theory and Practice", *GSPP Working Paper* 240, University of California, Berkeley.

Secretariat of the Convention on Biological Diversity (1996). *The Impact of Intellectual Property Rights Systems on the Conservation and Sustainable Use of Biological Diversity and on the Equitable Sharing of Benefits from its Use: A Preliminary Study*, CBD Secretariat, Montreal.

Sengupta, Nirmal (1980). "Indigenous Irrigation Organisation of South Bihar", *Indian Economic and Social History Review*, April.

———. (1995). "Salvaging 'Traditional' Knowledges", *Economic and Political Weekly*, Vol. 16 December.

———. (2005). "Traditional Value and Valuable Tradition", in D.P. Chattopadhyaya (ed.), *Self, Society and Science: Theoretical and Historical Perspectives*, in *History of Science, Philosophy and Culture in Indian Civilization*, Series 21(2), pp.433-445, New Delhi, Centre for Studies in Civilizations.

Sen, Geeti (ed.) (1992). *Indigenous Vision*, Sage and India International Centre, New Delhi.

Sengupta, Nirmal and Aparna Bhagirathy (2001). *Proceedings of the Round Table on Indigenous (Traditional) Knowledge*, Madras Institute of Development Studies, Chennai, India.

———. (2002). *Proceedings and Resolutions of the Workshop on Traditional Knowledge– Appreciation for Policy Making*, India International Centre.

Sewekow, Ulrich (1998). "Natural Dye-An Alternative To Synthetic Dye?" *Selezione Chimica Tintoria*, Vol. 6, pp.77-84, Leverkusen, Federal Republic of Germany.

Sharma, P.V. (1992). *History of Medicine in India*, Indian National Science Academy, New Delhi.

Sheikh, Rubeena, R. C. Sharma and G. P. Pandey (2002). "Biochemical Analysis of Natural Dyes: An Empirical Study", *Research Journal of Chemistry and Environment*, Vol. 6(4), pp.67-72, School of Future Studies, Indore, India.

Simpson, R.D., R.A. Sedjo and J.W. Reid (1996). "Valuing Biodiversity for Use in Pharmaceutical Research", *Journal of Political Economy*, Vol. 104(1), pp.163-85.

Small, A.A. (1998). "The Market for Genetic Resources: The Role of Research and Development in the Conservation of Biological Intellectual Capital", *Ph.D. Dissertation*, University of California Berkeley, USA.

Smith, R.B.W. and P. Kumar (2002). "Royalties and Benefit Sharing Contracts in Bioprospecting", *Working Paper* E/221/2002, Institute of Economic Growth, Delhi.

Steinhart, J.S. and C.E. Steinhart (1974). "Energy Use in the U.S. Food System", *Science*, Vol. 184, pp.307-316.

Stirrat, R.L. (1974). "Fish to Market: Traders in Rural Srilanka", *South Asian Review*, Vol. 7(3), pp.189-207.

Suster, J. (1980). "Under the Thumb while One Hand Washes the Other: Traditional Market Relations in a California Commercial Fishing Community", *Anthropological Quarterly*, Vol. 53(1), pp.4-11.

Talreja, Dheeraj, Priyanka Talreja and Monika Mathur (2003). "Eco-friendliness of Natural Dyes", *Colourage*, Vol. 50(7), pp.35-36, 38, 40-42, 44, Ciba Speciality Chemicals India Ltd., India.

Teli, M.D., Paul, Roshan and P.D. Pardeshi (2000). "Natural Dyes: Classification, Chemistry and Extraction Methods Part-I: Chemical Classes, Extraction Methods and Future Prospects", *Colourage*, Vol. 47(12), pp.43-48, Division of Technology of Fibres and Textile Processing, Department of Chemical Technology, University of Mumbai, Mumbai, India.

Thomson, K.T. (1989). *Political Economy of Fishing: A Study of an Indigenous Social System in Tamilnadu*, unpublished Ph.D thesis, Madras University, Madras.

Toky, O.P. and P.S. Ramakrishnan (1981a). "Cropping and Yields in Agricultural Systems of the North-Eastern Hill Region of India", *Agro Ecosystems*, Vol. 7, pp.11-25.

———. (1981b). "Run-off and Infiltration Losses Related To Shifting Agriculture (Jhum) in North-Eastern India", *Environmental Conservation*, Vol. 8(4), pp.313-321.

———. (1982). "A Comparative Study of the Energy Budget of Hill Agro-Ecosystems With Emphasis on the Slash and Burn System (Jhum) at Lower Elevations of North-Eastern India", *Agricultural Systems*, Vol. 9, pp.143-154.

———. (1983). "Secondary Succession Following Slash and Burn Agriculture in North-Eastern India", *Journal of Ecology*, Vol. 71, pp.735-745.

UNEP (1997). Document UNEP/CBD/TKBD/1/2, Note by the Executive Secretary, "Traditional Knowledge and Biological Diversity".

———. (1994). *Conserving Indigenous Knowledge: Integrating Two Systems of Innovation*, an independent study by the Rural Advancement Foundation International, New York.

UNESCO (1979). *Man and the Humid Tropics*, MAB Audio-Visual Series, I, Paris.

United States Congress (1993). *Biotechnology, Indigenous Peoples, and Intellectual Property Rights*, Congressional Research Service Report for US Congress, April 16, pp.11.

Vijayan and Kurien (1980). *Capitalist Relations in Traditional Fishing: The Case of the Goan Rampani*, PCO, Trivandrum.

Villegas-Navarrol, A., M.Y. Ramiez, M.S.B. Salvador and Y.M. Gallardo (2001). "Determination of Wastewater LC50 of the Different Process Stages of the Textile Industry", *Ecotoxicology and Environmental Safety*, pp.48, 56, 61.

von Oppen, M. and K. V. Subba Rao (1980). *Tank Irrigation in Semi-arid Tropical India*, Vols. 1, 2 and 3, ICRISAT , *Mimeo*, Patancheru, Andhra Pradesh.

WHO (2002). "Traditional Medicine Strategy, 2002-2005", *Document WHO/EDM/TRM/2002.1*, Geneva.

———. (2006). Factsheets, *www.who.int/mediacentre/factsheets/fs134/en*.

Williams, R. (1980). *Problems in Materialism and Culture*, Verso, London. p.170.

Wilson, Herbert M. (1903). *Irrigation in India*, Washington DC, reprinted by Daya Publishing House, Delhi, pp. 200.

WIPO (2001a). *Progress Report on the Status of Traditional Knowledge as Prior Art*. Intergovernmental Committee on Intellectual Property and Genetic Resources, Traditional Knowledge and Folklore, Second Session, Geneva 10-14 December.

———. (2001b). "Matters Concerning Intellectual Property and Genetic Resources, Traditional Knowledge and Folklore–An Overview", *WIPO/GRTKF/IC/1/3*.

———. (2002a). "Traditional Knowledge–Operational Terms and Definitions", *WIPO/GRTKF/IC/3/9*.

———. (2002b). "Review of Intellectual Property Protection of Traditional Knowledge", *WIPO/GRTKF/IC/3/7*.

———. (2002c). "Elements of a *Sui Generis* System for the Protection of Traditional Knowledge", *WIPO/GRTKF/IC/3/8*.

———. (2003). "Information on National Experiences with Intellectual Property Protection of Traditional Knowledge", *WIPO/GRTKF/IC/5/INF/2*.

WTO (2001). "Doha Ministerial Declaration", *Document WTO/MIN (01)/DEC/1*.

World Bank (1998). "Indigenous Knowledge for Development: A Framework for Action, Knowledge and Learning Center", Africa Region, World Bank, November 4.

Wynne-Edwards, V.C. (1962). *Animal Dispersion in Relation to Social Behaviour*, Oliver and Boyd, Edinburg, pp.653.

Index

G

H

I

M

N

P